THE
COMPLETE POEMS OF
Thomas Gray

THOMAS GRAY
From the painting by J. G. Eckhardt in the National Portrait Gallery, London

THE
COMPLETE POEMS OF
Thomas Gray

ENGLISH, LATIN AND GREEK

EDITED BY

H. W. STARR

AND

J. R. HENDRICKSON

DOMI NUS ILLU MINA TIO MEA

OXFORD

AT THE CLARENDON PRESS

1966

Oxford University Press, Ely House, London W. 1

GLASGOW NEW YORK TORONTO MELBOURNE WELLINGTON
CAPE TOWN SALISBURY IBADAN NAIROBI LUSAKA ADDIS ABABA
BOMBAY CALCUTTA MADRAS KARACHI LAHORE DACCA
KUALA LUMPUR HONG KONG

PRINTED IN GREAT BRITAIN
AT THE UNIVERSITY PRESS, OXFORD
BY VIVIAN RIDLER
PRINTER TO THE UNIVERSITY

CONTENTS

Contents

INTRODUCTION

THERE has never been a truly complete collection of Gray's verse. Mitford, Gosse, and Bradshaw include both English and Latin poems in their editions, but always with certain omissions; the texts of the first two are not beyond reproach, and all three have long been out of print. Tovey and Whibley, especially the latter, give the best texts of the English verse in their editions, but both omit all of the Latin and some of the English, particularly the translations of Statius, Propertius, and Dante. Of the two, only Whibley's Oxford edition is easily available, and, although the textual apparatus is excellent, the explanatory material is minimal.

For the Latin poems the situation has also been unfortunate. Although Bradshaw corrected the text as preserved by Mason and Mitford, this is the first edition to provide a thorough check of the extant poems against all available original manuscripts and early editions. In addition to a sound text, literal English translations have been provided for all the Latin poems. There have been, of course, other translations of many of the individual poems—they are listed in the Northup and Starr bibliographies—but they are scattered through a considerable number of publications, most of them periodicals not to be found in every college library, and they vary from reasonably literal translations to what can only be called, generously, 'imitations'.

ORDER OF THE POEMS

Tovey printed the poems in chronological order, but the method involves some difficulties, for the exact date when each poem was written is not always known. Consequently, the present editors have followed Gray's instructions for the edition of 1768 (see T & W no. 465) and have printed the first ten poems in the order that he indicated. The *Long Story*, which Gray wished omitted from the edition of 1768, and the *Ode for Music*, which was not published until 1769, follow. The satire on Lord Holland was never published with Gray's consent; but, since it did appear during his lifetime, it is placed at the end of this section although, save for the accident of its unauthorized printing in 1768, it would be more appropriately placed in the second division of the posthumous poems.

The posthumously published poems are arranged in groups according to their subject or nature. Within each group the order is, very roughly, chronological.

The translations (with which *The Fatal Sisters*, *The Descent of Odin*, and *The Triumphs of Owen* should be considered) illustrate the greatly increasing mastery which Gray developed as he grew older. The early translations of Statius, Propertius, Tasso, and Dante are at times weak and diffuse, at best reputable but not remarkable. Yet, although he knew little Welsh and Norse and consequently consulted Latin translations made by other scholars, his Celtic and Scandinavian poems are far superior in their ability to capture much of the fire of the original—and indeed to improve upon it at times. As may be seen from an examination of the explanatory notes, Gray shows a surprising, almost intuitive, ability now and then to avoid the pitfalls into which his superficial knowledge of the original tongues might easily have lured him.

Humorous verse, however—as Walpole commented—came much more easily to him at all times. It is true that the early poems do not have the compact venom of *The Candidate*, but even the *Ghost of Dennis* is superior to Gray's youthful translations. Unfortunately, Mason saw fit to destroy much of this verse and thus has obscured the toughness of soul and satirical, often ribald, humour that Gray's more serious works do not reveal. Indeed, had complete control of all Gray's poems rested in Mason's hands, it is unlikely that most of even those lighter poems which we now possess would have survived. It is a depressing truth that, although he certainly had access to some of them, of the humorous posthumous poems Mason printed merely the *Hymn to Ignorance* and Gray's *Sketch of His Own Character*—and the latter appeared only in a footnote designed to show that Gray's religious opinions were earnest and orthodox.

Two of the poems printed by Gosse and Bradshaw as possibly by Gray are omitted here from the Poems of Doubtful Authenticity. The first (*Ode*—'Seeds of poetry and rhime') may be eliminated since it is signed 'Celadon', a name now known to have been used by Horace Walpole in the 'Quadruple Alliance'. The second is the *Poetical Rondeau* ('First to love,—and then to part,') printed and attributed to Gray by John Young in his *Criticism on the Elegy* . . ., 1783. The *Rondeau* is so clearly nothing but a part of Young's burlesque of Samuel Johnson that there can be no serious consideration that Gray wrote it. (For a more detailed discussion see Hendrickson and Starr, *N & Q*, n.s. viii [Feb. 1961], 57–58.)

Titles from manuscript sources or contemporary printed works are given as they appear in the basic text of each poem (e.g. *From Propertius: To Mecænas*); titles supplied by later editors, including the editors of the present edition, are enclosed in square brackets and all letters are capitalized.

TEXT AND TEXTUAL NOTES

Since there is no one authoritative edition or manuscript of the poems, it has seemed best to select the text for each poem independently. For those few poems which survive in a manuscript draft that Gray prepared for the printer, the manuscript is the text adopted. For only three (*The Fatal Sisters*, *The Descent of Odin*, and *The Triumphs of Owen*) does there exist such a manuscript; and this, we believe, is the first edition of these poems in which Gray's own text has been carefully followed, for Dodsley made alterations in punctuation, capitalization, and spelling. In other instances, where there exists an edition published in Gray's lifetime which apparently was either supervised or at least approved by the poet, and consequently may be regarded as authoritative, this text has been adopted. Still other poems survived only in his manuscripts, in copies made by friends or scholars, or in editions published either after his death or without his authorization. In such cases a holograph manuscript, if extant, is the text followed; when the poem has been found in a manuscript letter the reference number for the Toynbee and Whibley *Correspondence* is added as a convenience for the reader, even though the editors have here retranscribed the manuscript. If no holograph is known, the most satisfactory printed text or written copy is adopted. Occasionally, certain of Gray's practices in spelling (his use of *sooth* for *soothe*, for example) seem likely to confuse a reader, and usually such a word has been altered to conform to modern usage, with the original reading indicated by either a textual note or the use of brackets. However, such emendations normally have been avoided; his confusion of *its* and *it's*, for instance, is hardly likely to lead to any misunderstanding. The notes for each poem indicate the text used and the versions collated.

In representing such headings as the titles of poems, the editors have to some extent standardized without textual comment certain of the variants in Gray's capitalization and punctuation.

The lines of poems, whether or not any numbers appeared in the original texts, have here been numbered in 5's; and, if misnumbered by Gray, the numbering has been corrected by the editors.

The textual notes, in general, record only those variants which seem to have some bearing on the meaning. Consequently, most variations in spelling, capitalization, punctuation, use of the ampersand, &c., are ignored. Gray's habits (as the reader may observe in the poems which follow the text of a holograph manuscript) in such matters varied greatly from the usual practice of eighteenth-century printers; and, if all such variants were recorded here, the length of the textual notes would exceed all reasonable bounds without adding materially to the enlightenment of the reader.

Certain basic principles followed in the notes should be mentioned:

1. When such a variant as

gray and repress'd] black and depress'd *CB, M.*

is noted, the reader should assume that—although both *CB* (Gray's Commonplace Book) and *M* (Mason) give the same wording—the spelling, capitalization, and punctuation recorded pertain to only the *first* source given: i.e. 'depress'd' is the spelling in *CB*, but the other source or sources noted do not necessarily follow this spelling; for example, in *M* the phrase may appear as 'Black, & depressed'.

2. Gray's customary way of indicating a revision is to underline the reading to be deleted in the text and to write the revised reading in the margin. Ordinarily, we have incorporated the revision into the text and printed the original reading in the notes.

Sometimes, however, Gray crossed out a word and wrote the revision above it. In such instances the abbreviation *del* is employed:

gray] black (*del*) *CB.*

Here the meaning is that 'black' was originally written in *CB*, then deleted, and the present reading, 'gray', substituted. Other types of revision, used occasionally, are described more fully in the notes to the individual poems.

3. The following abbreviations have been used for the most frequently cited manuscripts or editions. Others are explained in the notes to the individual poems.

CB   Gray's Commonplace Book, 3 v., at Pembroke College,
       Cambridge, the most valuable collection of holograph manu-
       scripts of the poems. Only the first [1,095] pages are in

Gray's hand; thus in reading the textual notes it should be understood that any drafts of poems which appear before p. [1,095] are holographs. Mason copied several additional poems culled from odd manuscripts into the third volume after Gray's death. For such a draft the abbreviation *CBM* is used.

B   *Designs by Mr. R. Bentley for Six Poems by Mr. T. Gray.* London, 1753.

Mt   See 'Nineteenth and Twentieth-century Editions' below.

P   *Poems by Mr. Gray.* London: Dodsley, 1768.

M   *The Poems of Mr. Gray, to which are prefixed Memoirs of his Life and Writing by W[illiam]. Mason.* York, 1775.

B and *P* are both editions in which Gray is known to have had a hand. (See the Toynbee and Whibley *Correspondence* cited below.) Mason (*M*), although most unreliable in his representation of the letters, seems to have been a little more careful with the text of the poems and, in fact, is the only source for several. Unhappily, however, he did destroy the only known copies of some of Gray's poems (see R. W. Ketton-Cremer's *Thomas Gray*, Cambridge, 1955, p. 204), apparently under the misguided notion that he was preserving Gray's reputation by burning some of the more frivolous or ribald verse.

Nineteenth and Twentieth-century Editions

Mt   *The Poetical Works of Thomas Gray*, ed. John Mitford. London: Pickering, 1836. The same abbreviation is used for Mitford's Note-books (British Museum Add. MS. 32561); a specific notation identifies this meaning whenever it is used.

Br   *The Poetical Works of Thomas Gray*, ed. John Bradshaw. London: Bell, 1898.

Tv   *Gray's English Poems, Original and Translated from the Norse and Welsh*, ed. D. C. Tovey. Cambridge, 1914.

T & W no. The number of the letter in *The Correspondence of Thomas Gray*, eds. Paget Toynbee and Leonard Whibley. Oxford: Clarendon Press, 1935, 3 v.

Wh   *The Poems of Thomas Gray*, ed. Austin Lane Poole, 4th ed. rev. by Leonard Whibley. London: Oxford, 1937, 1948.

Other editions occasionally referred to by their editors' surnames are *The Works of . . . Gray*, ed. Edmund Gosse (London: Macmillan, 1885, 4 v.; revised ed., 1902–6) and *Selections from . . . Gray*, ed. William Lyon Phelps (Boston: Ginn, 1894).

EXPLANATORY NOTES

In the explanatory notes the editors have attempted to supply the information which the average educated reader as well as the scholar would find useful for an understanding of the poems. Translations of phrases in a foreign language have been included; but, if the notes were not to become intolerably long, certain curtailments seemed necessary. Although elaborate parallel passages recording the possible sources are printed in the editions of Bradshaw and Mitford especially, most of them seem to the present editors of somewhat limited value. Consequently, unless the parallel has been the subject of some dispute among former editors, or was noted by Gray himself (usually either in a manuscript or in an edition over which he exercised some supervision), or seems particularly close or useful (as in the case of a mock heroic poem), those echoes have ordinarily been omitted. The reader who wishes to investigate them in detail should consult the editions of Mitford and Bradshaw and the sections on the individual poems in C. S. Northup's *A Bibliography of Thomas Gray*, New Haven: Yale University Press, 1917 (Cornell Studies in English, I), and H. W. Starr's *A Bibliography of Thomas Gray, 1917–1951* . . ., Philadelphia: University of Pennsylvania Press, 1953 (Temple University Publications).

The abbreviations employed in these notes are identical with those in the textual notes; see the introduction to the latter, pp. xii–xiv.

Certain notes (see, for example, explanatory notes 1, 3 to *Progress of Poesy*) which Gray designed to be printed in the particular text which we have adopted are preceded by a double dagger (‡) to distinguish them from other notes which he had written in texts which we have not followed. Both types of note are followed by the word '*Gray*'.

Finally, it is assumed that the reader who consults the explanatory notes will have already checked the corresponding entry in the textual notes, since it occasionally will have some bearing on the subject of the explanatory notes.

ACKNOWLEDGEMENTS

As far as the published works are concerned, any editor of Gray owes much to John Mitford, who, despite occasional errors, did important pioneer work in discovering and publishing many Gray manuscripts, and, above all, to Paget Toynbee and Leonard Whibley, whose meticulously accurate edition of the correspondence is the most important source for all kinds of information concerning Gray. Other debts are acknowledged in the notes to the individual poems.

The editors wish to acknowledge in particular the invaluable assistance over many years of Mr. M. J. C. Hodgart, Librarian of Pembroke College, Cambridge, without which this edition would have been entirely impossible, as well as the permission of the Master and Fellows of Pembroke College to draw upon the resources of the college's manuscript collection. Mr. Walter Hausdorfer of Temple University Library and his staff have done everything in their power to provide us with books and films. In addition, we should like to express our gratitude to the authorities of the British Museum, Miss Carolyn E. Jakeman of Harvard University Library, Mr. Tyrus G. Harmsen of Huntington Library, Mr. Tom Lyon of Eton College Library, and all the other library staffs cited in the notes. We have been given advice and help by Miss Mabel Zahn, the Marchioness of Crewe, Mrs. Eleanor D. Kewer of Harvard University Press, Mr. Charles G. Profitt of Columbia University Press, Mr. Cyril I. Nelson of Everyman's Library (E. P. Dutton), and the Oxford University Press. Professor Ames Johnston has helped to collate and prepare the manuscript, Professor James D. Powell has provided notes and translations for passages dealing with the Romance languages, and Messrs. William Powell Jones, Wilmarth S. Lewis, Guy Mermier, A. Dayle Wallace, A. Carson Simpson, A. R. Millbourn, J. C. Maxwell, Helge Kökeritz, Carl Anderson, Eric Partridge, and T. C. Hammond have all aided us. Mrs. H. W. Starr and Mrs. J. R. Hendrickson have assisted in the proof-reading. Finally, Temple University has done much to further our work by providing a research grant and a leave of absence.

ENGLISH POETRY

ODE
ON THE
SPRING.

Lo! Where the rosy-bosom'd Hours,
Fair VENUS' train appear,
Disclose the long-expecting flowers,
And wake the purple year!
The Attic warbler pours her throat,   5
Responsive to the cuckow's note,
The untaught harmony of spring:
While whisp'ring pleasure as they fly,
Cool Zephyrs thro' the clear blue sky
Their gather'd fragrance fling.   10

Where'er the oak's thick branches stretch
A broader browner shade;
Where'er the rude and moss-grown beech
O'er-canopies the glade
Beside some water's rushy brink   15
With me the Muse shall sit, and think
(At ease reclin'd in rustic state)
How vain the ardour of the Crowd,

ODE ON THE SPRING. First published anonymously in Dodsley's *Collection of Poems by Several Hands*, 1748, ii. 265.
   Text used: *P*. Texts collated: *CB*, i. 275, 278; *B*; *M*; *Wal* (Letter to Walpole, 20 Oct. 1746, Pembroke College MS. L.C. 2. 123, no. 42, T & W no. 125).

Title: Noon-Tide, An Ode. *CB*.   12 Their broadest brounest Shade: *CB*.

How low, how little are the Proud,
How indigent the Great!   20

Still is the toiling hand of Care:
The panting herds repose:
Yet hark, how thro' the peopled air
The busy murmur glows!
The insect youth are on the wing,   25
Eager to taste the honied spring,
And float amid the liquid noon:
Some lightly o'er the current skim,
Some shew their gayly-gilded trim
Quick-glancing to the sun.   30

To Contemplation's sober eye
Such is the race of Man:
And they that creep, and they that fly,
Shall end where they began.
Alike the Busy and the Gay   35
But flutter thro' life's little day,
In fortune's varying colours drest:
Brush'd by the hand of rough Mischance,
Or chill'd by age, their airy dance
They leave, in dust to rest.   40

Methinks I hear in accents low
The sportive kind reply:
Poor moralist! and what art thou?
A solitary fly!
Thy Joys no glittering female meets,   45
No hive hast thou of hoarded sweets,
No painted plumage to display:
On hasty wings thy youth is flown;
Thy sun is set, thy spring is gone—
We frolick, while 'tis May.   50

19–20   How low, how indigent the Proud,
          How little are the Great. *CB*, *Wal*, *Dodsley's* Collection.
At the end of the poem in CB appears the note: at Stoke, the beginning of June, 1742.
sent to Fav[onius]: not knowing he was then Dead.

ODE

ON THE DEATH OF A
FAVOURITE CAT,
Drowned in a Tub of Gold Fishes.

'TWAS on a lofty vase's side,
Where China's gayest art had dy'd
　　The azure flowers, that blow;
Demurest of the tabby kind,
The pensive Selima reclin'd,　　　　　　　　　5
　　Gazed on the lake below.

Her conscious tail her joy declar'd;
The fair round face, the snowy beard,
　　The velvet of her paws,
Her coat, that with the tortoise vies,　　　　　10
Her ears of jet, and emerald eyes,
　　She saw; and purr'd applause.

Still had she gaz'd; but 'midst the tide
Two angel forms were seen to glide,
　　The Genii of the stream:　　　　　　　　15
Their scaly armour's Tyrian hue
Thro' richest purple to the view
　　Betray'd a golden gleam.

The hapless Nymph with wonder saw:
A whisker first and then a claw,　　　　　　20
　　With many an ardent wish,

ODE ON THE DEATH OF A FAVOURITE CAT. First published in Dodsley's *Collection*,
1748, ii. 267.
　　Text used: *P*. Texts collated: *B*; *CB*, i. [381]; *M*; holograph letter (*Wh*) to Wharton
(T & W no. 135, 17 Mar. 1747, Brit. Mus. Egerton MS. 2400, f. 20).
　　See also T. C. Duncan Eaves, *PQ*, xxviii (1949), 512–15; xxx (1951), 91–94.

Title: On the Death of Selima, a favourite Cat, who fell into a China-Tub with Gold-
fishes in it, & was drown'd. *CB*; On a favourite Cat, call'd Selima, that . . . [*Remainder
as in CB*]. *Wh.*

4–5 *Lines transposed in Dodsley.*　　　10 Her] The *Dodsley*; *Foulis edition, Glasgow,*
1768.　　　　13 'midst] 'mid *CB*.　　　　14 angel] beauteous *CB*, *Dodsley*, *Foulis.*

She stretch'd in vain to reach the prize.
What female heart can gold despise?
What Cat's averse to fish?

Presumptuous Maid! with looks intent   25
Again she stretch'd, again she bent,
Nor knew the gulf between.
(Malignant Fate sat by, and smil'd)
The slipp'ry verge her feet beguil'd,
She tumbled headlong in.   30

Eight times emerging from the flood
She mew'd to ev'ry watry God,
Some speedy aid to send.
No Dolphin came, no Nereid stirr'd:
Nor cruel *Tom*, nor *Susan* heard.   35
A Fav'rite has no friend!

From hence, ye Beauties, undeceiv'd,
Know, one false step is ne'er retriev'd,
And be with caution bold.
Not all that tempts your wand'ring eyes   40
And heedless hearts, is lawful prize;
Nor all, that glisters, gold.

24 averse to] a foe to *Dodsley.*   25 looks] Eye *CB*; Eyes *Wh.*   35 *Susan*]
Harry *Wh*, *Dodsley.*   36 What fav'rite has a friend! *Dodsley.*   40 tempts]
strikes *CB*, *Wh.*   *At the end of the poem there is written in CB:* 1747. Cambr:

ODE
ON A DISTANT PROSPECT OF
ETON COLLEGE.

YE distant spires, ye antique towers,
That crown the watry glade,
Where grateful Science still adores
Her HENRY's holy Shade;
And ye, that from the stately brow   5
Of WINDSOR's heights th' expanse below
Of grove, of lawn, of mead survey,
Whose turf, whose shade, whose flowers among
Wanders the hoary Thames along
His silver-winding way.   10

Ah happy hills, ah pleasing shade,
Ah fields belov'd in vain,
Where once my careless childhood stray'd,
A stranger yet to pain!
I feel the gales, that from ye blow,   15
A momentary bliss bestow,
As waving fresh their gladsome wing,
My weary soul they seem to sooth[e],
And, redolent of joy and youth,
To breathe a second spring.   20

Say, Father THAMES, for thou hast seen
Full many a sprightly race
Disporting on thy margent green
The paths of pleasure trace,
Who foremost now delight to cleave   25
With pliant arm thy glassy wave?

ODE ON A DISTANT PROSPECT OF ETON COLLEGE. First published anonymously
by Dodsley in 1747, fol. (*D*).
    Text used: *P*. Texts collated: *CB*, i. 278-9, 284; *B*; *D*; *E* (Eton College holograph
MS. given to Wordsworth by Mason's nephew W. Dixon); *M*; *Ode* (1747).

Title: AN ODE ... *D*; Ode. on a distant Prospect of Windsor, & the adjacent Country.
CB; *with the omission of* distant *the same in E. After the title in M and in the margin of
CB, 279, appears the motto from Menander (see expl. notes).*

7 Of Grove & Lawn & Mead survey, *CB*.   22 sprightly] smileing, *CB, E*.   26 arm]
arms *Foulis edition, Glasgow, 1768.*

The captive linnet which enthrall?
What idle progeny succeed
To chase the rolling circle's speed,
Or urge the flying ball?   30

While some on earnest business bent
Their murm'ring labours ply
'Gainst graver hours, that bring constraint
To sweeten liberty:
Some bold adventurers disdain   35
The limits of their little reign,
And unknown regions dare descry:
Still as they run they look behind,
They hear a voice in every wind,
And snatch a fearful joy.   40

Gay hope is theirs by fancy fed,
Less pleasing when possest;
The tear forgot as soon as shed,
The sunshine of the breast:
Theirs buxom health of rosy hue,   45
Wild wit, invention ever-new,
And lively chear of vigour born;
The thoughtless day, the easy night,
The spirits pure, the slumbers light,
That fly th' approach of morn.   50

Alas, regardless of their doom,
The little victims play!
No sense have they of ills to come,
Nor care beyond to-day:
Yet see how all around 'em wait   55
The Ministers of human fate,
And black Misfortune's baleful train!
Ah, shew them where in ambush stand
To seize their prey the murth'rous band!
Ah, tell them, they are men!   60

29 To chase the Hoop's elusive Speed, *CB. See* Agrippina, *l. 194.*   55 'em]
them *E, Foulis.*   59 murth'rous] griesly *underlined,* murtherous *underlined in
margin, CB.*   60 them] 'em *CB, E, Foulis.*

These shall the fury Passions tear,
The vultur[e]s of the mind,
Disdainful Anger, pallid Fear,
And Shame that sculks behind;
Or pineing Love shall waste their youth, 65
Or Jealousy with rankling tooth,
That inly gnaws the secret heart,
And Envy wan, and faded Care,
Grim-visag'd comfortless Despair,
And Sorrow's piercing dart. 70

Ambition this shall tempt to rise,
Then whirl the wretch from high,
To bitter Scorn a sacrifice,
And grinning Infamy.
The stings of Falshood those shall try, 75
And hard Unkindness' alter'd eye,
That mocks the tear it forc'd to flow;
And keen Remorse with blood defil'd,
And moody Madness laughing wild
Amid severest woe. 80

Lo, in the vale of years beneath
A griesly troop are seen,
The painful family of Death,
More hideous than their Queen:
This racks the joints, this fires the veins, 85
That every labouring sinew strains,
Those in the deeper vitals rage:
Lo, Poverty, to fill the band,
That numbs the soul with icy hand,
And slow-consuming Age. 90

To each his suff'rings: all are men,
Condemn'd alike to groan,
The tender for another's pain;
Th' unfeeling for his own.
Yet ah! why should they know their fate? 95
Since sorrow never comes too late,
And happiness too swiftly flies.

71 this] That *CB, E, Foulis.*   75 those] These *CB.*   95 fate?] fate, *CB.*
97 flies.] flies? *CB.*

Thought would destroy their paradise.
No more; where ignorance is bliss,
'Tis folly to be wise.   100

ODE,
TO
ADVERSITY.

DAUGHTER of JOVE, relentless Power,
Thou Tamer of the human breast,
Whose iron scourge and tort'ring hour,
The Bad affright, afflict the Best!
Bound in thy adamantine chain   5
The Proud are taught to taste of pain,
And purple Tyrants vainly groan
With pangs unfelt before, unpitied and alone.

When first thy Sire to send on earth
Virtue, his darling Child, design'd,   10
To thee he gave the heav'nly Birth,
And bad[e] to form her infant mind.
Stern rugged Nurse! thy rigid lore
With patience many a year she bore:

At the end of the poem in CB is written at Stoke, Aug: 1742.

ODE, TO ADVERSITY. First published in *B*. Save for the title, the text used here is *P*.
   Texts collated: *B*; *CB*, i. 284–5; *M*; letter to Walpole (*Wal*), 8 Sept. 1751 (T & W
no. 161, Pembroke College MS. L.C. 2. 123, no. 52). A large *X* is drawn across the entire
poem in *Wal*.

Title: Hymn to Adversity *in B, Wal, and even P, although in his letter to Dodsley (T & W
no. 465, c. 1 Feb. 1768) Gray directed that it should be* Ode .... *Foulis (Glasgow, 1768).*
CB, and M read Ode. *In the margin of CB (p. 284) and after the title in P and M appears
the motto*

—Ζῆνα . . .
τὸν φρονεῖν βροτοὺς ὁδώ-
σαντα, τῷ [τὸν] πάθει μαθάν [μάθος]
Θέντα κυρίως ἔχειν.

[Zeus . . . who put mortals in the way of learning wisdom, who has fixed it as a law that
wisdom comes through suffering.—Aeschylus, *Agamemnon*, 173, 176–8]. *In CB a
second motto is added (as in Foulis, which has the misprint* ΣΤΕΝΟΥ):

— Ξυμφέρει
Σωφρονεῖν ὑπὸ στένει.

[It is profitable to learn wisdom through suffering.—Aeschylus, *Eumenid.*, 523].
8 unpitied and alone] & Misery not their own (*del*) *CB*.

What sorrow was, thou bad'st her know,   15
And from her own she learn'd to melt at others' woe.

Scared at thy frown terrific, fly
Self-pleasing Folly's idle brood,
Wild Laughter, Noise, and thoughtless Joy,
And leave us leisure to be good.   20
Light they disperse, and with them go
The summer Friend, the flatt'ring Foe;
By vain Prosperity received,
To her they vow their truth, and are again believed.

Wisdom in sable garb array'd   25
Immers'd in rapt'rous thought profound,
And Melancholy, silent maid
With leaden eye, that loves the ground,
Still on thy solemn steps attend:
Warm Charity, the gen'ral Friend,   30
With Justice to herself severe,
And Pity, dropping soft the sadly-pleasing tear.

Oh, gently on thy Suppliant's head,
Dread Goddess, lay thy chast'ning hand!
Not in thy Gorgon terrors clad,   35
Nor circled with the vengeful Band
(As by the Impious thou art seen)
With thund'ring voice, and threat'ning mien,
With screaming Horror's funeral cry,
Despair, and fell Disease, and ghastly Poverty.   40

Thy form benign, oh Goddess, wear,
Thy milder influence impart,
Thy philosophic Train be there
To soften, not to wound my heart,
The gen'rous spark extinct revive,   45
Teach me to love and to forgive,
Exact my own defects to scan,
What others are, to feel, and know myself a Man.

32 *Written in margin of CB appears* ἁ γλυκυδακρὺς [she who causes sweet tears]. *See
explanatory notes.* 42 Thy milder Influence deign to impart *CB, a variant which
avoids the present unnatural stress on the last syllable of* Influence. *At the end of the
poem there appears in CB:* at Stoke. Aug: 1742.

ADVERTISEMENT.

When the Author first published this and the following Ode, he was advised, even by his Friends, to
subjoin some few explanatory Notes: but had too
much respect for the understanding of his Readers
to take that liberty.

THE
PROGRESS of POESY.
A PINDARIC ODE.

I. i.

[Strophe 1.]

AWAKE, Æolian lyre, awake,
And give to rapture all thy trembling strings.
From Helicon's harmonious springs
A thousand rills their mazy progress take:
The laughing flowers, that round them blow,   5
Drink life and fragrance as they flow.
Now the rich stream of music winds along
Deep, majestic, smooth, and strong,

THE PROGRESS OF POESY. First published by Walpole, Strawberry Hill, 1757.
Advertisement and notes added in 1768. The text followed here is *P* with the exception
of headings in brackets (*Strophe, Antistrophe, Epode*), which follow the autograph MSS.
(*CB, Wh, Bed*).

    Texts collated: *CB*, ii. 727–8; *M*; *Odes* (printed by Walpole at Strawberry Hill, 1757,
here indicated by *O*); Letter to Wharton (T & W no. 194), 26 Dec. 1754 (*Wh*), Brit.
Mus. Egerton MS. 2400, ff. 67–68ᵛ; Letter to Bedingfield (ll. 1–24), 29 Dec. 1756
(T & W no. 231), Huntington Library MS. 21913 (*Bed*).

    Title: Ode. in the Greek manner. *CB, Wh. In P the poem is preceded by the motto:*
        φωνᾶντα συνετοῖσιν· ἐς
        Δὲ τὸ πᾶν ἑρμηνέων χατίζει.
[*For translation see explanatory notes.*] The Powers of Poetry (*the title given in the
Receipt to Dodsley, 29 June 1757, T & W no. 243, n. 1*).

1 Awake my Lyre, my Glory, wake, *CB with present reading in margin.*   2 rapture]
transport *CB, Wh.*   strings.] strings! *CB, Wh.*

Thro' verdant vales, and Ceres' golden reign:
Now rowling down the steep amain,   10
Headlong, impetuous, see it pour:
The rocks, and nodding groves rebellow to the roar.

I. 2.
[Antistrophe 1.]

Oh! Sovereign of the willing soul,
Parent of sweet and solemn-breathing airs,
Enchanting shell! the sullen Cares,   15
And frantic Passions hear thy soft controul.
On Thracia's hills the Lord of War,
Has curb'd the fury of his car,
And drop'd his thirsty lance at thy command.
Perching on the scept'red hand   20
Of Jove, thy magic lulls the feather'd king
With ruffled plumes, and flagging wing:
Quench'd in dark clouds of slumber lie
The terror of his beak, and light'nings of his eye.

I. 3.
[Epode 1.]

Thee the voice, the dance, obey,   25
Temper'd to thy warbled lay.
O'er Idalia's velvet-green
The rosy-crowned Loves are seen
On Cytherea's day
With antic Sports, and blue-eyed Pleasures,   30
Frisking light in frolic measures;
Now pursuing, now retreating,
Now in circling troops they meet:
To brisk notes in cadence beating
Glance their many-twinkling feet.   35
Slow melting strains their Queen's approach declare:
Where'er she turns the Graces homage pay.

10 rowling] rushing *Bed.*   11 Headlong, impetuous,] With torrent-rapture *CB*,
Wh; Impetuous, headlong, *Bed.*   12 The rocks,] While rocks *Bed.*   23 dark]
black *CB*, *Wh*, *Bed.*   34 in] the *CB*, *Wh.*

With arms sublime, that float upon the air,
In gliding state she wins her easy way:
O'er her warm cheek, and rising bosom, move   40
The bloom of young Desire, and purple light of Love.

II. 1.

[Strophe 2.]

Man's feeble race what Ills await,
Labour, and Penury, the racks of Pain,
Disease, and Sorrow's weeping train,
And Death, sad refuge from the storms of Fate!   45
The fond complaint, my Song, disprove,
And justify the laws of Jove.
Say, has he giv'n in vain the heav'nly Muse?
Night, and all her sickly dews,
Her Spectres wan, and Birds of boding cry,   50
He gives to range the dreary sky:
Till down the eastern cliffs afar
Hyperion's march they spy, and glitt'ring shafts of war.

II. 2.

[Antistrophe 2.]

In climes beyond the solar road,
Where shaggy forms o'er ice-built mountains roam,   55
The Muse has broke the twilight-gloom
To chear the shiv'ring Native's dull abode.
And oft, beneath the od'rous shade
Of Chili's boundless forests laid,

42 await,] await? *CB.*   45 Fate!] Fate? *Wh.*
52–53   Till o'er the eastern cliffs from far
                Hyperion hurls around his glittering shafts of war.
The above is underlined and crossed out in CB and in the margin is written
                Till fierce Hyperion from afar
                Hurls *at their flying* rear his glitt'ring shafts of war.
                     on   scatter'd.
                                shadowy.
In Wh the lines read
                Till fierce Hyperion from afar
                Pours on their scatter'd rear his glitt'ring shafts of war.
57 shiv'ring] buried *but* shivering *in margin, both underlined, CB;* shivering *Wh, M.*
dull] chill *but* dull *in margin, both underlined, CB.*

She deigns to hear the savage Youth repeat 60
In loose numbers wildly sweet
Their feather-cinctured Chiefs, and dusky Loves.
Her track, where'er the Goddess roves,
Glory pursue, and generous Shame,
Th' unconquerable Mind, and Freedom's holy flame. 65

II. 3.
[Epode 2.]

Woods, that wave o'er Delphi's steep,
Isles, that crown th' Egæan deep,
Fields, that cool Ilissus laves,
Or where Mæander's amber waves
In lingering Lab'rinths creep, 70
How do your tuneful Echoes languish,
Mute, but to the voice of Anguish?
Where each old poetic Mountain
Inspiration breath'd around:
Ev'ry shade and hallow'd Fountain 75
Murmur'd deep a solemn sound:
Till the sad Nine in Greece's evil hour
Left their Parnassus for the Latian plains.
Alike they scorn the pomp of tyrant-Power,
And coward Vice, that revels in her chains. 80
When Latium had her lofty spirit lost,
They sought, oh Albion! next thy sea-encircled coast.

III. 1.
[Strophe 3.]

Far from the sun and summer-gale,
In thy green lap was Nature's Darling laid,
What time, where lucid Avon stray'd, 85
To Him the mighty Mother did unveil
Her aweful face: The dauntless Child
Stretch'd forth his little arms, and smiled.

69 Or] And *CB.*   71 Echoes] Echo's *O, P. Noted by Gray in letter to Walpole,
10 Aug. 1757 (T & W no. 243), but still uncorrected in P.*   76 deep a solemn sound:]
a celestial sound: *with present reading in margin, both underlined, CB.*

This pencil take (she said) whose colours clear
Richly paint the vernal year: 90
Thine too these golden keys, immortal Boy!
This can unlock the gates of Joy;
Of Horrour that, and thrilling Fears,
Or ope the sacred source of sympathetic Tears.

III. 2.
[Antistrophe 3.]

Nor second He, that rode sublime 95
Upon the seraph-wings of Extasy,
The secrets of th' Abyss to spy.
He pass'd the flaming bounds of Place and Time:
The living Throne, the saphire-blaze,
Where Angels tremble, while they gaze, 100
He saw; but blasted with excess of light,
Closed his eyes in endless night.
Behold, where Dryden's less presumptuous car,
Wide o'er the fields of Glory bear
Two Coursers of ethereal race, 105
With necks in thunder cloath'd, and long-resounding pace.

III. 3.
[Epode 3.]

Hark, his hands the lyre explore!
Bright-eyed Fancy hovering o'er
Scatters from her pictur'd urn
Thoughts, that breath[e], and words, that burn. 110
But ah! 'tis heard no more—
Oh! Lyre divine, what daring Spirit
Wakes thee now? tho' he inherit
Nor the pride, nor ample pinion,
That the Theban Eagle bear 115
Sailing with supreme dominion
Thro' the azure deep of air:

89–94 *Preceded by double and single quotation marks respectively in CB and Wh.*
93 Horrour] Terror *Wh and, underlined, in margin of CB.* 108 Bright-eyed] Full-
plumed *CB, Wh.*

Yet oft before his infant eyes would run
Such forms, as glitter in the Muse's ray
With orient hues, unborrow'd of the Sun: 120
Yet shall he mount, and keep his distant way
Beyond the limits of a vulgar fate,
Beneath the Good how far—but far above the Great.

118–22   Yet, when they first were open'd on the day,
                 Before his visionary eyes would run
                 Such Forms, as glitter in the Muse's ray
                 With orient hues unborrow'd of the sun:
                 Yet never can he fear a vulgar fate
CB with the present version written below. Shapes, *underlined, is written in margin beside*
l. 119 to replace Forms, *underlined. At the end of the poem in CB appears* Finish'd in
1754. printed together with the Bard, an Ode. Aug: 8. 1757.

ADVERTISEMENT.

The following Ode is founded on a Tradition
current in Wales, that EDWARD THE FIRST, when
he compleated the Conquest of that country,
ordered all the Bards, that fell into his hands, to
be put to death.

THE
BARD.
A PINDARIC ODE.

I. 1.

[Strophe 1.]

'RUIN seize thee, ruthless King!
'Confusion on thy banners wait,
'Tho' fann'd by Conquest's crimson wing
'They mock the air with idle state.
'Helm, nor Hauberk's twisted mail,   5
'Nor even thy virtues, Tyrant, shall avail
'To save thy secret soul from nightly fears,
'From Cambria's curse, from Cambria's tears!'
Such were the sounds, that o'er the crested pride
Of the first Edward scatter'd wild dismay,   10

THE BARD. First published by Walpole at Strawberry Hill, 1757 (*O*). The text followed
here is *P*, although the designations *Strophe*, *Antistrophe*, &c., for which the MSS.
show a preference, have been added in brackets and the capitalization of l. 62 has been
corrected. The only explanatory notes in *O* were variants of those printed below to
ll. 77, 99, 121. The note to l. 110 read merely: 'Accession of the line of Tudor.'

Texts collated: *M*; *Odes*, Strawberry Hill, 1757 (*O*); letters to Wharton (T & W
no. 205), 21 Aug. 1755 (*Wh-1*); Wharton (T & W no. 205A), Brit. Mus. Egerton MS.
2400, ff. 75–76—ll. 57–144 (*Wh-2*); Bedingfield (T & W no. 222), Huntington Library
MS. HM 21917, 27 Aug. 1756—ll. 23–56 (*Bed*); Mason (T & W no. 238), 24 or 31 May
1757 (*Ma-1*); Mason (T & W no. 239), 11 June 1757 (*Ma-2*).

Advertisement. The following Ode] This Ode *M*.
Title: ODE / VI. / THE / BARD. / PINDARIC. *M*.
6 even] e'en *M*.

As down the steep of Snowdon's shaggy side
He wound with toilsome march his long array.
Stout Glo'ster stood aghast in speechless trance:
To arms! cried Mortimer, and couch'd his quiv'ring lance.

I. 2.
[Antistrophe 1.]

On a rock, whose haughty brow   15
Frowns o'er old Conway's foaming flood,
Robed in the sable garb of woe,
With haggard eyes the Poet stood;
(Loose his beard, and hoary hair
Stream'd, like a meteor, to the troubled air)   20
And with a Master's hand, and Prophet's fire,
Struck the deep sorrows of his lyre.
'Hark, how each giant-oak, and desert cave,
'Sighs to the torrent's aweful voice beneath!
'O'er thee, oh King! their hundred arms they wave,   25
'Revenge on thee in hoarser murmurs breath[e];
'Vocal no more, since Cambria's fatal day,
'To high-born Hoël's harp, or soft Llewellyn's lay.

I. 3.
[Epode 1.]

'Cold is Cadwallo's tongue,
'That hush'd the stormy main: 30
'Brave Urien sleeps upon his craggy bed:
'Mountains, ye mourn in vain
'Modred, whose magic song
'Made huge Plinlimmon bow his cloud-top'd head.
'On dreary Arvon's shore they lie,   35
'Smear'd with gore, and ghastly pale:
'Far, far aloof th' affrighted ravens sail;

17–18   With fury pale, & pale with woe,
               Secure of fate, the Poet stood &c:
*Wh-1. Gray agreed to this revision but it does not appear in the later versions. Secure is
used here in the sense of the Latin* securus—*i.e. 'fearless'.*
28 Hoël's. *The " is omitted in P.*   29 Cadwallo's] Caswallo's *Bed.*   30 stormy]
roaring *Bed.*   31 Brave] Great *Bed.*

'The famish'd Eagle screams, and passes by.
'Dear lost companions of my tuneful art,
'Dear, as the light that visits these sad eyes,   40
'Dear, as the ruddy drops that warm my heart,
'Ye died amidst your dying country's cries—
'No more I weep. They do not sleep.
'On yonder cliffs, a griesly band,
'I see them sit, they linger yet,   45
'Avengers of their native land:
'With me in dreadful harmony they join,
'And weave with bloody hands the tissue of thy line.'

II. 1.

[Strophe 2.]

"Weave the warp, and weave the woof,
"The winding-sheet of Edward's race.   50
"Give ample room, and verge enough
"The characters of hell to trace.
"Mark the year, and mark the night,
"When Severn shall re-eccho with affright
"The shrieks of death, thro' Berkley's roofs that ring,   55
"Shrieks of an agonizing King!
"She-Wolf of France, with unrelenting fangs,
"That tear'st the bowels of thy mangled Mate,
"From thee be born, who o'er thy country hangs
"The scourge of Heav'n. What Terrors round him wait!   60
"Amazement in his van, with Flight combined,
"And Sorrow's faded form, and Solitude behind.

II. 2.

[Antistrophe 2.]

"Mighty Victor, mighty Lord,
"Low on his funeral couch he lies!
"No pitying heart, no eye, afford   65
"A tear to grace his obsequies.

43 They] ye *Bed.*   62 Sorrow's . . . Solitude] sorrow's . . . solitude *O, P, but
in a letter to Walpole (T & W no. 243, 10 Aug. 1757) Gray stated his preference for
capitals.*   63 Victor] Conqueror (*del*) *Wh-2.*   64 his] the (*del*) *Wh-2.*   65 No...,
no] What . . ., what (*del*) *Wh-2.*   66 obsequies.] obsequies? *Wh-2.*

"Is the sable Warriour fled?
"Thy son is gone. He rests among the Dead.
"The Swarm, that in thy noon-tide beam were born?
"Gone to salute the rising Morn.   70
"Fair laughs the Morn, and soft the Zephyr blows,
"While proudly riding o'er the azure realm
"In gallant trim the gilded Vessel goes;
"Youth on the prow, and Pleasure at the helm;
"Regardless of the sweeping Whirlwind's sway,   75
"That, hush'd in grim repose, expects his evening-prey.

II. 3.
[Epode 2.]

"Fill high the sparkling bowl,
"The rich repast prepare,
"Reft of a crown, he yet may share the feast:
"Close by the regal chair   80
"Fell Thirst and Famine scowl
"A baleful smile upon their baffled Guest.
"Heard ye the din of battle bray,
"Lance to lance, and horse to horse?
"Long Years of havock urge their destined course,   85
"And thro' the kindred squadrons mow their way.
"Ye Towers of Julius, London's lasting shame,
"With many a foul and midnight murther fed,
"Revere his Consort's faith, his Father's fame,
"And spare the meek Usurper's holy head.   90
"Above, below, the rose of snow,
"Twined with her blushing foe, we spread:

69 in thy noon-tide beam were born] hover'd in thy noontide ray (*del*) *Wh-2*.
70 Morn] day (*del*) *Wh-2*.
71–76   Mirrors of Saxon truth & loyalty,
               Your helpless old expiring Master view
               They hear not. scarce Religion dares supply
               Her mutter'd Requiems, & her holy Dew.
               Yet thou, proud Boy, from Pomfret's walls shalt send
               A sigh, & envy oft thy happy Grandsire's end.
These lines are crossed out and present reading with in *for* on (*l.* 74) *appears on back of Wh-2*.
82 baleful smile upon] smile of horror on *Wh-2*.   84 horse?] horse! *Wh-2*.
87 Ye] Grim (*del*) *Wh-2*.   88 murther] murder *M*.   90 holy] hallow'd *Wh-2*.

"The bristled Boar in infant-gore
"Wallows beneath the thorny shade.
"Now, Brothers, bending o'er th' accursed loom   95
"Stamp we our vengeance deep, and ratify his doom.

III. 1.
[Strophe 3.]

"Edward, lo! to sudden fate
"(Weave we the woof. The thread is spun)
"Half of thy heart we consecrate.
"(The web is wove. The work is done.)"   100
'Stay, oh stay! nor thus forlorn
'Leave me unbless'd, unpitied, here to mourn:
'In yon bright track, that fires the western skies,
'They melt, they vanish from my eyes.
'But oh! what solemn scenes on Snowdon's height   105
'Descending slow their glitt'ring skirts unroll?
'Visions of glory, spare my aching sight,
'Ye unborn Ages, crowd not on my soul!
'No more our long-lost Arthur we bewail.
'All-hail, ye genuine Kings, Britannia's Issue, hail!   110

III. 2.
[Antistrophe 3.]

'Girt with many a Baron bold
'Sublime their starry fronts they rear;
'And gorgeous Dames, and Statesmen old
'In bearded majesty, appear.

101 thus] here (*del*) *Wh-2*.   102 'Leave your despairing Caradoc to mourn! (*del*)
Wh-2.   103 track] clouds (*del*) *Wh-2*.   104 melt] sink (*del*) *Wh-2*.   105 'But
ah! what scenes of heav'n on Snowdon's height *Wh-2 with* of heav'n *del and* solemn
written above scenes.   106 glitt'ring skirts unroll?] golden skirts unroll! *with* golden
del Wh-2.
109–10   From Cambria's thousand hills a thousand strains
          Triumphant tell aloud, another Arthur reigns. (*del*) *Wh-2*.
111 Youthful Knights & Barons bold (*del*) *Wh-2*; Haughty Knights, & Barons bold
Ma-1.   112 With dazzling helm & horrent spear *Ma-1*, (*del*) *Wh-2*.   114 'In]
Of *Ma-1*. *In Ma-2 Gray explains,* 'In bearded majesty *was alter'd to* of, *only because
the next line begins with* In *the midst &c:*' *The revision does not appear in other texts.*

'In the midst a Form divine! 115
'Her eye proclaims her of the Briton-Line;
'Her lyon-port, her awe-commanding face,
'Attemper'd sweet to virgin-grace.
'What strings symphonious tremble in the air,
'What strains of vocal transport round her play! 120
'Hear from the grave, great Taliessin, hear;
'They breathe a soul to animate thy clay.
'Bright Rapture calls, and soaring, as she sings,
'Waves in the eye of Heav'n her many-colour'd wings.

III. 3.

[Epode 3.]

'The verse adorn again 125
'Fierce War, and faithful Love,
'And Truth severe, by fairy Fiction drest.
'In buskin'd measures move
'Pale Grief, and pleasing Pain,
'With Horrour, Tyrant of the throbbing breast. 130
'A Voice, as of the Cherub-Choir,
'Gales from blooming Eden bear;
'And distant warblings lessen on my ear,
'That lost in long futurity expire.
'Fond impious Man, think'st thou, yon sanguine cloud, 135
'Rais'd by thy breath, has quench'd the Orb of day?
'To-morrow he repairs the golden flood,
'And warms the nations with redoubled ray.
'Enough for me: With joy I see

116 of the Briton-Line;] born of Arthur's line, *Ma-1.* 117 Her . . ., her] A . . .,
an (*del*) *Wh-2.* 119 air,] air! *Wh-2*; air? *Ma-1.* 120 play!] play? *Ma-1.*
123 calls] wakes *Ma-1.* 125 *In Ma-2 Gray wrote,* 'I understand what you mean
about the *Verse* adorn again, but do not think it signifies much, for there is no mistaking
the sense, when one attends to it.' *T & W* (*no. 239, n. 3*) *add*: 'After "adorn again" Gray
originally wrote, and afterwards scored through: "you may read
                    Fierce War and faithful Love
                    Resume their".'
128 buskin'd] mystic *Ma-1.* 130 Tyrant of] that chills *Ma-1.* *In Ma-2 Gray
wrote,* '*That chills the throbbing* &c: I dislike, as much as you can do.'

'The different doom our Fates assign.   140
'Be thine Despair, and scept'red Care,
'To triumph, and to die, are mine.'
He spoke, and headlong from the mountain's height
Deep in the roaring tide he plung'd to endless night.

142 *In Ma-2 Gray wrote,* '. . . both somehow dislike the conclusion of the Bard, &
mutter something about Antithesis & Conceit in *To triumph, to die,* wch I do not com-
prehend, & am sure, it is alterd for the better. it was before
                    Lo! to be free, to die, are mine.
if you like it better so, so let it be. it is more abrupt, & perhaps may mark the action
better. or it may be, *Lo! Liberty & Death are mine,* w^chever you please.'   144 plung'd]
sunk *Wh-2, Ma-1. In n. 7 to Wh-2 T & W comment that in his copy of O Walpole wrote,*
'In the original this word was *sunk* but Mr Garrick suggested *plung'd* as a more emphatic
word on such an occasion.'

THE FATAL SISTERS,
THE DESCENT OF ODIN,
THE TRIUMPHS OF OWEN

The following three poems are Gray's renderings of Latin translations of Old Norse and Welsh poems. Although he copied the original as well as the Latin translation of *The Fatal Sisters*, for example, into *CB*, his limited knowledge of the original languages apparently led him to rely primarily on the Latin translations, since he has reproduced errors found in the Latin (see individual notes below). For the Scandinavian poems, he drew most of his data from the *Orcades* of Thormodus Torfaeus and from Thomas Bartholinus, *Antiquitatum Danicarum de causis contemptae . . . mortis* (Copenhagen, 1689). Mason reprints in his notes (ii. 99–102) the Latin translation used by Gray (see explanatory notes).

Gray told Beattie (T & W no. 466), 1 Feb. 1768, that the three poems were to be published in the 1768 editions 'to make up (in bulk) for the omission' of the *Long Story*.

ADVERTISEMENT.

The Author once had thoughts (in concert with a Friend) of giving *the History of English Poetry*: In the Introduction to it he meant to have produced some specimens of the Style that reigned in ancient times among the neighbouring nations, or those who had subdued the greater part of this Island, and were our Progenitors: the following three Imitations made a part of them. He has long since drop'd his design, especially after he had heard, that it was already in the hands of a Person well qualified to do it justice, both by his taste, and his researches into antiquity.

Preface.

In the eleventh century *Sigurd*, Earl of the Orkney-islands, went with a fleet of ships & a considerable body of troops into Ireland to the assistance of *Sictryg with the silken beard*, who was then making war on his Father-in-Law *Brian*, King of Dublin: the Earl & all his forces were cut to pieces, & *Sictryg* was in danger of a total defeat, but the Enemy had a greater loss by the death of *Brian*, their King, who fell in the action. on Christmas-day (the day of the battle) a Native of *Caithness* in Scotland saw at a distance a number of Persons on horseback riding full speed towards a hill, & seeming to enter into it. curiosity led him to follow them, till looking thro' an opening in the rocks he saw twelve gigantic figures resembling Women: they were all employ'd about a loom; & as they wove,

Preface. An earlier draft, very similar in phrasing, is in CB, iii. 1041 ff. Only the more important deviations are listed here:

12 ... employ'd about a loom; ...] they were all employ'd about a loom: the threads, that formed the texture, were the entrails of Men, the shuttles were so many swords, the weights were human heads, the warp was all of bloody spears. as they wove, they sung the following magic song. *Then appear four lines of the Norse original, a Latin translation, and several notes, the most important of which reads*: The People of these Islands were Christians, yet did not become so till after A:D: 966. probably it happen'd in 995. but tho' they & the other Gothic Nations no longer worship'd their Old

they sung the following dreadful song, wch when they had finish'd, they tore the web into twelve pieces, & (each taking her portion) gallop'd six to the north & as many to the south.

Divinities, yet they never doubted of their existence, or forgot their ancient mythology, as appears from the History of Olaus Tryggueson. (See Bartholin: L. 3. cii. pag: 615.) *Note. A similar note appears in CB, iii. 1044, but with this additional information:* Gunna, Gondula, & Hilda, are the names of three such divinities mention'd in the Edda (Gunnr, Gaundol, Hilldr). there were also Skaugol, Geirskaugol, Skulld, Sigrun, & others. they are often described as spinning, or flying thro' the air, dress'd in the skin of a swan: some of them were married to mortal Men, (as Svanhvitr, Aulrunr, & Alvitrar) with whom they cohabited for a few years. they also are call'd *Disir* (see Bartholin, L: 3. cap: i, & L: 2. cap: ii) [.] there were a great number more of these Valkyriur, as Hrist, Mist, Skeggiold, Thrudr, Hlokk, Herfiotur, Gaull, Geira, Hod, Ranngrid, Radgrid, Reginleif, &c: whose office it was to serve the departed Heroes with horns of Mead & Ale.

Valhalla] *Valkalla M, P (Dodsley evidently misread Gray's hand here, a natural error since this is supposedly the first use of the word in English). See Gray's explanatory note beginning 'The Valkyriur . . .'.*

[THE
FATAL SISTERS.]

Ode (from the *Norse*-tongue) in the *Orcades*
of Thormodus Torfæus. Hafniæ. 1697. Fol:
& also in Bartholinus.

Vitt er orpit fyrir valfalli &c:
[Wide is flung before the fall of the slain]

Now the storm begins to lower,
(Haste, the loom of hell prepare)
Iron-sleet of arrowy shower
Hurtles in the darken'd air.

Glitt'ring lances are the loom,   5
Where the dusky warp we strain,
Weaving many a Soldier's doom,
Orkney's woe, & *Randver*'s bane.

See the griesly texture grow,
('Tis of human entrails made)   10
And the weights, that play below
Each a gasping Warriour's head.

Shafts for shuttles, dipt in gore,
Shoot the trembling cords along.
Sword, that once a Monarch bore,   15
Keep the tissue close & strong!
   Mista black, terrific Maid,
Sangrida, & *Hilda* see

THE FATAL SISTERS. First published in *P*. The text used here is the MS. sent by Gray
to Dodsley, his publisher, who followed it fairly closely in *P*, *c*. 1 Feb. 1768 (T & W
no. 465), 'Autograph Directions', Brit. Mus. Add. MS. 38511, ff. 5–6 (*D*).

   Texts collated: *CB*, iii. 1041–3, 1067–8; *M*; *P*; *Wh* (transcript by Wharton, Brit.
Mus. Egerton MS. 2400, ff. 228, 228a, 229). The text followed in the 'Advertisement'
is *P*.

Title: THE / FATAL SISTERS. / AN ODE. *P*; ODE / VIII. / THE FATAL SISTERS. /
FROM THE NORSE TONGUE. *M*; The Song of the Valkyries. *CB*; The Song of the weird
Sisters translated from the Norwegian written about 1029. *Wh*.
15 Sword] Blade *Wh*.
17–18   Sangrida, terrific Maid,
                   Mista black, and Hilda see *Wh*.

Join the weyward work to aid:
'Tis the woof of victory.   20
 E'er the ruddy sun be set,
Pikes must shiver, javelins sing,
Blade with clattering buckler meet,
Hauberk crash, & helmet ring.
 (Weave the crimson web of war)   25
Let us go, & let us fly,
Where our Friends the conflict share,
Where they triumph, where they die.
 As the paths of fate we tread,
Wading thro' th' ensanguined field: 30
Gondula, & *Geira*, spread
O'er the youthful King your shield.
 We the reins to slaughter give,
Ours to kill, & ours to spare:
Spite of danger he shall live.   35
(Weave the crimson web of war)
 They, whom once the desart-beach
Pent within its bleak domain,
Soon their ample sway shall stretch
O'er the plenty of the plain.   40
 Low the dauntless Earl is laid,
Gor'd with many a gaping wound;
Fate demands a nobler head,
Soon a King shall bite the ground:
 Long his loss shall Eirin weep,   45
Ne'er again his likeness see,
Long her strains in sorrow steep,
Strains of immortality!
 Horror covers all the heath,
Clouds of carnage blot the sun.   50
Sisters, weave the web of death,
Sisters, cease. the work is done.
 Hail the task, & hail the hands!
Songs of joy & triumph sing,

23 Blade] Sword *Wh.*   28 triumph] triumph *del with* conquer *above it*, *CB*.
die.] die *D.*   31 Gunna & Gondula, spread *CB*, *Wh.*   33 slaughter] havock
CB.   38 its] it's *CB*, *D.*   44 shall] must *CB*, *Wh.*   45 his] her *CB*.
50 blot] veil *Wh.*

Joy to the victorious bands; 55
Triumph to the younger King.
    Mortal, thou that hear'st the tale,
Learn the tenour of our song.
Scotland, thro' each winding vale
Far & wide the notes prolong. 60
    Sisters, hence with spurs of speed:
Each her thundering faulchion wield,
Each bestride her sable steed.
Hurry, hurry to the field.

59 winding] ecchoing *Wh.*
        61–63 Sisters, hence! 'tis time to ride:
            Now your thund'ring faulchions wield,
            Now your sable steeds bestride,
CB, Wh, but faulchion *(l. 62) and* steed *(l. 63) in Wh.*   *In CB 1761 | is written at the end of the poem.*

[THE DESCENT OF ODIN.]

Ode (from the Norse-tongue) in Bartholinus,
de causis contemnendæ [*sic*] mortis. Hafniæ.
1689. 4to.

Upreis Odinn allda gautr &c:
[Upp reis Óðinn alda gautr
Up rose Odin creator of all]

Uprose the King of Men with speed,
And saddled strait his coal-black steed:
Down the yawning steep he rode
That leads to Hela's drear abode.
Him the Dog of darkness spied: 5
His shaggy throat he open'd wide,
While from his jaws with carnage fill'd
Foam & human gore distill'd:
Hoarse he bays with hideous din,
Eyes, that glow, & fangs, that grin,   10
And long pursues with fruitless yell
The Father of the powerful spell.
Onward still his way he takes,
(The groaning earth beneath him shakes)
Till full before his fearless eyes   15
The portals nine of hell arise.
  Right against the eastern gate
By the moss-grown pile he sate,
Where long of yore to sleep was laid
The dust of the prophetic Maid.   20
Facing to the northern clime
Thrice he traced the runic rhyme,
Thrice pronounc'd in accents dread
The thrilling verse, that wakes the Dead,

THE DESCENT OF ODIN. First published in *P*. The text followed here is *D* (see textual note to *The Fatal Sisters*). The editors have supplied terminal punctuation to l. 5.

Texts collated: *CB*, iii. 1043, 1069–70; *M*; *P*; *Wh* (Wharton's transcript, Brit. Mus. Egerton MS. 2400, ff. 230–1^v).

Title: THE / DESCENT of ODIN. / AN ODE. *P*; ODE / IX. / . . . / FROM THE NORSE-TONGUE. *M*; The Vegtams Kwitha, from Bartholinus. *Wh*; . . . tongue . . .] . . . tonque . . . *D*.

5 spied:] spied *D*.   11 fruitless] ceaseless *Wh*.   14 shakes] quakes *Wh*.
23 accents] murmurs *Wh*.

Till from out the hollow ground 25
Slowly breath'd a sullen sound.
    Pr: What call unknown, what charms presume
To break the quiet of the tomb?
Who thus afflicts my troubled sprite,
And drags me from the realms of night? 30
Long on these mould'ring bones have beat
The winter's snow, the summer's heat
The drenching dews, & driving rain!
Let me, let me sleep again.
Who is he with voice unblest, 35
That calls me from the bed of rest?
    O: A Traveller to thee unknown
Is he, that calls, a Warriour's Son.
Thou the deeds of light shalt know,
Tell me what is done below, 40
For whom yon glitt'ring board is spread,
Drest for whom yon golden bed.
    Pr: Mantling in the goblet see
The pure bev'rage of the bee,
O'er it hangs the shield of gold; 45
'Tis the drink of *Balder* bold:
Balder's head to death is giv'n.
Pain can reach the Sons of heav'n!
Unwilling I my lips unclose,
Leave me, leave me to repose. 50
    O: Once again my call obey.
Prophetess, arise & say,
What dangers *Odin*'s Child await,
Who the Author of his fate.
    Pr: In *Hoder*'s hand the Heroe's doom: 55
His Brother sends him to the tomb.
Now my weary lips I close.
Leave me, leave me to repose.
    O: Prophetess, my spell obey,
Once again arise & say, 60

27 call] voice *Wh.*   29 my troubled] a weary *Wh.*   35 he] this *Wh.*   41 yon]
the *CB, Wh.*   42 yon] the *Wh.*   47 *Balder*'s] Balder's *D.*   48 reach]
touch *Wh.*   51 Once again] Prophetess *Wh.*   52 Prophetess] Once again *Wh.*
59–60   Once again my call obey,
                Prophetess, arise and say *Wh.*

Who th' Avenger of his guilt,
By whom shall *Hoder*'s blood be spilt.
 Pr: In the caverns of the west
By *Odin*'s fierce embrace comprest
A wond'rous Boy shall *Rinda* bear,   65
Who ne'er shall comb his raven-hair,
Nor wash his visage in the stream,
Nor see the sun's departing beam:
Till he on *Hoder*'s coarse shall smile
Flaming on the fun'ral pile.   70
Now my weary lips I close;
Leave me, leave me to repose.
 O: Yet a while my call obey.
Prophetess, awake & say,
What Virgins these in speechless woe,   75
That bend to earth their solemn brow,
That their flaxen tresses tear,
And snowy veils, that float in air.
Tell me, whence their sorrows rose:
Then I leave thee to repose.   80
 Pr: Ha! no Traveller art thou,
King of Men, I know thee now,
Mightiest of a mighty line—
 O: No boding Maid of skill divine
Art thou, nor Prophetess of good;   85
But Mother of the giant-brood!
 Pr: Hie thee hence & boast at home,
That never shall Enquirer come
To break my iron-sleep again:
Till *Lok* has burst his tenfold chain.   90
Never, till substantial Night
Has reassum'd her ancient right;
Till wrap'd in flames, in ruin hurl'd,
Sinks the fabrick of the world.

61–62 *Lines transposed in Wh.* 64 *Odin*'s] Odin's *D.* 65 wond'rous] giant *Wh.*
69 *Hoder*'s] Hoder's *D.* 74 awake] arise *Wh.* 76 That] Who *Wh.* 77 Who
their flowing tresses tear, *Wh.* 79 Tell me] Say from *Wh.* sorrows] sorrow *CB.*
83 The Mightiest of the mighty line *Wh.* 87 hence &] Odin, *Wh.* 90 has]
have *Wh.* 92 Has reassum'd] Reassumes *Wh.* *At the end of the poem in*
CB is written 1761.

[ADVERTISEMENT.]

Owen succeeded his Father Griffin in the princi-
pality of North-Wales, A:D: 1120. this battle was
fought near forty years afterwards. (from M^r
Evans's Specimens of the Welch poetry. Lond:
1764. 4to)

[THE
TRIUMPHS of OWEN.
A FRAGMENT.]

Owen's praise demands my song,
Owen swift, & Owen strong,
Fairest flower of Roderic's stem,
Gwyneth's shield, & Britain's gem.
He nor heaps his brooded stores,   5
Nor on all profusely pours;
Lord of every regal art,
Liberal hand, & open heart.
  Big with hosts of mighty name
Squadrons three against him came;   10
This the force of Eirin hiding,
Side by side as proudly riding
On her shadow long & gay
Lochlin plows the watry way,
There the Norman sails afar   15
Catch the winds, & join the war:
Black & huge along they sweep,
Burthens of the angry deep.

THE TRIUMPHS OF OWEN. First published in *P*. The text followed here is *D* (see
textual note to *The Fatal Sisters*).
  Texts collated: *CB*, iii. [1064] or [1068] (the pagination is faulty); *M*; *P*.

Title: . . . Fragment from the Welch. *CB, M. The present title is the one Gray gave
Dodsley in T & W no. 465.*

Dauntless on his native sands
The Dragon-Son of Mona stands;   20
In glitt'ring arms & glory drest
High he rears his ruby crest.
There the thund'ring strokes begin,
There the press, & there the din,
Talymalfra's rocky shore   25
Ecchoing to the battle's roar.
[Check'd by the torrent-tide of blood
Backward Meinai rolls his flood:
While heap'd his Master's feet around
Prostrate Warriors gnaw the ground.]   30
Where his glowing eyeballs turn,
Thousand banners round him burn.
Where he points his purple spear,
Hasty, hasty Rout is there,
Marking with indignant eye   35
Fear to stop & shame to fly.
There Confusion, Terror's child,
Conflict fierce, & Ruin wild,
Agony, that pants for breath,
Despair, & honourable Death.   40

23–24 *Transposed in D, but present order indicated by numbers in margin.*   27–30 *Omitted from D and P, but in CB and M; the text is from CB and the location that given in M.*

ELEGY
Written in a Country Church Yard.

THE Curfew tolls the knell of parting day,
The lowing herd wind slowly o'er the lea,
The plowman homeward plods his weary way,
And leaves the world to darkness and to me.

Now fades the glimmering landscape on the sight,   5
And all the air a solemn stillness holds,
Save where the beetle wheels his droning flight,
And drowsy tinklings lull the distant folds;

ELEGY WRITTEN IN A COUNTRY CHURCH YARD. First printed by Dodsley in 1751
(*Q1*). Some of the errors which Gray pointed out were corrected in the third edition
(*Q3*). The eighth quarto (*Q8*) of 1753, according to Dodsley, was corrected by Gray,
although this claim makes it difficult to account for the persistence of one of the most
obvious of the errors (see note to l. 11) which Gray had mentioned in his letter of
3 Mar. 1751 to Walpole (T & W no. 159): see notes to ll. 11, 96, 105. The text followed
here, save where otherwise noted (Gray's explanatory notes to ll. 1, 92, 127 are supplied
from *P*), is the one recommended by Gray to Dodsley, *c.* 1 Feb. 1768 (T & W no. 465)—
B. Dodsley followed *B* closely in *P*. The three extant holograph MSS. are the one at
Eton College (*E*), probably the earliest; the one sent to Wharton (*Wh*) in Gray's letter
of 18 Dec. 1750 (T & W no. 156), Brit. Mus. Egerton MS. 2400, ff. 45–46; and the one
in *CB*, ii. 617–18. Although in his letter to Walpole, 11 Feb. 1751 (T & W no. 157),
Gray had asked that the poem be printed 'without an Interval between the Stanza's
because the Sense is in some Places continued beyond them' (this was done in *Q1*
although the first line of each stanza was indented), he does not seem to have repeated
this request for *B* and *P*; he either had overlooked the issue or had concluded that
closing up the intervals was not necessary or desirable. With some editorial hesitation,
the poem is printed here with the customary intervals.

    Texts collated: *CB*, *E*, *M*, *Q1*, *Q3*, *Q8*, *P*, *Wh*, and *F* (Foulis ed., Glasgow, 1768):
i.e. the holograph MSS., Mason's edition, and the ones in which it seems likely that
Gray may have had a hand. For a detailed bibliographical description and collation of
all the variants in the MSS. and the editions published in Gray's lifetime, see Francis G.
Stokes's edition of the *Elegy* (Oxford: Clarendon Press, 1929) and the edition by Rintaro
Fukuhara and Henry Bergen (Primrose Hill, London: Edward Walters & Geoffrey
Miller, 1933).

Title: Stanza's wrote in a . . . *E*; AN ELEGY WROTE IN A . . . *Q1*; . . . written ORI-
GINALLY in a . . . / . . . Corrected by the AUTHOR. *Q8*.

1 parting *was originally* dying *according to Norton Nicholls* (*see T & W Appendix Z,
p. 1297*), *but changed* 'to *parting* to avoid the *concetto*'.   2 wind] winds *Q1*, *Q3*.
6 all] now *E*.   7 droning] drony *F*.   8 And] Or *CB*, *E*, *Wh*, *Q3*.

Save that from yonder ivy-mantled tow'r
The mopeing owl does to the moon complain   10
Of such, as wand'ring near her secret bow'r,
Molest her ancient solitary reign.

Beneath those rugged elms, that yew-tree's shade,
Where heaves the turf in many a mould'ring heap,
Each in his narrow cell for ever laid,   15
The rude Forefathers of the hamlet sleep.

The breezy call of incense-breathing Morn,
The swallow twitt'ring from the straw-built shed,
The cock's shrill clarion, or the ecchoing horn,
No more shall rouse them from their lowly bed.   20

For them no more the blazing hearth shall burn,
Or busy houswife ply her evening care:
No children run to lisp their sire's return,
Or climb his knees the envied kiss to share.

Oft did the harvest to their sickle yield,   25
Their furrow oft the stubborn glebe has broke;
How jocund did they drive their team afield!
How bow'd the woods beneath their sturdy stroke!

Let not Ambition mock their useful toil,
Their homely joys, and destiny obscure;   30
Nor Grandeur hear with a disdainful smile,
The short and simple annals of the poor.

The boast of heraldry, the pomp of pow'r,
And all that beauty, all that wealth e'er gave,
Awaits alike th' inevitable hour.   35
The paths of glory lead but to the grave.

11 wand'ring] stray too *is written above in E.*   secret] sacred *Q1, Q8* [*an erratum
noted by Gray in T & W no. 159*].   12 Molest her ancient] & pry into *written above
in E.*   16 hamlet] Village (*del*) *E.*   17 For ever sleep. the breezy Call of Morn,
E.   18 The swallow] Or Swallow *E.*   19 The cock's shrill clarion, or the] Or
Chaunticleer so shrill or *E.*   or] & *CB, Wh.*   20 rouse] wake *Q1.*   24 Or]
Nor *CB, E, Wh.*   envied] coming *but* envied *written above and* doubtful? *in margin, E.*
25 sickle] Sickles *Wh.*   27 they] they they [*a misprint*] *Q1.*   29 useful] *underlined with* homely *in margin, E.*   30 homely] rustic *E.*   35 Awaits] Await *M.*
36 paths ... lead] path ... leads *F.*

Nor you, ye Proud, impute to These the fault,
If Mem'ry o'er their Tomb no Trophies raise,
Where thro' the long-drawn isle and fretted vault
The pealing anthem swells the note of praise.   40

Can storied urn or animated bust
Back to its mansion call the fleeting breath?
Can Honour's voice provoke the silent dust,
Or Flatt'ry sooth the dull cold ear of Death?

Perhaps in this neglected spot is laid   45
Some heart once pregnant with celestial fire,
Hands, that the rod of empire might have sway'd,
Or wak'd to extasy the living lyre.

But Knowledge to their eyes her ample page
Rich with the spoils of time did ne'er unroll;   50
Chill Penury repress'd their noble rage,
And froze the genial current of the soul.

Full many a gem of purest ray serene,
The dark unfathom'd caves of ocean bear:
Full many a flower is born to blush unseen,   55
And waste its sweetness on the desert air.

Some village-Hampden, that with dauntless breast
The little Tyrant of his fields withstood;
Some mute inglorious Milton here may rest,
Some Cromwell guiltless of his country's blood.   60

Th' applause of list'ning senates to command,
The threats of pain and ruin to despise,
To scatter plenty o'er a smiling land,
And read their hist'ry in a nation's eyes

37–38   Forgive, ye Proud, th' involuntary Fault
               If Memory to These no Trophies raise,
CB, E, Wh, Q1. The present text is underlined in the margin of CB.   43 provoke]
awake *with* provoke *in margin, E.*   44 Death?] Death! *B.*   47 rod] Reins *CB,
E, Wh, Q1, Q3. CB has* Rod *in the margin.*   49–60 *In E these lines are written in
this order:* 57–60, 49–56, *but the numbers* 1–4 *beside them indicate the present order.*
51 repress'd] had damp'd *with* depress'd repress'd *written above, E.*   57 Hamp-
den] Cato *E.*   58 *In CB* Fields *is written above a deleted word, probably* Lands.
59 Milton] Tully *E.*   60 Cromwell] Caesar *E.*

Their lot forbad: nor circumscrib'd alone   65
Their growing virtues, but their crimes confin'd;
Forbad to wade through slaughter to a throne,
And shut the gates of mercy on mankind,

The struggling pangs of conscious truth to hide,
To quench the blushes of ingenuous shame,   70
Or heap the shrine of Luxury and Pride
With incense kindled at the Muse's flame.

Far from the madding crowd's ignoble strife,
Their sober wishes never learn'd to stray;
Along the cool sequester'd vale of life   75
They kept the noiseless tenor of their way.

Yet ev'n these bones from insult to protect
Some frail memorial still erected nigh,
With uncouth rhimes and shapeless sculpture deck'd,
Implores the passing tribute of a sigh.   80

65 lot] Fate *with* Lot *written above*, E.   66 growing] struggling *with* growing
written above, E.   68 And] Or *CB*, *Wh*.   71 Or heap] And at *with* crown
written above at E.   shrine] Shrines *Wh*.   72 With] Burn (*del*) E.   incense
                                          by
kindled at] Incense hallowd in *with* kindled at *written below*, E.   72 ff. *After l. 72
in E there appear the following lines with an irregular line drawn down the margin beside
them:*

> The thoughtless World to Majesty may bow
> Exalt the brave, & idolize Success
> But more to Innocence their Safety owe
> Than Power & Genius e'er conspired to bless
>
> And thou, who mindful of the unhonour'd Dead
>   eir
> Dost in these Notes thy artless Tale relate
> By Night & lonely Contemplation led
> To linger in the gloomy Walks of Fate
>
> Hark how the sacred Calm, that broods around
> Bids ev'ry fierce tumultuous Passion cease
> In still small Accents whisp'ring from the Ground
> A grateful Earnest of eternal Peace
>
> No more with Reason & thyself at Strife;
> Give anxious Cares & endless Wishes room
> But thro' the cool sequester'd Vale of Life
> Pursue the silent Tenour of thy Doom.

74 learn'd] knew *E.*   76 Noiseless] silent *with* noiseless *written above*, E.   79 With]
Written above a deleted word, perhaps In *E.*   rhimes] Rhime *E.*

Their name, their years, spelt by th' unletter'd muse,
The place of fame and elegy supply:
And many a holy text around she strews,
That teach the rustic moralist to die.

For who to dumb Forgetfulness a prey,   85
This pleasing anxious being e'er resign'd,
Left the warm precincts of the chearful day,
Nor cast one longing ling'ring look behind?

On some fond breast the parting soul relies,
Some pious drops the closing eye requires;   90
Ev'n from the tomb the voice of Nature cries,
Ev'n in our Ashes live their wonted Fires.

For thee, who mindful of th' unhonour'd Dead
Dost in these lines their artless tale relate;
If chance, by lonely contemplation led,   95
Some kindred Spirit shall inquire thy fate,

Haply some hoary-headed Swain may say,
'Oft have we seen him at the peep of dawn
'Brushing with hasty steps the dews away
'To meet the sun upon the upland lawn.   100

82 elegy] Epitaph *CB, E.*   84 die] dye *B.*   90 *In CB l. 90 is mistakenly numbered*
100, *an error which is carried through the rest of the poem.*   92 And buried Ashes glow
with social Fires *E*; Awake, and faithful to her wonted Fires. [*This is the version given
by Gray in his instructions to Walpole* (*T & W no. 157*). *His later comment to Walpole
was* 'I humbly propose, for the benefit of Mr. Dodsley and his matrons, that take *awake*
for a verb, that they should read *asleep*, and all will be right.' (*T & W no. 159*)] *Q1, Q3*;
And in our Ashes glow their . . . *CB, Wh, with* Ev'n *and* live *in margin of CB*; *Wh adds
the note* Even in our ashes live &c: 93–96 *In E there appears only* For Thee,
who mindful &c: as above [*a reference back to the second stanza quoted in the note to
ll. 72 ff.*], *after which is written*:
> If chance that e'er some pensive Spirit more,
> By sympathetic Musings here delay'd,
> With vain, tho' kind, Enquiry shall explore
> Thy once-loved Haunt, this long-deserted Shade.

96 kindred] hidden *Q1* [*a misprint*].   97 may] shall *E.*   99 'Brushing with
hasty steps] With hasty Footsteps brush *E.*   100 On the high Brow of yonder
hanging Lawn *E.*   100 ff. *In E the following lines appear here*:
> Him have we seen the Green-wood Side along,
> While o'er the Heath we hied, our Labours done,
> Oft as the Woodlark piped her farewell Song
> With whistful Eyes pursue the setting Sun.

'There at the foot of yonder nodding beech
'That wreathes its old fantastic roots so high,
'His listless length at noontide wou'd he stretch,
'And pore upon the brook that babbles by.

'Hard by yon wood, now smiling as in scorn,   105
'Mutt'ring his wayward fancies he wou'd rove,
'Now drooping, woeful wan, like one forlorn,
'Or craz'd with care, or cross'd in hopeless love.

'One morn I miss'd him on the custom'd hill,
'Along the heath and near his fav'rite tree;   110
'Another came; nor yet beside the rill,
'Nor up the lawn, nor at the wood was he,

'The next with dirges due in sad array
'Slow thro' the church-way path we saw him born[e].
'Approach and read (for thou can'st read) the lay,   115
'Grav'd on the stone beneath yon aged thorn.'

101 There] Oft *E.*   nodding] hoary *with* spreading *written above and* nodding *in margin,*
E.   105 Hard . . . wood] With Gestures quaint *E.*   smiling] frowning [*a mis-*
print] *Q1.*
                    wayward fancies l̶o̶v̶e̶d̶ would he
106 Mutt'ring his fond Conceits he w̶e̶n̶t̶-̶t̶e̶ rove: *E.*   he would] would he *CB, Wh.*
            drooping,
107 Now woeful wan, h̶e̶-̶d̶r̶o̶o̶p̶'̶d̶, as one forlorn *E.*
109 I] we *E.*   on] from *CB.*   custom'd] accustom'd *E.*
        Along the   near
110 By the Heath-s̶i̶d̶e̶, & at his fav'rite Tree. *E.*   112 f. *After l. 112 is written but*
deleted There scatter'd oft, the earliest *E.*   113 due] meet *E.*   114 thro'] thro
with by *written above, E.*   116 Grav'd] Wrote *with* Graved carved *written above,*
E.   the] his *F.*   yon] that *with* yon *written above, E.*   aged] ancient *E,* ancient
(*del*) *CB*; aged *is the variant preferred by Gray in his instructions* (*T & W no. 157*).
thorn.'] thorn. *B.*   116 f. The EPITAPH. The *is omitted in CB and Wh, and* The
Epitaph *is written in the margin of E.*   116 ff. *At the bottom of the page there*
appears in CB:
                Insert.
                There scatter'd oft, the earliest of the Year,
                By Hands unseen, are Show'rs of Violets found:
                The Red-breast loves to build, & warble there,
                And little Footsteps lightly print the Ground. Omitted in 1753.
It first appears in print in Q3 and in E is placed after l. 116 with the following variants:
            1. Year] Spring (*del*).
            2. Show'rs of] frequent *with* Showers of *written above.*
            3. Red-breast] Robin *with* Redbreast *written above.*

The EPITAPH.

HERE *rests his head upon the lap of Earth*
A Youth to Fortune and to Fame unknown,
Fair Science frown'd not on his humble birth,
And Melancholy mark'd him for her own.   120

Large was his bounty, and his soul sincere,
Heav'n did a recompence as largely send:
He gave to Mis'ry all he had, a tear,
He gain'd from Heav'n ('twas all he wish'd) a friend.

No farther seek his merits to disclose,   125
Or draw his frailties from their dread abode,
(There they alike in trembling hope repose)
The bosom of his Father and his God.

A LONG STORY.

IN BRITAIN'S Isle, no matter where,
An ancient pile of building stands:
The Huntingdons and Hattons there
Employ'd the power of Fairy hands

think

121 soul] Heart *E.*   126 Or draw his frailties] Nor seek to draw them *E.*
127 There they alike] His Frailties there *E.*

A LONG STORY. First published in *B*, the text followed here. *B* is the only text to be printed with Gray's approval, though in some respects *CB* (and perhaps even *Gt*) may more closely approach his preference. Terminal quotation marks have been added to ll. 128, 134, 140.

Texts collated: *CB*, ii. 651–2; *Gt*; *M*, i. 214–20. *Gt* is an earlier holograph than *CB* and was formerly in the possession of the late John Garrett of Baltimore (see Whibley, 'Gray's Own Copy of *A Long Story*', *Essays and Studies by Members of the English Association, 1937*, ed. S. C. Roberts, xxiii [Oxford, 1938], 55–57, in which a few of the more interesting variations are noted). At present it is in the John Work Garrett Library of the Johns Hopkins University (The Evergreen House Foundation, Inc.). It is now for the first time collated in an edition of Gray's poems.

Although there are no noticeable gaps between the stanzas, the first line of each stanza (save ll. 1, 81, 142 in CB and ll. 1, 49, 97 in Gt) is indented in CB, Gt, and M. In CB Aug: 1750 *is written in the upper right corner of p. 651, although the Aug: is probably a slip of memory; see explanatory notes, Whibley's article cited above, and textual note to l. 120.*

3 *Expl. note in margin of Gt*: N: B: the House was built by the Earls of Huntingdon, & came from them to Sr Christopher[,] afterwards Ld Keeper, Hatton, prefer'd by Q: Elizabeth for his graceful Person & fine Dancing.

To raise the cieling's fretted height,   5
Each pannel in achievements cloathing,
Rich windows that exclude the light,
And passages, that lead to nothing.

Full oft within the spatious walls,
When he had fifty winters o'er him,   10
My grave Lord-Keeper led the Brawls:
The Seal, and Maces, danc'd before him.

His bushy beard, and shoe-strings green,
His high-crown'd hat, and sattin-doublet,
Mov'd the stout heart of England's Queen,   15
Tho' Pope and Spaniard could not trouble it.

What, in the very first beginning!
Shame of the versifying tribe!
Your Hist'ry whither are you spinning?
Can you do nothing but describe?   20

A House there is, (and that's enough)
From whence one fatal morning issues
A brace of Warriors, not in buff,
But rustling in their silks and tissues.

The first came cap-a-pee from France   25
Her conqu'ring destiny fulfilling,
Whom meaner Beauties eye askance,
And vainly ape her art of killing.

The other Amazon kind Heaven
Had arm'd with spirit, wit, and satire: 30
But COBHAM had the polish given,
And tip'd her arrows with good-nature.

To celebrate her eyes, her air - - - - -
Coarse panegyricks would but teaze her.
Melissa is her Nom de Guerre.   35
Alas, who would not wish to please her!

5–8 *Omitted in Gt, probably by an oversight, for in CB they are written in the margin with
the present position indicated by an asterisk.*   11 *Expl. note attached to* Brawls *in
Gt*: an old-fashion'd Dance.   20 you] ye *Gt.*   33 eyes] Looks *Gt.*   35 *Expl.
note attached to* Melissa, *Gt*: She had been call'd by that Name in Verse before.

With bonnet blue and capucine,
And aprons long they hid their armour,
And veil'd their weapons bright and keen
In pity to the country-farmer.   40

Fame in the shape of Mr. P - - - t
(By this time all the Parish know it)
Had told, that thereabouts there lurk'd
A wicked Imp they call a Poet,

Who prowl'd the country far and near,   45
Bewitch'd the children of the peasants,
Dried up the cows, and lam'd the deer,
And suck'd the eggs, and kill'd the pheasants.

My Lady heard their joint petition,
Swore by her coronet and ermine,   50
She'd issue out her high commission
To rid the manour of such vermin.

The Heroines undertook the task,
Thro' lanes unknown, o'er stiles they ventur'd,
Rap'd at the door, nor stay'd to ask,   55
But bounce into the parlour enter'd.

The trembling family they daunt,
They flirt, they sing, they laugh, they tattle,
Rummage his Mother, pinch his Aunt,
And up stairs in a whirlwind rattle.   60

Each hole and cupboard they explore,
Each creek and cranny of his chamber,
Run hurry-skurry round the floor,
And o'er the bed and tester clamber,

Into the Drawers and China pry,   65
Papers and books, a huge Imbroglio!
Under a tea-cup he might lie,
Or creased, like dogs-ears, in a folio.

41 P - - - t] Purt *CB, Gt. Expl. note, Gt*: A Clergyman, Tutor to the Duke of Bridge-
water, who had first mention'd me to them, as their Neighbour.

On the first marching of the troops
The Muses, hopeless of his pardon,   70
Convey'd him underneath their hoops
To a small closet in the garden.

So Rumor says. (Who will, believe.)
But that they left the door a-jarr,
Where, safe and laughing in his sleeve,   75
He heard the distant din of war.

Short was his joy. He little knew,
The power of Magick was no fable.
Out of the window, whisk, they flew,
But left a spell upon the table.   80

The words too eager to unriddle
The Poet felt a strange disorder:
Transparent birdlime form'd the middle,
And chains invisible the border.

So cunning was the Apparatus,   85
The powerful pothooks did so move him,
That, will he, nill he, to the Great-house
He went, as if the Devil drove him.

Yet on his way (no sign of grace,
For folks in fear are apt to pray)   90
To Phœbus he prefer'd his case,
And beg'd his aid that dreadful day.

The Godhead would have back'd his quarrel,
But with a blush on recollection
Own'd, that his quiver and his laurel   95
'Gainst four such eyes were no protection.

The Court was sate, the Culprit there,
Forth from their gloomy mansions creeping
The Lady *Janes* and *Joans* repair,
And from the gallery stand peeping: 100

72 in] near *Gt.*   73 (Who will, believe.)] who will, may believe. *CB, Gt.*
87 *Expl. note to* Great-house, *Gt:* So the Country People call it.   91 prefer'd]
explain'd *CB, Gt.*   95 Own'd, that] He own'd, *Gt.*   97 Culprit] Prisoner *Gt.*
100 from] in *Gt.*

Such as in silence of the night
Come (sweep) along some winding entry
(*Styack* has often seen the sight)
Or at the chappel-door stand sentry;

In peaked hoods and mantles tarnish'd,   105
Sour visages, enough to scare ye,
High Dames of honour once, that garnish'd
The drawing-room of fierce Queen Mary!

The Peeress comes. The Audience stare,
And doff their hats with due submission: 110
She curtsies, as she takes her chair,
To all the People of condition.

The Bard with many an artful fib,
Had in imagination fenc'd him,
Disproved the arguments of *Squib*,   115
And all that *Groom* could urge against him.

But soon his rhetorick forsook him,
When he the solemn hall had seen;
A sudden fit of ague shook him,
He stood as mute as poor *Macleane*.   120

Yet something he was heard to mutter,
'How in the park beneath an old-tree
'(Without design to hurt the butter,
'Or any malice to the poultry,)

'He once or twice had pen'd a sonnet;   125
'Yet hoped, that he might save his bacon:
'Numbers would give their oaths upon it,
'He ne'er was for a conj'rer taken.'

The ghostly Prudes with hagged face
Already had condemn'd the sinner,   130
My Lady rose, and with a grace - - - -
She smiled, and bid him come to dinner.

103 *Expl. note to* Styack, *Gt*: Lady C:ˢ House-keeper.   115 *Expl. note to* Squib,
Gt: Her Groom of the Chambers.   116 could] might *CB*, *Gt*.   *Expl. note to*
Groom, *Gt*: Her Keeper.   120 *Gray's expl. note in Gt reads simply* hanged last
Week.   123 hurt] spoil *Gt*.   126 Yet] But *CB*.

'Jesu-Maria! Madam Bridget,
'Why, what can the Vicountess mean?'
(Cried the square Hoods in woful fidget)   135
'The times are alter'd quite and clean!

'Decorum's turn'd to mere civility;
'Her air and all her manners shew it.
'Commend me to her affability!
'Speak to a Commoner and Poet!'   140

[*Here* 500 *Stanzas are lost.*]

And so God save our noble King,
And guard us from long-winded Lubbers,
That to eternity would sing,
And keep my Lady from her Rubbers.

[ODE FOR MUSIC.]

AIR.

"HENCE, avaunt, ('tis holy ground)
"Comus, and his midnight-crew,
"And Ignorance with looks profound,
"And dreaming Sloth of pallid hue,
"Mad Sedition's cry profane,   5
"Servitude that hugs her chain,
"Nor in these consecrated bowers
"Let painted Flatt'ry hide her serpent-train in flowers.

---

137 turn'd] chang'd *Gt.*   140 f. [*Here* 500 *Stanzas are lost.*]] (Here 500 Stanzas
are lost, the last only remaining.) *Gt.*   143 That] Who *Gt.*

ODE FOR MUSIC. First printed anonymously in 1769, the text followed here: Ode /
performed in the / Senate-House at Cambridge, / July 1, 1769, / at the installation of
His Grace / Augustus-Henry Fitzroy, / Duke of Grafton, / Chancellor of the University. / Set to music by / Dr. Randal, / Professor of Music. / Cambridge, / Printed
by J. Archdeacon Printer to the University. / M.DCC.LXIX. On the first page of text
the title is simply ODE FOR MUSIC. It was reprinted in *M*, ii. [37]-43, as ODE /
VII. / FOR MUSIC. / IRREGULAR. and with the substitution of Roman numerals for the
headings AIR, RECITATIVE, &c. Terminal quotation marks have been added to ll. 12,
34, 64, 94.

CHORUS.

"Nor Envy base, nor creeping Gain
"Dare the Muse's walk to stain, 10
"While bright-eyed Science watches round:
"Hence, away, 'tis holy Ground!"

RECITATIVE.

From yonder realms of empyrean day
Bursts on my ear th' indignant lay:
There sit the sainted Sage, the Bard divine, 15
The Few, whom Genius gave to shine
Through every unborn age, and undiscovered clime.
Rapt in celestial transport they, (*accomp.*)
Yet hither oft a glance from high
They send of tender sympathy 20
To bless the place, where on their opening soul
First the genuine ardor stole.
'Twas *Milton* struck the deep-toned shell,
And, as the choral warblings round him swell,
Meek *Newton's* self bends from his state sublime, 25
And nods his hoary head, and listens to the rhyme.

AIR.

"Ye brown o'er-arching Groves,
"That Contemplation loves,
"Where willowy *Camus* lingers with delight!
"Oft at the blush of dawn 30
"I trod your level lawn,
"Oft woo'd the gleam of *Cynthia* silver-bright
"In cloisters dim, far from the haunts of Folly,
"With Freedom by my Side, and soft-ey'd Melancholy."

RECITATIVE.

But hark! the portals sound, and pacing forth 35
With solemn steps and slow
High Potentates and Dames of royal birth
And mitred Fathers in long order go:

Great *Edward* with the lillies on his brow
From haughty *Gallia* torn,   40
And sad *Chatillon*, on her bridal morn
That wept her bleeding Love, and princely *Clare*,
And *Anjou's* Heroïne, and the paler Rose,
The rival of her crown, and of her woes,
And either *Henry* there,   45
The murther'd Saint, and the majestic Lord,
That broke the bonds of *Rome*.
(Their tears, their little triumphs o'er,   (*accomp.*)
Their human passions now no more,
Save Charity, that glows beyond the tomb)   50
All that on *Granta's* fruitful plain
Rich streams of regal bounty pour'd,
And bad these aweful fanes and turrets rise,
To hail their *Fitzroy's* festal morning come;
And thus they speak in soft accord   55
The liquid language of the skies.

QUARTETTO.

"What is Grandeur, what is Power?
"Heavier toil, superior pain.
"What the bright reward we gain?
"The grateful mem'ry of the Good.   60
"Sweet is the breath of vernal shower,
"The bee's collected treasures sweet,
"Sweet music's melting fall, but sweeter yet
"The still small voice of Gratitude."

RECITATIVE.

Foremost and leaning from her golden cloud   65
The venerable *Marg'ret* see!
"Welcome, my noble Son, (she cries aloud)
"To this, thy kindred train, and me:
"Pleas'd in thy lineaments we trace
"A *Tudor's* fire, a *Beaufort's* grace.   70

AIR.

"Thy liberal heart, thy judging eye,
"The flower unheeded shall descry,
"And bid it round heaven's altars shed
"The fragrance of it's blushing head:
"Shall raise from earth the latent gem   75
"To glitter on the diadem.

RECITATIVE.

"Lo, *Granta* waits to lead her blooming band,
"Not obvious, not obtrusive, She
"No vulgar praise, no venal incense flings;
"Nor dares with courtly tongue refin'd   80
"Profane thy inborn royalty of mind:
"She reveres herself and thee.
"With modest pride to grace thy youthful brow
"The laureate wreath, that *Cecil* wore, she brings,
"And to thy just, thy gentle hand   85
"Submits the Fasces of her sway,
"While Spirits blest above and Men below
"Join with glad voice the loud symphonious lay.

GRAND CHORUS.

"Thro' the wild waves as they roar
"With watchful eye and dauntless mien   90
"Thy steady course of honor keep,
"Nor fear the rocks, nor seek the shore:
"The Star of *Brunswick* smiles serene,
"And gilds the horrors of the deep."

FINIS.

[EPITAPH ON MRS. CLERKE.]

Lo! where this silent marble weeps,
A friend, a wife, a mother sleeps:
A heart, within whose sacred cell
The peaceful virtues lov'd to dwell,
Affection warm, and faith sincere,   5
And soft humanity were there.
In agony, in death resign'd,
She felt the wound she left behind.
Her infant image, here below,
Sits smiling on a father's woe: 10
Whom what awaits, while yet he strays
Along the lonely vale of days?
A pang, to secret sorrow dear;
A sigh; an unavailing tear;
Till time shall every grief remove,   15
With life, with memory, and with love.

EPITAPH ON MRS. CLERKE. First printed in Fawkes and Woty, *The Poetical Calendar*, 2nd ed., London: Dryden Leach, 1763, viii. 121. The text used here is that inscribed in St. George's parish church at Beckenham, Kent (*BK*), but on the tablet (examined by the editors and rechecked by the Revd. T. C. Hammond, Rector of Beckenham) the inscription is cut in capital letters throughout and there are no marks of punctuation. Consequently, lower-case letters and punctuation have been supplied. The only holograph MS. is the letter to Bedingfield (T & W no. 266), 31 Jan. 1758, Huntington Library MS. HM 21912 (*Bed*).
   Texts collated: *Bed*, *M*.

Title: *In BK the inscription is headed* JANE CLERKE / DIED APRIL XXVII, MDCCLVII. AGED XXXI.
1 silent] little *Bed*.   4 The peaceful virtues] Each peaceful Virtue *Bed*.
7–10   To hide her cares her only art,
                             Her pleasure pleasures to impart
                             In ling'ring pain, in death resign'd,
                             Her latest agony of mind
                             Was felt for him, who could not save
                             His All from an untimely grave:
Bed, also noted as variant in M.   13 secret] silent *Bed*.

On L[or]d H[ollan]d[s] Seat near
M[argat]e. K[en][t]

Old and abandon'd by each venal friend
    Here H[olland]. took the pious resolution
To smuggle some few years and strive to mend
    A broken character and constitution.
On this congenial spot he fix'd his choice,   5
    Earl Godwin trembled for his neighbouring sand,
Here Seagulls scream and cormorants rejoice,
    And Mariners tho' shipwreckt dread to land,
Here reign the blustring north and blighting east,
    No tree is heard to whisper, bird to sing,   10
Yet nature cannot furnish out the feast,
    Art he invokes new horrors still to bring;
Now mouldring fanes and battlements arise,
    Arches and turrets nodding to their fall,
Unpeopled palaces delude his eyes,   15
    And mimick desolation covers all.
Ah, said the sighing Peer, had Bute been true
    Nor Shelburn's, Rigby's, Calcraft's friendship vain,
Far other scenes than these had bless'd our view
    And realis'd the ruins that we feign.   20
Purg'd by the sword and beautifyed by fire,
    Then had we seen proud London's hated walls,
Owls might have hooted in S[t] Peters Quire,
    And foxes stunk and litter'd in S[t] Pauls.

ON LORD HOLLAND'S SEAT NEAR MARGATE, KENT. First printed (anonymously)
without Gray's consent in *The New Foundling Hospital for Wit*, London, 1769, iii. 34–
35 (*NF*). There is a copy by Wharton in Brit. Mus. Egerton MS. 2400, f. 232 (*Wh*),
the text followed here. Mitford (*Mt*) follows the text in Stephen Jones's edition (London,
1800). The names of individuals are filled in with dashes or asterisks in *NF* and *Mt*.
    Texts collated: *Mt, NF*.

Title: Inscription for the Villa of a decay'd Satesman [sic] *on the Sea-Coast. NF.*
2 took] form'd *NF, Mt.*   3 some] a *Mt.*   6 Godwin] Goodwin *NF, Mt.*
8 dread] fear *is recorded by Mt as an earlier printed variant.*   9 reign] reigns *NF.*
11 cannot] could not *Mt.*   13 Now] Here *Mt.*   14 Arches and turrets]
Turrets and arches *Mt.*   15 palaces delude his] monast'ries delude our *Mt.*
18 Shelburn's . . . Calcraft's] M—'s, R—'s, B—'s *Mt, where the explanation given in
a note is* Mungo's, Rigby's, Bradshaw's. *Mt also notes another early printed variant:*
Nor C—'s, nor B—d's promises been vain. Calcraft's] Calcrofts *Wh.*   19 other]
better *Mt.*   bless'd] crown'd *NF.*   20 ruins that] beauties which *Mt.*   21
beautifyed] purified *Mt.*   23 might] would *Mt.*

POSTHUMOUS POEMS

TRANSLATIONS

[TRANSLATION OF
A PASSAGE FROM STATIUS,]
E LIB: 6ᵗᵒ THEBAIDOS

[ll. 646–88.]

Then thus the King, 'whoe'er the Quoit can wield,   Adrastus
And furthest send its weight athwart the field;
Let him stand forth his brawny arm to boast.'
Swift at the word, from out the gazing host
Young Pterelas with strength unequal drew   5
Labouring the Disc, & to small distance threw:
The Band around admire the mighty Mass,
A slipp'ry weight, & form'd of polish'd Brass;
The love of honour bad[e] two Youths advance,
Achaians born, to try the glorious chance;   10
A third arose, of Acarnania he,
Of Pisa one, & three from Ephyre;
Nor more for now Nesimachus's Son,   Hippomedon
By Acclamations roused, came towring on;
Another Orb upheaved his strong right hand,   15
Then thus, "Ye Argive flower, ye warlike band,
Who trust your arms shall rase the Tyrian towers,
And batter Cadmus' Walls with stony Showers,
Receive a worthier load; yon puny Ball
Let Youngsters toss:"   20

TRANSLATION OF A PASSAGE FROM STATIUS, *Thebaid*, vi. 646–88. First published by Mitford in his *Gray–Mason Correspondence*, 1853. The only extant holograph MS. is the letter to West (T & W no. 22), 8 May 1736, which is the text followed here. Quotation marks are supplied in ll. 16, 20.

1, 13 Adrastus *and* Hippomedon *are written in the margin.*

He said, & scornful flung th' unheeded weight
Aloof; the champions trembling at the sight
Prevent disgrace, the palm despair'd resign;
All, but two youths, th' enormous Orb decline,
These conscious Shame withheld, & pride of noble line: } 25
As bright & huge the spatious circle lay
With doubled light it beam'd against the Day;
So glittering shews the Thracian Godheads shield,
With such a gleam affrights Pangæa's field,
When blazing 'gainst the Sun it shines from far, 30
And clash'd rebellows with the Din of war:
 Phlegyas the long-expected play began,
Summon'd his strength, & call'd forth all the Man;
All eyes were bent on his experienced hand,
For oft in Pisa's sports his native land 35
Admired that arm, oft on Alpheus' Shore
The pond'rous brass in exercise he bore;
Where flow'd the widest Stream he took his stand; }
Sure flew the Disc from his unerring hand; }
Nor stop'd till it had cut the further strand: } 40
And now in Dust the polish'd Ball he roll'd,
Then grasp'd its weight, elusive of his hold;
Now fitting to his gripe, & nervous Arm
Suspends the crowd with expectation warm;
Nor tempts he yet the plain, but hurl'd upright 45
Emits the mass, a prelude of his might;
Firmly he plants each knee, & o'er his head,
Collecting all his force, the circle sped;
It towers to cut the clouds; now thro' the Skies
Sings in its rapid way, & strengthens, as it flies; 50
Anon with slack'ned rage comes quivering down,
Heavy & huge, & cleaves the solid ground.
 So from th' astonish'd Stars, her nightly train,
The Sun's pale sister, drawn by magic strain,
Deserts precipitant [her] darken'd Sphere; 55
In vain the Nations [wi]th officious fear
Their cymbals toss, & sounding brass explore; }
Th' Æmonian Hag enjoys her dreadful hour, }
And smiles malignant on the labouring Power. }

55–56 *The MS. is damaged.*

[TRANSLATION OF
A PASSAGE FROM STATIUS,
Thebaid, VI. 704–24.]

Third in the labours of the Disc came on,
With sturdy step and slow, Hippomedon;
Artful and strong he pois'd the well-known weight, ⎫
By Phlegyas warn'd, and fir'd by M[e]nestheus' fate, ⎬
That to avoid, and this to emulate. ⎭   5
His vigorous arm he try'd before he flung,
Brac'd all his nerves, and every sinew strung;
Then with a tempest's whirl and wary eye,
Pursu'd his cast, and hurl'd the orb on high;
The orb on high tenacious of its course,   10
True to the mighty arm that gave it force,
Far overleaps all bound, and joys to see
Its antient lord secure of victory.
The theatre's green height and woody wall
Tremble ere it precipitates its fall,   15
The ponderous mass sinks in the cleaving ground,
While vales and woods and echoing hills rebound.
As when from Ætna's smoking summit broke,
The eyeless Cyclops heav'd the craggy rock;
Where Ocean frets beneath the dashing oar,   20
And parting surges round the vessel roar;
'Twas there he aim'd the meditated harm,
And scarce Ulysses scap'd his giant arm.
A tyger's pride the victor bore away,
With native spots and artful labour gay,   25
A shining border round the margin roll'd,
And calm'd the terrors of his claws in gold.

Cambridge, May 8, 1736.

TRANSLATION OF A PASSAGE FROM STATIUS, *Thebaid*, vi. 704-24. The only extant text is *M*, i. 9-10, which is followed here.

[TRANSLATION FROM STATIUS,
Thebaid, IX. 319–26.]

Crenæus, whom the Nymph Ismenis bore
To Faunus on the Theban Rivers shore
With new-born heat amidst his native stream
Exults in arms, which cast an iron gleam.
In this clear wave he first beheld the day   5
On the green bank first taught his steps to stray,
To skim the parent flood & on the margin play:
Fear he disdains & scorns the power of fate,
Secure within his mothers watry state.
The youth exulting stems the bloody tide,   10
Visits each bank & stalks with martial pride,
While old Ismenus' gently-rolling wave,
Delights the favourite youth within its flood to lave.

TRANSLATION FROM STATIUS, *Thebaid*, ix. 319–26. First printed by Paget Toynbee
in *The Correspondence of Gray, Walpole, West, and Ashton* (Oxford, 1915), ii. [299]–300,
with a facsimile. Printed in the 1917 Poole edition, it was omitted by Whibley in his
1937 revision. The text followed here is that of the holograph MS. at Pembroke College
(L.C. 2. 123, p. 106). The rough draft is written first.

Crenæus, whom the Nymph Ismenis bore
To Faunus, on the Theban rivers shore
       new-born
With ~~youthful~~ heat amidst his native stream,
    He shines   [illeg.] ~~his fury~~
~~Exults~~ in arms, ~~which cast a meet~~
              which cast an iron gleam
In this clear wave he first beheld the day
On the green bank first taught his steps to stray
To skim the parent flood & on the margin play
hḛ²   Disdains ~~all~~ feȧr & scorns the power of fate
      Secure within his mothers watry state
youth   stems   e.   ~~liquid plain~~
The   ~~While~~ he exulting ~~cross'd~~ th ~~indulgent wave~~
                  bloody tide
~~And~~ [illeg.]   Visits   pride
~~While old Ismenes~~ each bank, & stalks with martial
         ~~with~~ e   ing
While old Ismenus gently rolls ~~his~~ wave,
Delights ~~his~~ the favoured youth within its
~~And loves his offspring in his~~ flood to lave

Whither the youth obliquely steers his course
Or cuts the downward stream with equal force   15
Th' indulgent river strives his steps to aid.

[TRANSLATION]
From Tasso
[*Gerusalemme liberata*]
Canto, 14, Stanza, 32.

Preser commiato, e si 'l desir gli sprona, &c:
[They took their leave, and so does desire spur them, &c.]

Dismiss'd at length they break thro' all delay
To tempt the dangers of the doubtful way;
And first to Ascalon their steps they bend,
Whose walls along the neighbouring Sea extend:
Nor yet in prospect rose the distant shore,   5
Scarce the hoarse waves from far were heard to roar;
When thwart the road a River roll'd its flood
Tempestuous, and all further course withstood:
The torrent-stream his ancient bounds disdains,
Swoll'n with new force, & late-descending rains.   10

After this, ll. 1–13 appear with the Latin of Statius below them:

> Gaudebat Fauno, Nymphaq̄ Ismenide natus
> Maternis bellare tener Crenæus in undis[,]
> Crenæus, cui prima dies in gurgite fido
> Et natale vadum et virides cunabula ripæ[.]
> Ergo ratus nihil Elysias ibi posse sorores
>
> Lætus adulantem nunc hoc, nunc margine in illo
> Transit avum—

This is followed by ll. 14–16, but l. 14 has been revised:

> ~~the~~[?] the youth obliquely steers his course
> Whither ~~with course direct~~ he

Below there is written very faintly in Walpole's hand:

> This written when he was very young.

The editors have inserted full stops at the ends of ll. 4 and 16.

TRANSLATION FROM TASSO. First published by Mathias, 1814, ii. 90–92 (*Ma*).
  Text used: *CB*, i. 95–96. Text collated: *Ma*.

Irresolute they stand, when lo! appears
The wondrous Sage; vigorous he seem'd in years,
Awful his mien; low as his feet there flows
A vestment unadorn'd, tho' white as new-fal'n Snows:
Against the stream the waves secure he trod,   15
His head a chaplet bore, his hand a Rod.
　As on the Rhine when Boreas' fury reigns,
And Winter binds the floods in icy chains
Swift shoots the Village-maid in rustick play
Smooth, without step, adown the shining way: 20
Fearless in long excursion loves to glide,
And sports, & wantons o'er the frozen tide.
　So moved the Seer, but on no harden'd plain:
The river boil'd beneath & rush'd towards the Main.
Where fixed in wonder stood the warlike pair,   25
His course he turn'd, & thus relieved their care.
　"Vast, oh my friends, & difficult the toil
To seek your Hero in a distant Soil!
No common helps, no common guide ye need,
Art it requires, and more than winged speed.   30
What length of sea remains, what various lands,
Oceans unknown, inhospitable Sands!
For adverse fate the captive chief has hurl'd
Beyond the confines of our narrow world.
Great things and full of wonder in your ears   35
I shall unfold; but first dismiss your fears;
Nor doubt with me to tread the downward road,
That to the grotto leads, my dark abode."
　Scarce had he said, before the warriours' eyes,
When mountain-high the waves disparted rise: 40
The flood on either hand its billows rears,
And in the midst a spacious arch appears.
Their hands he seized and down the steep he led
Beneath the obedient river's inmost bed.
The watry glimmerings of a fainter day   45
Discover'd half, & half conceal'd their way.
As when athwart the dusky woods by night
The uncertain Crescent gleams a sickly light.

---

23 plain:] plain *CB*.　　24 towards] toward *Ma*.　　27 "Vast, oh] Vast oh *CB*.
38 abode."] abode. *CB*.

Thro' subterraneous passages they went
Earth's inmost cells, & caves of deep descent.   50
Of many a flood they view'd the secret source
The birth of rivers, riseing to their course;
Whate'er with copious train its channel fills,
Floats into Lakes, or bubbles into rills.
The Po was there to see, Danubius' bed,   55
Euphrates' fount, & Nile's mysterious head.
Further they pass; where ripening minerals flow,
And embryon metals undigested glow:
Sulphureous veins & liveing silver shine,
Which soon the parent Sun's warm powers refine;   60
In one rich mass unite the precious store,
The parts combine & harden into Ore.
Here gems break thro' the night with glitt'ring beam,
And paint the margin of the costly stream.
All stones of lustre shoot their vivid ray,   65
And mix attemper'd in a various day.
    Here the soft emerald smiles of verdant hue,
And rubies flame, with sapphires heavenly blue;
The diamond there attracts the wond'ring sight
Proud of its thousand dies, & luxury of light.   70

54 or] *Ma and most modern editions, including Br, read* and *but it is clearly* or *in CB.*
69 wond'ring] wondrous *Ma.*   *At the end of the poem in CB is written* *1738.

[TRANSLATION FROM]
Dante, Canto 33 dell' Inferno.

From his dire food the greisly Fellon raised
His gore-dyed lips, which on the clotter'd locks
Of th' half devoured Head he wiped, & thus
Began; "Wouldst thou revive the deep despair
The Anguish, that unutter'd nathless wrings   5
My inmost Heart? yet if the telling may
Beget the Traitour's infamy, whom thus
I ceaseless gnaw insatiate, thou shalt see me
At once give loose to Utterance & to Tears.

I know not who thou art nor on what errand   10
Sent hither; but a Florentine my ear
Won by thy tongue, declares thee. Know, thou seest
In me Count Ugolino, & Ruggieri
Pisa's perfidious Prelate, this: now hear
My Wrongs & from them judge of my revenge.   15

That I did trust him, that I was betrayd
By trusting, & by Treachery slain, it rekes not
That I advise Thee; that which yet remains

DANTE. Fifteen lines published in *The Gentleman's Magazine*, N.S. xxxii (Oct. 1849), 343. First published in full by Gosse in Gray's *Works*, 1884. The text here followed is that from Mitford's Note-book, vol. iii, and the variants recorded by Mitford (ff. 70–73, 123). No holograph MS. is known. W. P. Jones in his *Thomas Gray, Scholar* (Cambridge: Harvard, 1937), p. 181, records a MS. ('84 lines on two quarto sheets') now supposedly in the collection of the late Marquess of Crewe which Lady Crewe has been unable to find. It is possible that this MS. is merely a copy of the version in Mitford's Note-book, for Professor Jones has transcribed a note from it which is identical with the one that heads the version in the Note-book: 'It is uncertain when Mr. Gray translated the following Story from Dante; but most probably very early, and when he was making himself Master of the Italian language.' Gosse's account is rather puzzling. In his preface (I. xvi) he states that he prints the translation 'for the first time, from a MS. *of the poet's* [our italics] in the possession of Lord Houghton. This is undated, and no one knows anything of its history; but from the peculiarities of its spelling, I have no hesitation in attributing it to the period from 1742 to 1744. Such a fact as this may be allowed to justify exactitude.' This account surely implies a holograph MS. Yet on p. 157 he describes the MS. as 'in the handwriting of Mitford'. In that event, it is difficult to understand how one could assign the poem to 1742–4 on the basis of its spelling with any 'exactitude' at all—even if one could with confidence date Gray's verse by his spelling. A more probable date would be 1738 (see explanatory notes).

The editors have inserted the single and double quotation marks (ll. 4, 56, 57, 65, 68, 81) and the terminal punctuation for ll. 20, 67, 69.

1 Fellon raised] father raisd *Variant*.   8 insatiate,] insatiate; *Mt*.   10 art]
art; *Mt*.

To thee & all unknown (a horrid Tale)
The bitterness of Death, I shall unfold.   20
Attend, & say if he have injurd me.
   Thro' a small Crevice opening, what scant light
That grim & antique Tower admitted (since
Of me the Tower of Famine hight & known
To many a Wretch) already 'gan the dawn   25
To send; the whilst I slumbring lay, A Sleep
Prophetic of my Woes with direful Hand
Oped the dark Veil of fate. I saw methought
Toward Pisa's Mount, that intercepts the view
Of Lucca chas'd by Hell-hounds gaunt & bloody   30
A Wolf full grown; with fleet & equal speed
His young ones ran beside him, Lanfranc there
And Sigismundo & Gualandi rode
Amain, my deadly foes! headed by this
The deadliest; he their Chief, the foremost he   35
Flashed to pursue & chear the eager Cry:
Nor long endured the Chase: the panting Sire
Of Strength bereft, his helpless offspring soon
Oerta'en beheld, & in their trembling flanks
The hungry Pack their sharp-set Fangs embrued.   40
   The Morn had scarce commencd, when I awoke:
My Children (they were with me) Sleep as yet
Gave not to know their Sum of Misery
But yet in low & uncompleated Sounds
I heard 'em wail for bread. oh! thou art cruel   45
Or thou dost mourn to think, what my poor Heart
Foresaw, foreknew: oh! if thou weep not now,
Where are thy Tears? too soon they had arousd them
Sad with the fears of Sleep, & now the Hour
Of timely food approached: when at the gate   50
Below I heard the dreadful Clank of bars,
And fastning bolts; then on my Children's eyes
Speechless my Sight I fix'd, nor wept, for all
Within was Stone: they wept, unhappy boys!
They wept, & first my little dear Anselmo   55
Cried, 'Father, why, why do you gaze so sternly?

31 grown;] grown, *Mt.*   32 him.] him, *Mt.*   35 deadliest;] deadliest, *Mt.*
foremost he] foremost he, *Mt.*   36 Flashed] Fleshed *Mt.*

What would you have?' yet wept I not, or answerd
All that whole day, or the succeeding Night
Till a new Sun arose with weakly gleam
And wan, such as mought entrance find within   60
That house of Woe: but oh! when I beheld
My sons & in four faces saw my own
Despair reflected, either hand I gnawed
For Angeuish, which they construed Hunger; straight
Ariseing all they cried, 'far less shall be   65
Our sufferings, Sir, if you resume your gift;
These miserable limbs with flesh you cloathed;
Take back what once was yours.' I swallowd down
My struggling Sorrow, nor to heighten theirs.
That day & yet another, mute we sate   70
And motionless: O! Earth! couldst thou not gape
Quick to devour me? yet a fourth day came
When Gaddo at my feet outstretchd, implor'ng
In vain my Help, expir'd: ee'r the sixth Morn
Had dawnd, my other three before my eyes   75
Died one by one; I saw 'em fall: I heard
Their doleful Cries; for three days more I grop'd
About among their cold remains (for then
Hunger had reft my eyesight) often calling
On their dear Names, that heard me now no more: 80
The fourth, what Sorrow could not, Famine did."
   He finished; then with unrelenting eye
Askaunce he turn'd him, hasty to renew
The hellish feast, & rent his trembling Prey.

73 Implor'ng] implor'd'ng *Mt.*   82 unrelenting] unbending *Variant.*   83
Askaunce] Askfaunce *Mt.*   hasty] haply *Variant.   At the end of the poem is
written by Mitford:* N.B. The above is not in Grays Writing, but in a clear large hand.
perhaps Mr. Stonehewer's (yes.)

[IMITATED]

From Propertius. Lib: 2: Eleg: 1.
To Mecænas.

You ask, why thus my Loves I still rehearse,
Whence the soft Strain & ever-melting Verse?
From Cynthia all, that in my Numbers shines:
She is my Genius, she inspires the Lines;
No Phœbus else, no other Muse I know;   5
She tunes my easy Rhime, & gives the Lay to flow.
If the loose Curls around her Forehead play,
Or lawless o'er their Ivory Margin stray:
If the thin Coan Web her Shape reveal,
And half disclose those Limbs it should conceal: 10
Of those loose Curls, that Ivory front I write;
Of the dear Web whole Volumes I indite:
Or if to Musick she the Lyre awake,
That the soft Subject of my Song I make,
And sing with what a careless Grace she flings   15
Her artful hand across the sounding Strings.
If sinking into Sleep she seem to close
Her languid Lids, I favour her repose
With lulling Notes, & thousand beauties see,
That Slumber brings to aid my Poetry.   20
When less averse, & yielding to Desires
She half accepts, & half rejects my Fires;
While to retain the envious Lawn she tries,
And struggles to elude my longing Eyes:
The fruitful Muse from that auspicious Night   25
Dates the long Iliad of the amorous Fight.

IMITATED FROM PROPERTIUS: TO MECAENAS. First published by Mathias, 1814,
ii. 87–89 (*Ma*).

Text used: *CB*, i. 254–5. Texts collated: *Ma*; *We*, letter to West (T & W no. 105),
23 Apr. 1742; *Mt*, Mitford's copy (Note-book, vol. iii, ff. 77–78). Mitford and Mathias
did not print the first 30 lines.

Title: *Possibly* Eleg: 5: *in CB, but* Eleg: I: *in We and Mt.* (*The correct number is* 1.)
Mecænas *is Gray's spelling* (*as it is also Milton's*).

     10 those] the *We, Mt.*   18 Lids] limbs *Mt.*

In brief whate'er she do, or say, or look:
'Tis ample Matter for a Lover's Book:
And many a copious Narrative you'll see
Big with the important Nothing's History.   30
 Yet would the Tyrant Love permit me raise
My feeble Voice to sound the Victor's Praise,
To paint the Hero's Toil, the Ranks of War,
The laurel'd Triumph, & the sculptured Carr:
No Giant-Race, no Tumult of the Skies,   35
No Mountain-Structures in my Verse should rise,
Nor Tale of Thebes, or Ilium there should be,
Or how the Persian trod the indignant Sea;
Not Marius' Cimbrian Wreaths would I relate;
Nor lofty Carthage struggleing with her Fate.   40
Here should Augustus great in Arms appear,
And Thou, Mecænas, be my second Care:
Here Mutina from flames & famine free,
And there th' ensanguined Wave of Sicily:
And sceptred Alexandria's captive Shore;   45
And sad Philippi red with Roman Gore:
Then, while the vaulted Skies loud Io's rend,
In golden Chains should loaded Monarchs bend,
And hoary Nile with pensive Aspect seem
To mourn the Glories of his sevenfold Stream   50
While Prows, that late in fierce Encounter mett,
Move thro' the Sacred Way, and vainly threat.
Thee too the Muse should consecrate to Fame,
And with his Garlands weave thy ever-faithful Name.
But nor Callimachus' enervate Strain   55
May tell of Jove, & Phlegra's blasted Plain:
Nor I with unaccustom'd Vigour trace
Back to it's Source divine the Julian Race.
Sailors to tell of Winds & Seas delight,

32 sound] sing *We.* 36 Structures] Structure *We.* 37 or] not *Mt*; nor *Ma.*
38 Or] Nor *We, Mt, Ma.* 45–46 *These lines are written in the margin of CB with
their position in the poem indicated by a caret after* Sicily: *in l. 44.*
50 *After l. 50 there appears in We alone:*
    The long-contended World's old Discords cease,
    And Actium's Terrours grace the Pomp of Peace;
See expl. note to ll. 43–46.
51 Prows] Beaks *We.* 58 it's] its *We, Mt, Ma.* 59 Winds & Seas] Seas &
Winds *We.*

The Shepherd of his flocks, the Soldier of the Fight,　　60
A milder Warfare I in Verse display;
Each in his proper Art should waste the Day:
Nor thou my gentle Calling disapprove;
To die is glorious in the Bed of Love.
Happy the Youth, & not unknown to Fame,　　65
Whose heart has never felt a second flame.
Oh, might that envied Happiness be mine!
To Cynthia all my Wishes I confine,
Or if, alas! it be my Fate to try
Another Love, the quicker let me die.　　70
But she, the Mistress of my faithful breast,
Has oft the Charms of Constancy confest,
Condemns her fickle Sexe's fond Mistake,
And hates the Tale of Troy for Helen's Sake.
Me from myself the soft Enchantress stole;　　75
Ah! let her ever my Desires controul,
Or if I fall the Victim of her Scorn,
From her loved Door may my pale Coarse be born[e].
The Power of Herbs can other Harms remove,
And find a Cure for every Ill, but Love.　　80
The Melian's Hurt Machaon could repair,
Heal the slow Chief, & send again to War;
To Chiron Phœnix owed his long-lost Sight,
And Phœbus' Son recall'd Androgeon to the Light.
Here Arts are vain, even Magick here must fail,　　85
The powerful Mixture, & the midnight Spell:
The Hand, that can my captive heart release,
And to this bosom give it's wonted Peace,
May the long Thirst of Tantalus allay,
Or drive the infernal Vulture from his Prey.　　90
For Ills unseen what Remedy is found,
Or who can probe the undiscover'd Wound?
The Bed avails not, or the Leeche's Care,
Nor changeing Skies can hurt, nor sultry Air.
'Tis hard th' elusive Symptoms to explore.　　95

---

78 Door] Doors *We.*　　80 Love.] Love *CB.*　　81 *CB, We, Ma, Mt all have*
Lemnian's *in text, but in CB* Melian's *is substituted in margin.*　　84 recall'd] restored
We.　　85 Arts are] Skill is *We.* even] e'en *Ma.*　　88 it's] its *We, Mt, Ma.*
90 Or] And *We.*

To day the Lover walks, tomorrow is no more:
A Train of mourning Friends attend his Pall,
And wonder at the sudden Funeral.
   When then my Fates, that breath they gave, shall claim;
When the short Marble but preserves a Name,   100
A little Verse, my All, that shall remain:
Thy passing Courser's slacken'd Speed retain;
(Thou envied Honour of thy Poet's Days,
Of all our Youth the Ambition, & the Praise!)
Then to my quiet Urn awhile draw near,   105
And say, while o'er the Place You drop a Tear,
Love & the Fair were of his Life the Pride;
He lived, while she was kind; & when she frown'd, he died.

Imitated from Propertius,
Lib: 3: Eleg: 5:

Pacis amor Deus est, &c:
[Love is a God of peace, &c.]

Love, gentle Power! to Peace was e'er a friend:
Before the Goddess' shrine we too, love's vot'ries, bend.
Still may his Bard in softer fights engage;
Wars hand to hand with Cynthia let me wage.

*   *   *   *

Long as of youth the joyous hours remain;   5
Me may Castalia's sweet recess detain,
Fast by th' umbrageous Vale lull'd to repose,
Where Aganippe warbles as it flows;

99 my] the *Ma.*   100 When] And *Ma.*   but] shall *We*   preserves] preserve
We, Mt, Ma.   102 retain] restrain *Ma, Mt, and most modern editions including Br*;
detain *We.*   106 the Place] that place *Ma.*   a Tear] the tear *Ma.*   107 Life]
youth *Ma.*   *At the end of the poem in CB is written* **April. 1742.

IMITATED FROM PROPERTIUS, Lib: 3: Eleg: 5. First published by Mathias, 1814,
ii. 85–87 (*Ma*), and erroneously numbered as Elegy 4.
  Text used: *CB*, i. 96–97. Text collated: *Ma*.

1–4 *Omitted in Ma.*   2 love's] loves' *CB*.

Or roused by sprightly sounds from out the trance
I'd in the ring knit hands, & joyn the Muses' Dance.   10
Give me to send the laughing bowl around,
My soul in Bacchus' pleasing fetters bound:
Let on this head unfadeing flowers reside
There bloom the vernal rose's earliest pride;
And when, our flames commission'd to destroy,   15
Age step 'twixt love & me, and intercept the joy;
When my changéd head these locks no more shall know,
And all it's jetty honours turn to Snow:
Then let me rightly spell of nature's ways
To Providence, to Him my thoughts I'd raise   20
Who taught this vast machine its stedfast laws,
That first, eternal, universal Cause:
Search to what regions yonder Star retires,
Who monthly waneing hides her paly fires;
And whence anew revived, with silver light   25
Relumes her crescent Orb to chear the dreary Night.
How riseing winds the face of Ocean sweep:
Where lie th' eternal fountains of the deep:
And whence the cloudy Magazines maintain
Their wintry war, or pour the autumnal rain: 30
How flames perhaps with dire confusion hurl'd
Shall sink this beauteous fabric of the world:
What colours paint the vivid arch of Jove:
What wondrous force the solid earth can move;
When Pindus' self approaching ruin dreads,   35
Shakes all his Pines, & bows his hundred heads:
Why does yon Orb, so exquisitely bright
Obscure his radiance in a short-lived night:
Whence the seven Sisters' congregated fires;
And what Bootes' lazy waggon tires: 40
How the rude Surge its sandy Bounds controul;
Who measured out the year, & bad[e] the seasons roll:
If realms beneath those fabled torments know;
Pangs without respite, fires that ever glow;
Earth's monster-brood stretch'd on their iron bed;   45
The hissing terrours round Alecto's head;
Scarce to nine acres Tityus' bulk confined;

24 Who] That *Ma*.

The triple dog, that scares the shadowy kind;
All angry heaven inflicts, or hell can feel,
The pendent rock, Ixion's whirling wheel,   50
Famine at feasts, & thirst amid the stream:
Or are our fears th' enthusiast's empty dream,
And all the scenes, that hurt the grave's repose,
But pictured horrour, & poëtic woes.
   These soft, inglorious joys my hours engage;   55
Be love my youth's pursuit, & science crown my Age.
You whose young bosoms feel a nobler flame
Redeem, what Crassus lost, & vindicate his name.

[The DEATH of HOËL.]
From Aneurin, Monarch of the Bards,
extracted from the Gododin.

Had I but the torrent's might,
With headlong rage & wild affright
Upon Deïra's squadrons hurl'd,
To rush, & sweep them from the world!
   Too, too secure in youthful pride   5
By them my Friend, my Hoël, died,
Great Cian's Son: of Madoc old
He ask'd no heaps of hoarded gold;
Alone in Nature's wealth array'd
He ask'd, & had the lovely Maid.   10
   To Cattraeth's vale in glitt'ring row
Twice two hundred Warriors goe;
Every Warriors manly neck
Chains of regal honour deck,

51 &] or *Ma.*   57–58 *Omitted in Ma.*   *In CB at the end of the poem is written* *December, 1738.*

THE DEATH OF HOËL. First published in *M.* The only holograph MS. is *CB*, iii. 1070, which is followed here.

Title: THE DEATH OF HOEL. *M* (From Aneurin . . . *is reworded as a footnote by M but is the only title in CB*).
12 Twice] *So in both CB and M, although given as* Thrice *by Mt, Br, and Wh.*

Wreath'd in many a golden link: 15
From the golden cup they drink
Nectar, that the bees produce,
Or the grape's extatic juice.
Flush'd with mirth & hope they burn:
But none from Cattraeth's vale return,   20
Save Aeron brave, & Conan strong,
(Bursting thro' the bloody throng)
And I, the meanest of them all,
That live to weep, & sing their fall.

17 bees] bee's *mistakenly in CB but corrected by M.*

[CARADOC.]

Have ye seen the tusky Boar,
Or the Bull, with sullen roar,
On surrounding Foes advance?
So Carádoc bore his lance.

CARADOC. First printed in *M*, ii. 106, the text followed here. There is no MS. copy.

[CONAN.]

Conan's name, my lay, rehearse,
Build to him the lofty verse,
Sacred tribute of the Bard,
Verse, the Hero's sole reward.
As the flame's devouring force;   5
As the whirlwind in its course;
As the thunder's fiery stroke,
Glancing on the shiver'd oak;
Did the sword of Conan mow
The crimson harvest of the foe.   10

CONAN. First printed in *M*, ii. 106–7, the text followed here. There is no MS. copy.

HUMOROUS AND
SATIRIC VERSE

[LINES SPOKEN BY
THE GHOST OF JOHN DENNIS AT
THE DEVIL TAVERN.]

From purling Streams & the Elysian Scene,
From Groves, that smile with never-fading Green
I reascend; in Atropos' despight
Restored to Celadon, & upper light:
Ye gods, that sway the Regions under ground,   5
Reveal to mortal View your realms profound;
At his command admit the eye of Day;
When Celadon commands, what God can disobey?
Nor seeks he your Tartarean fires to know,
The house of Torture, & th' Abyss of Woe;   10
But happy fields & Mansions free from Pain,
Gay Meads, & springing flowers best please yᵉ gentle Swain:
 That little, naked, melancholy thing
My Soul, when first she tryed her flight to wing;
Began with speed new Regions to explore,   15
And blunder'd thro' a narrow Postern door:
First most devoutly having said its Prayers,
It tumbled down a thousand pair of [Stairs],
Thro' Entries long, thro' Cellars vast & deep,
Where ghostly Rats their habitations keep,   20

LINES SPOKEN BY THE GHOST OF JOHN DENNIS. First printed by Paget Toynbee
in the *Correspondence of Gray, Walpole, West, and Ashton*, 1915, i. 13–15, from Gray's
holograph letter to Walpole (T & W no. 4), 8 Dec. 1734 (Pembroke College MS.
L.C. 2. 123, no. 5), the text followed here.

18 *A fragment has been cut out of the letter, but* Stairs *in what appears to be Walpole's
hand has been written below.*

Where Spiders spread their Webs, & owlish Goblins sleep.
After so many Chances had befell,
It came into a mead of Asphodel:
Betwixt the Confines of ye light & dark
It lies, of 'Lyzium ye St James's park: 25
Here Spirit-Beaux flutter along the Mall,
And Shadows in disguise scate o'er ye Iced Canal:
Here groves embower'd, & more sequester'd Shades,
Frequented by ye Ghosts of Ancient Maids,
Are seen to rise: the melancholy Scene   30
With gloomy haunts, & twilight walks between
Conceals the wayward band: here spend their time
Greensickness Girls, that died in youthful prime,
Virgins forlorn, all drest in Willow-green-i
With Queen Elizabeth and Nicolini.   35
    More to reveal, or many words to use
Would tire alike your patience & my muse.
Believe, that never was so faithful found
Queen Proserpine to Pluto under ground,
Or Cleopatra to her Marc-Antony   40
As Orozmades to his Celadony.
    P:S: Lucrece for half a crown will shew you fun,
But Mrs Oldfield is become a Nun.
Nobles & Cits, Prince Pluto & his Spouse
Flock to the Ghost of Covent-Garden house: 45
Plays, which were hiss'd above, below revive;
When dead applauded, that were damn'd alive:
The People, as in life, still keep their Passions,
But differ something from the world in Fashions.
Queen Artemisia breakfasts on Bohea,   50
And Alexander wears a Ramilie.

[HYMN TO IGNORANCE.
A FRAGMENT.]

HAIL, Horrors, hail! ye ever gloomy bowers,
Ye gothic fanes, and antiquated towers,
Where rushy Camus' slowly-winding flood
Perpetual draws his humid train of mud:
Glad I revisit thy neglected reign,   5
Oh take me to thy peaceful shade again.
   But chiefly thee, whose influence breath'd from high
Augments the native darkness of the sky;
Ah Ignorance! soft salutary Power!
Prostrate with filial reverence I adore.   10
Thrice hath Hyperion roll'd his annual race,
Since weeping I forsook thy fond embrace.
Oh say, successful do'st thou still oppose
Thy leaden Ægis 'gainst our antient foes?
Still stretch, tenacious of thy right divine,   15
The massy sceptre o'er thy slumb'ring line?
And dews Lethean thro' the land dispense
To steep in slumbers each benighted sense?
If any spark of Wit's delusive ray
Break out, and flash a momentary day,   20
With damp, cold touch forbid it to aspire,
And huddle up in fogs the dangerous fire.
   Oh say—she hears me not, but careless grown,
Lethargic nods upon her ebon throne.
Goddess! awake, arise, alas my fears!   25
Can powers immortal feel the force of years?

HYMN TO IGNORANCE. First published in *M*, i. 176–7. There is no holograph MS.,
but in *CB*, iii. [1103–5], there is a copy in Mason's hand (*CBM*).
   Text used: *M*. Text collated: *CBM*.

Title: Fragment of an address or Hymn to Ignorance. *CBM. There is no title in M,
although in the introductory material on p. 175 Mason refers to the poem as a* Hymn *or*
Address to Ignorance.
3 Camus'] Camus *CBM.*
17–18   Oer all the land Lethæan showers dispense
                       And steep . . .
CBM, with present reading on opposing page.

Not thus of old, with ensigns wide unfurl'd,
She rode triumphant o'er the vanquish'd world;
Fierce nations own'd her unresisted might,
And all was Ignorance, and all was Night.   30
   Oh sacred Age! Oh Times for ever lost!
(The School-man's glory, and the Church-man's boast.)
For ever gone—yet still to Fancy new, ⎫
Her rapid wings the transient scene pursue, ⎬
And bring the buried ages back to view. ⎭   35
   High on her car, behold the Grandam ride
Like old Sesostris with barbaric pride;
* * * * a team of harness'd monarchs bend
                                        * * * * *

[LINES ON
DR. ROBERT SMITH.]

Do you ask why old Focus Silvanus defies,
   And leaves not a chestnut in being?
'Tis not that old Focus himself has got eyes,
   But because he has writ about Seeing.

At the end of the poem in CBM there appears
                The pondrous Waggon lumberd slowly on x x
Below it in CBM is written
  Note:
    Thrice hath Hyperion etc.
  This line marks the time when this poem was written viz: on his return to the University after he came from abroad. about the year 1743[.]

LINES ON DR. ROBERT SMITH. The poem first appeared in *The Works of Thomas Gray in Prose and Verse*, ed. Edmund Gosse, vol. i: *Poems, Journals, and Essays*, revised edition (London: Macmillan, 1902), p. 142, the text followed here and the only text known.

[TOPHET.]

Inscription on a portrait.

Such *Tophet* was; so looked the grinning Fiend
Whom many a frighted Prelate calld his friend;
I saw them bow & while they wishd him dead
With servile simper nod the mitred head.
Our Mother-Church with half-averted sight   5
Blushd as she blesst her griesly proselyte:
Hosannahs rung thro Hells tremendous borders
And Satans self had thoughts of taking orders.

TOPHET. First published in the *London Magazine*, lii (June 1783), 296 (*L*), and later
by Bion in *The Gentleman's Magazine*, lv, ii (Oct. 1785), 759 (*G*). There are three
copies, none in Gray's hand, at Cambridge: (1) in *CB*, iii. 1106, which is followed here;
(2) accompanied by Mason's sketch in the Cole MSS. and reproduced by Whibley in
the Oxford Gray (*C*); and (3) also accompanied by the sketch in Pembroke College
MS. 74 (*Pe*).

Texts collated: *C*, *G*, *L*, *Pe*. The editors have provided terminal punctuation for
ll. 2 and 4.

Title: Mʳ. Etough, Rector of Therfeild [*sic*] in Hartfordshire, who had been a dissenting
Teacher in a Barn at Debden in Essex, died in August 1757 [*followed by Mason's sketch*]
Pe; Mʳ. Etough of Therfeild in Hartfordshire. obiit 1757. [*also followed by sketch*] *C*;
On Mr. E - - -'s being ordained. [*in italics*] *L*.

1 Such Tophet was — so grin'd the bawling Fiend, *C*, *Pe*, *also L with* grum'd *for* grin'd;
Thus Tophet look'd; so grinned the brawling fiend *G*.   2 While frighted Prelates
bow'd and called him Friend: *C*, *G*, *L*, *Pe*.   3-4 *Omitted in C*, *G*, *L*, *Pe, but
written at the bottom of the page in CB and marked* addition in the first copy.   4 *Below*
servile *in CB there is a blotted word which is possibly* civil.   *At the end of C and Pe*
Gray *and* Tho: Gray *respectively are written followed by notes of slightly different wording
indicating that Mason made the sketch and Tyson engraved it.*

SATIRE ON THE HEADS OF HOUSES;
OR, NEVER A BARREL THE
BETTER HERRING.

O CAMBRIDGE, attend
To the Satire I've pen'd
On the Heads of thy Houses,
Thou Seat of the Muses!

Know the Master of Jesus   5
Does hugely displease us;
The Master of Maudlin
In the same dirt is dawdling;
The Master of Sidney
Is of the same kidney;   10
The Master of Trinity
To him bears affinity;
As the Master of Keys
Is as like as two pease,
So the Master of Queen's   15
Is as like as two beans;
The Master of King's
Copies them in all things;
The Master of Catherine
Takes them all for his pattern;   20
The Master of Clare
Hits them all to a hair;
The Master of Christ
By the rest is enticed;
But the Master of Emmanuel   25
Follows them like a spaniel;

SATIRE ON THE HEADS OF HOUSES. First printed by Gosse, 1884, from a MS. owned by Lord Houghton, the text followed here. There is a copy by Mitford (*Mt*) in his Note-book, vol. iii, ff. 129–31.

Title: Lines on the Heads of Houses. Never a barrell better Herring. *Mt*.

2 I've pen'd] I penn'd *Mt*. 3 thy] the *Mt*. 6 hugely] largely *Mt*. 12 him] these *Mt*. 13 As the Master] The Master *Mt*. 15 So the Master] The Master *Mt*. 20 his] a *Mt*. 25 But the Master] The Master *Mt*.

The Master of Benet
Is of the like tenet;
The Master of Pembroke
Has from them his system took;　　30
The Master of Peter's
Has all the same features;
The Master of St. John's
Like the rest of the Dons.

P.S.—As to Trinity Hall　　35
We say nothing at all.

[SKETCH OF HIS OWN CHARACTER.]

Too poor for a bribe, and too proud to importune;
He had not the method of making a fortune:
Could love, and could hate, so was thought somewhat odd;
No very great Wit, he believ'd in a God.
A Post or a Pension he did not desire,　　5
But left Church and State to Charles Townshend and Squire.

28 the] a *Mt.*　　　29 Pembroke] Pembroke *Mt.*　　　30 system] system *Mt.*
35 *P.S. —* As to] As to *Mt.*

Sketch of his own character. First published in *M*, i. 264 n. (the text followed here), where Mason explains that the poem was written in 1761 and found by him in one of Gray's pocket-books. A copy in Mason's hand is in *CB*, iii. 1111–12 (*CBM*).

4 Wit, he] Wit: for he *CBM.*
5 *In the margin opposite* Post (*which is underlined*) *in CBM is written:*

　　first word
　　Place [*underlined*]

followed by a note in Mason's hand: wch authenticates these lines. *Mitford reads* Post *in the text as do the two Mason copies, but Bradshaw and Whibley prefer* Place.

THE CANDIDATE

BY

MR. GRAY.

WHEN sly Jemmy Twitcher had smugg'd up his face
With a lick of court white-wash, and pious grimace,
A wooing he went, where three Sisters of old
In harmless society guttle and scold.
    Lord! Sister, says Physic to Law, I declare   5
Such a sheep-biting look, such a pick-pocket air,

THE CANDIDATE. Written in 1764 during Sandwich's candidacy for the High Steward-ship at Cambridge. There are two MS. copies in Walpole's hand: (1) at the Yale University Library (*WY*) and (2) at the Pierpont Morgan Library (*WM*). What possibly was the first edition of the poem survives in several printed copies, two of them at Eton, from which the text followed here (*E*) is taken. Whibley believed that it was published by Walpole at Strawberry Hill after Sept. 1774 (see T & W, Appendix P), and that the title may have been given to the poem by Walpole, for in only *E*, *WM*, and *WY* is it entitled 'The Candidate'. On the other hand, Mr. Allen Hazen (*Walpole-Mason Corres.*, Yale ed., ii. 377, Appendix 7) states that the Headmaster of Eton, Mr. Robert Birley, 'who is a student of the S[trawberry] H[ill] Press, does not believe *The Candidate* was printed there . . .'. Consequently, Mr. Hazen suggests 'that HW made one or more manuscript copies in 1774, and that from one of these the *London Evening Post* derived its text in 1777; the separate printing was more probably prepared in London, very possibly as late as 1787'. The testimony of Mr. Birley is doubtless conclusive evidence that the separate copies were not printed at Strawberry Hill, but the present editors are less certain about the 1787 dating, for, as an examination of the textual notes will reveal, there are two basic texts for *The Candidate*: (1) the text appearing in the two periodicals (see below), which differ only very slightly, and (2) the text in the two Walpole MSS. and in the separate printing. The three last are almost identical but differ very noticeably in phrasing from the text given by the periodicals. One might, therefore, suspect that at some undetermined time between 1774 and 1787 Walpole either had the poem printed by an unknown printer or permitted someone to take a very accurate copy of his own MS. from which *E* was printed. In any event the poem was published without any title but prefaced by the following letter in the *London Evening Post* (*LP*), Feb. 1777 (Brit. Mus. Burney MS. 654*b*):

The following verses are said to be the production of the late celebrated Mr. Gray. They were written on the occasion of Jemmy Twitcher's standing a candidate for the ——, at ——, and in whose favour the gentlemen of the gown took a very active part. As they are in but a few hands, and I think them too good to be lost, you are at liberty to print them, if you shall think them worth a corner of your paper.

Anti-Twitcher.

A very similar text, also from an unidentified source, was published by 'Adurfi' in the *Gentleman's Magazine*, lii (Jan. 1782), 39–40 (*GM*), where it was entitled 'Jemmy Twitcher, or The Cambridge Courtship'. *GM* and *LP* are for the first time collated here.

Texts collated: *GM*, *LP*, *WM*, *WY*.

4 *Mason* (*Walpole-Mason Corres.*, ii. 171, 2 Oct. 1774) *wrote to Walpole, who had just sent him a copy of the poem, 'I remember when he repeated them to me (for I never before saw them in writing) that the epithet in the fourth line was* awkward *society, which I think better than* harmless.'

Not I, for the Indies! you know I'm no prude;
But his nose is a shame, and his eyes are so lewd!
Then he shambles and straddles so oddly, I fear—
No; at our time of life, 'twould be silly, my dear.   10

I don't know, says Law, now methinks, for his look,
'Tis just like the picture in Rochester's book.
But his character, Phyzzy, his morals, his life;
When she died, I can't tell, but he once had a wife.

They say he's no Christian, loves drinking and whoring, 15
And all the town rings of his swearing and roaring,
His lying, and filching, and Newgate-bird tricks:—
Not I, —for a coronet, chariot and six.

Divinity heard, between waking and dozing,
Her sisters denying, and Jemmy proposing;   20
From dinner she rose with her bumper in hand,
She stroked up her belly, and stroked down her band.

What a pother is here about wenching and roaring!
Why David loved catches, and Solomon whoring.
Did not Israel filch from th' Ægyptians of old   25
Their jewels of silver, and jewels of gold?
The prophet of Bethel, we read, told a lie:
He drinks; so did Noah: he swears; so do I.
To refuse him for such peccadillos, were odd;
Besides, he repents, and he talks about G - - .   30

Never hang down your head, you poor penitent elf!
Come, buss me, I'll be Mrs. Twitcher myself.
D - - n ye both for a couple of Puritan bitches!
He's Christian enough, that repents, and that - - - - - - - -.

8 nose] name *GM*.   9 Then he] He *WY*.   11 now] but *GM, LP*.   12 *See expl. notes*.   13 But] Then *GM, LP*.   14 can't tell, but he once] can't tell— he once *GM, LP. See expl. notes also*.   17 His lying, and filching] And filching and lying *GM, LP. An asterisk follows* filching *in LP and the following foot-note is appended*: When this genius presided at the *********, in 1763, about three months only, he —— every appointment that then became vacant; which example, *famous* as it was, was strictly followed by his compeer, his successor in office, to the injury of merit and faithful services.   19 between] betwixt *WY*.   21 dinner] table *GM, LP*.   with her bumper] , and with bumper *GM*; , with a bumper *LP, WY*.   22 She] And *LP*.   23 wenching] drinking *WY*.   24 *See expl. notes*.   25 Did not] Did'nt *LP*.   27 read,] know *WY*.   29 refuse] reject *GM, LP*.   30 , and] — for *GM, LP*.   *After l. 30 there is printed in GM [*To Jemmy*] and in italics in LP* (Speaking to Jemmy.).   33–34 *Both lines are omitted from GM, LP, and WY, but appear, although crossed out, in WM, where the final word is clearly* stitches. *See expl. note to line 34*.

William Shakespeare
To Mrs Anne, Regular Servant
to the Revd Mr Precentor
of York.

A MOMENT'S patience, gentle Mistris Anne!
(But stint your clack for sweet St Charitie)
'Tis Willy begs, once a right proper Man,
Tho' now a Book, and interleav'd, you see.
  Much have I born[e] from canker'd Critick's spite, 5
From fumbling Baronets, and Poets small,
Pert Barristers, & Parsons nothing bright:
But, what awaits me now, is worst of all!
  'Tis true, our Master's temper natural
Was fashion'd fair in meek & dovelike guise: 10
But may not honey's self be turn'd to gall
By residence, by marriage, & sore eyes?
  If then he wreak on me his wicked will:
Steal to his closet at the hour of prayer,
And (when thou hear'st the organ piping shrill) 15
Grease his best pen, & all he scribbles, tear.
  Better to bottom tarts & cheesecakes nice,
Better the roast-meat from the fire to save,
Better be twisted into caps for spice,
Than thus be patch'd, & cobbled in one's grave! 20

WILLIAM SHAKESPEARE TO MRS. ANNE. First published by Mitford in the *Correspondence of Gray and Mason*, 1853, pp. 339-40.
  Text used: Gray's letter to Mason (T & W no. 407), *c.* 8 July 1765 (*G-2*). Texts collated: Gray notebook owned by Lt.-Col. Sir John Murray (*G-1*), probably the first draft; copy by Mitford in his Note-book, vol. iii, f. 127 (*Mt*).

           Anne regular
Title: Verses from Wm Shakspeare to Mrs. Mcg, Servant to the Revd Mr Mason [Mason *del*, Precentor *substituted*] of York. *Mt.*
2 But] And *G-1*. your] thy *G-1, Mt.* sweet] dear *G-1*. 5 canker'd Critick's] crabbed Critics' *Mt.* 7 Barristers] Baronets *Mt.* 8 worst of] worse than *Mt.* *Ll. 17-20 appear after l. 8 in Mt.* 9 'Tis . . . Master's] True, the Precentor's *G-1*. 10 fashion'd fair] moulded soft *G-1*. dovelike] lowly *with* dovelike *as alternative, G-1*. 12 sore eyes?] Mince Pies. *Mt.* 14 at] in *Mt.* 17 cheesecakes] puddings *with* biscuits *substituted, G-1*. 17, 19 *transposed in G-1*. 20 one's] my *G-1*.

So York shall taste, what Clouët never knew;
So from *our* works sublimer fumes shall rise:
While Nancy earns the praise to Shakespear due
For glorious puddings, & immortal pies.

[IMPROMPTUS.]

Extempore by M.ʳ Gr[ay]. on D.ʳ K[eene].
B[ishop]. of C[hester].

The Bishop of Chester
Tho' wiser than Nestor
And fairer than Esther,
If you scratch him will fester.

one day the Bishop having offered to
give a Gentleman a Goose M.ʳ
Gr[ay]. composed his Epitaph,
thus.

Here lies Edmund Keene Lord Bishop of Chester,
He eat a fat Goose and could not digest her—

And this upon his Lady—

Here lies M.ʳˢ Keene the Bishop of Chester,
She had a bad face which did sadly molest her.

22 *our*] thy (*del*) *G-1*.   works] work *Mt*.   fumes] *illeg. possibly* buns *Mt*.
23 earns] reaps *G-1*.   24 For] To *Mt*.   puddings] Cheese cakes *Mt*.   *At the
end of G-2 Gray added*, Tell me, if you don't like this, and I'll send you a worse.

IMPROMPTUS. The text followed here, the only known MS., is that of Wharton's copy
in the British Museum, Egerton MS. 2400, ff. 233–4. See explanatory notes. First
published by Gosse, 1884.

'One day the Bishop having offered . . .'
Title: composed] wrote (*del*).
'And this upon his Lady'
1 the] *Illeg. word, possibly* Lord, *del*.

Impromptu by M.ʳ Gray going out of
Raby Castle

Here lives Harry Vane,
Very good claret and fine Champaign

A Couplet by M.ʳ Gray

When you rise from your dinner as light as before
'Tis a sign you have eat just enough and no more.

[PARODY ON AN EPITAPH.]

Now clean, now hideous, mellow now, now gruff,
She swept, she hiss'd, she ripen'd & grew rough,
At Broom, Pendragon, Appleby & Brough.

[INVITATION TO MASON.]

Prim *Hurd* attends your call, & *Palgrave* proud,
Stonhewer the lewd, & *Delaval* the loud.
For thee does *Powel* squeeze, & *Marriot* sputter,
And *Glyn* cut phizzes, & Tom *Nevile* stutter.
Brown sees thee sitting on his nose's tip,   5
The *Widow* feels thee in her aching hip
For thee fat *Nanny* sighs, & handy *Nelly*,
And *Balguy* with a Bishop in his belly!

PARODY ON AN EPITAPH. The text is the holograph copy in the British Museum, Egerton MS. 2400, f. 181, on which Wharton has noted 'Extempore Epitaph on Ann Countess of Dorset, Pembroke, and Montgomery, made by M.ʳ. Gray on reading the Epitaph on her mothers tomb in the Church at Appleby composed by the Countess in the same manner'. First published by Gosse, 1884.

INVITATION TO MASON. First published by Mitford in his *Gray and Mason* correspondence, 1853, and under the title of 'Comic Lines', by Gosse in 1884. The text adopted here is that of Gray's letter to Mason, 8 Jan. 1768 (T & W no. 461). There is a copy by Mitford (*Mt*) in his Note-book, vol. iii.

1 Prim *Hurd*] Weddell *Mt variant*.   6 in] on *Mt*.

[LINES WRITTEN AT BURNHAM.]

And, as they bow their hoary Tops, relate
In murm'ring Sounds the dark Decrees of Fate;
While Visions, as Poetic eyes avow,
Cling to each Leaf, & swarm on ev'ry Bough:

*   *   *

—the tim'rous Hare, & sportive Squirrel   5
Gambol around me — — — —

LINES WRITTEN AT BURNHAM. First published by Mason, i. 24. The text followed
here is that of the letter to Walpole (T & W no. 26, Aug. 1736), Pembroke College MS.
L.C. 2. 123, no. 24.

AGRIPPINA, a TRAGEDY.

DRAMATIS PERSONÆ.

AGRIPPINA, the Empress mother.
NERO, the Emperor.
POPPÆA, believed to be in love with OTHO.
OTHO, a young man of quality, in love with POPPÆA.
SENECA, the Emperor's preceptor.
ANICETUS, Captain of the guards.
DEMETRIUS, the Cynic, friend to SENECA.
ACERONIA, Confidant to AGRIPPINA.

SCENE, the Emperor's villa at BAIÆ.

[ARGUMENT.]

The drama opens with the indignation of Agrippina, at receiving her son's orders from Anicetus to remove from Baiæ, and to have her guard taken from her. At this time Otho having conveyed Poppæa from the house of her husband Rufus Crispinus, brings her to Baiæ, where he means to conceal her among the croud; or, if his fraud is discovered, to have recourse to the Emperor's authority; but, knowing the lawless temper of Nero, he determines not to have recourse to that expedient, but on the utmost necessity. In the meantime he commits her to the care of Anicetus, whom he takes to be his friend, and in whose age he thinks he may safely

AGRIPPINA. First printed in *M*, i. 125–35. Mason wrote: 'But let me . . . give the reader what little insight I can into Mr. Gray's plan, as I find, and select it from two detached papers' (p. 125). Gray composed the Argument himself: 'The argument drawn out by him [Gray], in these two papers, under the idea of a plot and underplot, I shall here unite; as it will tend to show that the action itself was possest of sufficient unity' (p. 126).

Since it had been objected that the speech of Agrippina was too long, Mason made certain revisions: 'The Editor has obviated this objection, not by retrenching, but by putting part of it into the mouth of Aceronia, and by breaking it in a few other places. Originally it was one continued speech from the line "Thus ever grave[,] and undisturbed Reflection" [l. 82] to the end of the scene; which was undoubtedly too long for the lungs of any Actress' (p. 136 n.). Bradshaw and Tovey attempted to restore the original text and Whibley follows their restoration (Oxford, 1937), for there are no known MSS. nor any other early printed texts. However, since even this ingenious restoration is necessarily somewhat conjectural, the text of *M* is followed here and the Tovey-Whibley (*T-W*) variants are indicated in the notes.

confide. Nero is not yet come to Baiæ; but Seneca, whom he sends before him, informs Agrippina of the accusation concerning Rubellius Plancus, and desires her to clear herself, which she does briefly; but demands to see her son, who, on his arrival, acquits her of all suspicion, and restores her to her honours. In the meanwhile Anicetus, to whose care Poppæa had been entrusted by Otho, contrives the following plot to ruin Agrippina: He betrays his trust to Otho, and brings Nero, as it were by chance, to the sight of the beautiful Poppæa; the Emperor is immediately struck with her charms, and she, by a feigned resistance, increases his passion; tho', in reality, she is from the first dazzled with the prospect of empire, and forgets Otho: She therefore joins with Anicetus in his design of ruining Agrippina, soon perceiving that it will be for her interest. Otho hearing that the Emperor had seen Poppæa, is much enraged; but not knowing that this interview was obtained thro' the treachery of Anicetus, is readily persuaded by him to see Agrippina in secret, and acquaint her with his fears that her son Nero would marry Poppæa. Agrippina, to support her own power, and to wean the Emperor from the love of Poppæa, gives Otho encouragement, and promises to support him. Anicetus secretly introduces Nero to hear their discourse; who resolves immediately on his mother's death, and, by Anicetus's means, to destroy her by drowning. A solemn feast, in honour of their reconciliation, is to be made; after which she being to go by sea to Bauli, the ship is so contrived as to sink or crush her; she escapes by accident, and returns to Baiæ. In this interval, Otho has an interview with Poppæa; and being duped a second time by Anicetus and her, determines to fly with her into Greece, by means of a vessel which is to be furnished by Anicetus; but he, pretending to remove Poppæa on board in the night, conveys her to Nero's apartment: She there encourages and determines Nero to banish Otho, and finish the horrid deed he had attempted on his mother. Anicetus undertakes to execute his resolves; and, under pretence of a plot upon the Emperor's life, is sent with a guard to murder Agrippina, who is still at Baiæ in imminent fear, and irresolute how to conduct herself. The account of her death, and the Emperor's horrour and fruitless remorse, finishes the drama.

I refer the reader to the 13th and 14th books of the annals of Tacitus for the facts on which this story is founded: By turning to that author, he will easily see how far the poet thought it necessary to deviate from the truth of history. I shall only further observe,

that as such a fable could not possibly admit of any good character,
it is terror only and not pity that could be excited by this tragedy,
had it been completed. [Mason, i. 126–8.]

ACT I. SCENE I.

AGRIPPINA, ACERONIA.

AGRIPPINA.

'T is well, begone! your errand is perform'd:

　　　　　　　　　　　　[Speaks as to Anicetus entering.

The message needs no comment. Tell your master,
His mother shall obey him. Say you saw her
Yielding due reverence to his high command:
Alone, unguarded, and without a Lictor,　　　　　　　　　5
As fits the daughter of Germanicus.
Say, she retired to Antium; there to tend
Her houshold cares, a woman's best employment.
What if you add, how she turn'd pale, and trembled;
You think, you spied a tear stand in her eye,　　　　　10
And would have drop'd, but that her pride restrain'd it?
(Go! you can paint it well) 'twill profit you,
And please the stripling. Yet 'twould dash his joy
To hear the spirit of Britannicus
Yet walks on earth; at least there are who know　　　15
Without a spell to raise, and bid it fire
A thousand haughty hearts, unus'd to shake
When a boy frowns, nor to be lur'd with smiles
To taste of hollow kindness, or partake
His hospitable board: They are aware　　　　　　　　20
Of th' unpledg'd bowl, they love not Aconite.

ACERONIA.

He's gone; and much I hope these walls alone,
And the mute air are privy to your passion.
Forgive your servant's fears, who sees the danger
Which fierce resentment cannot fail to raise　　　　25
In haughty youth, and irritated power.

AGRIPPINA.

And dost thou talk to me, to me, of danger,
Of haughty youth, and irritated power,
To her that gave it being, her that arm'd
This painted Jove, and taught his novice hand   30
To aim the forked bolt; while he stood trembling
Scar'd at the sound, and dazzled with its brightness?
    'Tis like, thou hast forgot, when yet a stranger
To adoration, to the grateful steam
Of flattery's incense, and obsequious vows   35
From voluntary realms, a puny boy,
Deck'd with no other lustre, than the blood
Of Agrippina's race, he liv'd unknown
To fame, or fortune; haply eyed at distance
Some edileship, ambitious of the power   40
To judge of weights, and measures; scarcely dar'd
On expectation's strongest wing to soar
High as the consulate, that empty shade
Of long-forgotten liberty: When I
Oped his young eye to bear the blaze of greatness;   45
Shew'd him, where empire tower'd, and bad[e] him strike
The noble quarry. Gods! then was the time
To shrink from danger; fear might then have worn
The mask of prudence: but a heart like mine,
A heart that glows with the pure Julian fire,   50
If bright Ambition from her craggy seat
Display the radiant prize, will mount undaunted,
Gain the rough heights, and grasp the dangerous honour.

ACERONIA.

Thro' various life I have pursued your steps,
Have seen your soul, and wonder'd at its daring: 55
Hence rise my fears. Nor am I yet to learn
How vast the debt of gratitude, which Nero
To such a mother owes; the world, you gave him,
Suffices not to pay the obligation.
    I well remember too (for I was present)   60
When in a secret and dead hour of night,
Due sacrifice perform'd with barb'rous rites

Of mutter'd charms, and solemn invocation,
You bad[e] the Magi call the dreadful powers,
That read futurity, to know the fate   65
Impending o'er your son: Their answer was,
If the son reign, the mother perishes.
Perish (you cry'd) the mother! reign the son!
He reigns, the rest is heav'n's; who oft has bad[e],
Ev'n when its will seem'd wrote in lines of blood,   70
Th' unthought event disclose a whiter meaning.
Think too how oft in weak and sickly minds
The sweets of kindness lavishly indulg'd
Rankle to gall; and benefits too great
To be repaid, sit heavy on the soul,   75
As unrequited wrongs. The willing homage
Of prostrate Rome, the senate's joint applause,
The riches of the earth, the train of pleasures,
That wait on youth, and arbitrary sway;
These were your gift, and with them you bestow'd   80
The very power he has to be ungrateful.

AGRIPPINA.

Thus ever grave, and undisturb'd reflection
Pours its cool dictates in the madding ear
Of rage, and thinks to quench the fire it feels not.
Say'st thou I must be cautious, must be silent,   85
And tremble at the phantom I have rais'd?
Carry to him thy timid counsels. He
Perchance may heed 'em: Tell him too, that one,
Who had such liberal power to give, may still
With equal power resume that gift, and raise   90
A tempest, that shall shake her own creation
To its original atoms—tell me! say
This mighty Emperor, this dreaded Hero,
Has he beheld the glittering front of war?
Knows his soft ear the Trumpet's thrilling voice,   95
And outcry of the battle? Have his limbs
Sweat under iron harness? Is he not
The silken son of dalliance, nurs'd in Ease
And Pleasure's flowery lap?—Rubellius lives,

And Sylla has his friends, tho' school'd by fear   100
To bow the supple knee, and court the times
With shows of fair obeisance; and a call,
Like mine, might serve belike to wake pretensions
Drowsier than theirs, who boast the genuine blood
Of our imperial house.   105

ACERONIA.

Did I not wish to check this dangerous passion,
I might remind my mistress that her nod
Can rouse eight hardy legions, wont to stem
With stubborn nerves the tide, and face the rigour
Of bleak Germania's snows. Four, not less brave,   110
That in Armenia quell the Parthian force
Under the warlike Corbulo, by you
Mark'd for their leader: These, by ties confirm'd,
Of old respect and gratitude, are yours.
Surely the Masians too, and those of Egypt,   115
Have not forgot your sire: The eye of Rome
And the Prætorian camp have long rever'd
With custom'd awe, the daughter, sister, wife,
And mother of their Cæsars.

AGRIPPINA.

Ha! by Juno,   120
It bears a noble semblance. On this base
My great revenge shall rise; or say we sound
The trump of liberty; there will not want,
Even in the servile senate, ears to own
Her spirit-stirring voice; Soranus there,   125
And Cassius; Vetus too, and Thrasea,
Minds of the antique cast, rough, stubborn souls,
That struggle with the yoke. How shall the spark
Unquenchable, that glows within their breasts,
Blaze into freedom, when the idle herd   130

105–8   Of our imperial house. [Cannot my nod]
               Rouse [up] eight hardy . . . *T-W*.
110 . . . snows. Four . . .] . . . snows [?] Four . . . *T-W*.   112 you] me *T-W*.
114 yours] mine *T-W*.   116 your] my *T-W*.
119–20   And mother of their Caesars.
               Ha! by Juno, *T-W*.

(Slaves from the womb, created but to stare,
And bellow in the Circus) yet will start,
And shake 'em at the name of liberty,
Stung by a senseless word, a vain tradition,
As there were magic in it? wrinkled beldams   135
Teach it their grandchildren, as somewhat rare
That anciently appear'd, but when, extends
Beyond their chronicle—oh! 'tis a cause
To arm the hand of childhood, and rebrace
The slacken'd sinews of time-wearied age.   140
  Yes, we may meet, ingrateful boy, we may!
Again the buried genius of old Rome
Shall from the dust uprear his reverend head,
Rous'd by the shout of millions: There before
His high tribunal thou and I appear.   145
Let majesty sit on thy awful brow,
And lighten from thy eye: Around thee call
The gilded swarm that wantons in the sunshine
Of thy full favour; Seneca be there
In gorgeous phrase of labour'd eloquence   150
To dress thy plea, and Burrhus strengthen it
With his plain soldier's oath, and honest seeming.
Against thee, liberty and Agrippina:
The world, the prize; and fair befall the victors.
  But soft! why do I waste the fruitless hours   155
In threats unexecuted? Haste thee, fly
These hated walls, that seem to mock my shame,
And cast me forth in duty to their lord.

ACERONIA.

'Tis time we go, the sun is high advanc'd
And, ere mid-day, Nero will come to Baiæ.   160

AGRIPPINA.

My thought aches at him; not the basilisk
More deadly to the sight, than is to me
The cool injurious eye of frozen kindness.
I will not meet its poison. Let him feel
Before he sees me.   165

  159–60 ACERONIA. / 'Tis . . . / . . . Baiæ. / AGRIPPINA. *deleted in T-W.*

ACERONIA.

Why then stays my sovereign,
Where he so soon may—

AGRIPPINA.

             Yes, I will be gone,
But not to Antium—all shall be confess'd
Whate'er the frivolous tongue of giddy fame   170
Has spread among the crowd; things, that but whisper'd
Have arch'd the hearer's brow, and riveted
His eyes in fearful extasy: No matter
What; so't be strange, and dreadful.—Sorceries,
Assassinations, poisonings—the deeper   175
My guilt, the blacker his ingratitude.
    And you, ye manes of ambition's victims,
Enshrined Claudius, with the pitied ghosts
Of the Syllani, doom'd to early death,
(Ye unavailing horrours, fruitless crimes!)   180
If from the realms of night my voice ye hear,
In lieu of penitence, and vain remorse,
Accept my vengeance. Tho' by me ye bled,
He was the cause. My love, my fears for him
Dried the soft springs of pity in my heart,   185
And froze them up with deadly cruelty.
Yet if your injur'd shades demand my fate,
If murder cries for murder, blood for blood,
Let me not fall alone; but crush his pride,
And sink the traitor in his mother's ruin.   *Exeunt.* 190

SCENE II.

OTHO, POPPÆA.

OTHO.

Thus far we're safe. Thanks to the rosy queen
Of amorous thefts: And had her wanton son
Lent us his wings, we could not have beguil'd
With more elusive speed the dazzled sight

166-7 ACERONIA. / Why . . . / . . . may— / AGRIPPINA. *deleted in T-W*.

Of wakeful jealousy. Be gay securely; 195
Dispell, my fair, with smiles, the tim'rous cloud
That hangs on thy clear brow. So Helen look'd,
So her white neck reclin'd, so was she borne
By the young Trojan to his gilded bark
With fond reluctance, yielding modesty, 200
And oft reverted eye, as if she knew not
Whether she fear'd, or wish'd to be pursued.

* * * * * * *

Sonnet.
[On the Death of Richard West.]

In vain to me the smileing Mornings shine,
And redning Phœbus lifts his golden Fire:
The Birds in vain their amorous Descant joyn;
Or chearful Fields resume their green Attire:
These Ears, alas! for other Notes repine, 5
A different Object do these Eyes require.
My lonely Anguish melts no Heart, but mine;
And in my Breast the imperfect Joys expire.
Yet Morning smiles the busy Race to chear,
And new-born Pleasure brings to happier Men: 10
The Fields to all their wonted Tribute bear:
To warm their little Loves the Birds complain:
I fruitless mourn to him, that cannot hear,
And weep the more, because I weep in vain.

SONNET. First published in *M*, ii. 60.
    Text used: *CB*, i. 284. Text collated: *M*.

Title: SONNET / ON THE DEATH OF / MR. RICHARD WEST. *M*.
At the end of the poem *at Stoke, Aug: 1742 *CB*.

[THE ALLIANCE OF
EDUCATION AND GOVERNMENT.
A FRAGMENT.]

COMMENTARY.

The Author's subject being (as we have seen) THE NECESSARY
ALLIANCE BETWEEN A GOOD FORM OF GOVERNMENT AND A GOOD
MODE OF EDUCATION, IN ORDER TO PRODUCE THE HAPPINESS OF
MANKIND, the Poem opens with two similes; an uncommon kind
of exordium: but which I suppose the Poet intentionally chose, to
intimate the analogical method he meant to pursue in his subsequent
reasonings. 1st, He asserts that men without education are like
sickly plants in a cold or barren soil (line 1 to 5, and 8 to 12;) and,
2dly, he compares them, when unblest with a just and well regulated
government, to plants that will not blossom or bear fruit in an
unkindly and inclement air (l. 5 to 9, and l. 13 to 22). Having thus
laid down the two propositions he means to prove, he begins by
examining into the characteristics which (taking a general view of
mankind) all men have in common one with another (l. 22 to 39);
they covet pleasure and avoid pain (l. 31); they feel gratitude for
benefits (l. 34); they desire to avenge wrongs, which they effect
either by force or cunning (l. 35); they are linked to each other by
their common feelings, and participate in sorrow and in joy (l. 36,
37). If then all the human species agree in so many moral particulars,
whence arises the diversity of national characters? This question
the Poet puts at line 38, and dilates upon to l. 64. Why, says he,
have some nations shewn a propensity to commerce and industry;
others to war and rapine; others to ease and pleasure? (l. 42 to 46)
Why have the Northern people overspread, in all ages, and prevailed over the Southern? (l. 46 to 58) Why has Asia been, time out
of mind, the seat of despotism, and Europe that of freedom? (l. 59
to 64) Are we from these instances to imagine men necessarily en-
slaved to the inconveniences of the climate where they were born?

THE ALLIANCE OF EDUCATION AND GOVERNMENT. First published in *M*, i. 193–
200, from which the 'Commentary' is taken. There are two copies in Gray's hand,
CB, ii. 619–20, and the letter to Wharton of 19 Aug. 1748, containing ll. 1–57 in Gray's
hand (*Wh-1*) and the remainder in Wharton's (*Wh-2*)—both in Brit. Mus. Egerton
MS. 2400, ff. 30–32 (T & W no. 146). Gray has added at the end of *Wh-1*: 'I desire your
Judgement upon so far, before I proceed any farther.'
Text used: *CB*. Texts collated: *M*, *Wh-1*, *Wh-2*.

(l. 64 to 72) Or are we not rather to suppose there is a natural strength in the human mind, that is able to vanquish and break through them? (l. 72 to 84) It is confest, however, that men receive an early tincture from the situation they are placed in, and the climate which produces them (l. 84 to 88). Thus the inhabitants of the mountains, inured to labour and patience, are naturally trained to war (l. 88 to 96); while those of the plain are more open to any attack, and softened by ease and plenty (l. 96 to 99). Again, the Ægyptians, from the nature of their situation, might be the inventors of home-navigation, from a necessity of keeping up an intercourse between their towns during the inundation of the Nile (l. 99 to ****). Those persons would naturally have the first turn to commerce, who inhabited a barren coast like the Tyrians, and were persecuted by some neighbouring tyrant; or were drove to take refuge on some shoals, like the Venetian and Hollander; their discovery of some rich island, in the infancy of the world, described. The Tartar hardened to war by his rigorous climate and pastoral life, and by his disputes for water and herbage in a country without land-marks, as also by skirmishes between his rival clans, was consequently fitted to conquer his rich Southern neighbours, whom ease and luxury had enervated: Yet this is no proof that liberty and valour may not exist in Southern climes, since the Syrians and Carthaginians gave noble instances of both; and the Arabians carried their conquests as far as the Tartars. Rome also (for many centuries) repulsed those very nations, which, when she grew weak, at length demolished her extensive Empire. [Mason, i. 193–200.]

ESSAY I.

πόταγ', ὦ 'γαθέ· τὰν γὰρ ἀοιδάν
οὔτι πω [πα] εἰς Ἀΐδαν γε τὸν ἐκλελάθοντα φυλαξεῖς.
Theoc[rítus, *Idyll* i. 62–63].

[Come, gentle sir; surely you will not keep your song
for Hades, who causes forgetfulness.]

As sickly Plants betray a niggard Earth,
Whose barren Bosom starves her gen'rous Birth
Nor genial Warmth, nor genial Juice retains
Their Roots to feed, & fill their verdant Veins:

2 barren] flinty *Wh-1.*

And as in Climes, where Winter holds his Reign,   5
The Soil, tho' fertile, will not teem in vain,
Forbids her Gems to swell, her Shades to rise,
Nor trusts her Blossoms to the churlish Skies.
So draw Mankind in vain the vital Airs,
Unform'd, unfriended, by those kindly Cares,   10
That Health & Vigour to the Soul impart,
Spread the young Thought, & warm the opening Heart.
So fond Instruction on the growing Powers
Of Nature idly lavishes her Stores,
If equal Justice with unclouded Face   15
Smile not indulgent on the rising Race,
And scatter with a free, tho' frugal, Hand
Light golden Showers of Plenty o'er the Land:
But Tyranny has fix'd her Empire there   ⎫
To check their tender Hopes with chilling Fear,   ⎬   20
And blast the blooming Promise of the Year.   ⎭
    This spacious animated Scene survey,
From where the rolling Orb, that gives the Day,
His sable Sons with nearer Course surrounds
To either Pole, & Life's remotest Bounds.   25
How rude soe'er th' exterior Form we find,
Howe'er Opinion tinge the varied Mind,
Alike to all the Kind impartial Heav'n
The Sparks of Truth & Happiness has given:
With Sense to feel, with Mem'ry to retain,   30
They follow Pleasure, & they fly from Pain;
Their Judgement mends the Plan their Fancy draws,
Th' Event presages, & explores the Cause;
The soft Returns of Gratitude they know,
By Fraud elude, by Force repell the Foe;   35
While mutual Wishes, mutual Woes, endear
The social Smile & sympathetic Tear.
    Say then, thro' Ages by what Fate confined
To diff'rent Climes seem different Souls assign'd?
Here measured Laws & philosophic Ease   40
Fix, & improve the polish'd Arts of Peace.
There Industry & Gain their Vigils keep,
Command the Winds, & tame th' unwilling Deep.

19 Tyranny has] gloomy Sway have *Wh-1*.   21 blooming] vernal *Wh-1*.

Here Force & hardy Deeds of Blood prevail;
There languid Pleasure sighs in every Gale.   45
Oft o'er the trembling Nations from afar
Has Scythia breath'd the living Cloud of War;
And, where the Deluge burst, with sweepy Sway
Their Arms, their Kings, their Gods, were roll'd away.
As oft have issued, Host impelling Host,   50
The blue-eyed Myriads from the Baltick Coast.
The prostrate South to the Destroyer yields
Her boasted Titles, & her golden Fields:
With grim Delight the Brood of Winter view
A brighter Day, & Heavens of azure Hue,   55
Scent the new Fragrance of the breathing Rose,
And quaff the pendent Vintage, as it grows.
Proud of the Yoke, & pliant to the Rod,
Why yet does Asia dread a Monarch's nod,
While European Freedom still withstands   60
Th' encroaching Tide, that drowns her less'ning Lands,
And sees far off with an indignant Groan
Her native Plains, & Empires once her own.
Can opener Skies & Suns of fiercer Flame
O'erpower the Fire, that animates our Frame;   65
As Lamps, that shed at Ev'n a chearful Ray,
Fade & expire beneath the Eye of Day?
Need we the Influence of the Northern Star
To string our Nerves & steel our Hearts to War?
And, where the Face of Nature laughs around,   70
Must sick'ning Virtue fly the tainted Ground?
Unmanly Thought! what Seasons can controul,
What fancied Zone can circumscribe the Soul,
Who, conscious of the Source from whence she springs,
By Reason's Light, on Resolution's Wings,   75
Spite of her frail Companion, dauntless goes
O'er Libya's Deserts & thro' Zembla's snows?
She bids each slumb'ring Energy awake,
Another Touch, another Temper take,
Suspends th' inferiour Laws, that rule our Clay: 80

51 *Illeg. word, probably* Nations, *del. below* Myriads *Wh-1.*   55 Heavens] Skies
Wh-1.   56 Scent] Catch *Wh-1.*   75 Resolution's] *illeg. word, probably* resolution's, *with* resolution's *in margin Wh-2.*

The stubborn Elements confess her Sway;
Their little Wants, their low Desires, refine,
And raise the Mortal to a Height divine.
　　Not but the human Fabrick from the Birth
Imbibes a Flavour of it's parent Earth   85
As various Tracts enforce a various Toil,
The Manners speak the Idiom of their Soil.
An Iron-Race the Mountain-Cliffs maintain,
Foes to the gentler Genius of the Plain:
For where unwearied Sinews must be found   90
With sidelong Plough to quell the flinty Ground,
To turn the Torrent's swift-descending Flood,
To brave the Savage rushing from the Wood,
What wonder, if to patient Valour train'd
They guard with Spirit, what by Strength they gain'd?   95
And while their rocky Ramparts round they see,
The rough Abode of Want & Liberty,
(As lawless Force from Confidence will grow)
Insult the Plenty of the Vales below?
What wonder, in the sultry Climes, that spread,   100
Where Nile redundant o'er his summer-bed
From his broad bosom life & verdure flings,
And broods o'er Egypt with his watry wings,
If with advent'rous oar & ready sail
The dusky people drive before the gale,   105
Or on frail floats to distant cities ride,
That rise & glitter o'er the ambient tide.

106 distant] neighb'ring *M*.

Mason's note, M, i. 203 n.: I find also among these papers a single couplet much too
beautiful to be lost, though the place where he meant to introduce it cannot be ascer-
tained; it must, however, have made a part of some description of the effect which the
reformation had on our national manners:

　　　When Love could teach a monarch to be wise,
　　　And Gospel-light first dawn'd from BULLEN's Eyes.

STANZAS to Mr. BENTLEY.

IN silent gaze the tuneful choir among,
  Half pleas'd, half blushing let the muse admire,
While Bentley leads her sister-art along,
  And bids the pencil answer to the lyre.
See, in their course, each transitory thought   5
  Fix'd by his touch a lasting essence take;
Each dream, in fancy's airy colouring wrought,
  To local Symmetry and life awake!
The tardy rhymes that us'd to linger on,
  To censure cold, and negligent of fame,   10
In swifter measures animated run,
  And catch a lustre from his genuine flame.
Ah! could they catch his strength, his easy grace,
  His quick creation, his unerring line;
The energy of Pope they might efface,   15
  And Dryden's harmony submit to mine.
But not to one in this benighted age
  Is that diviner inspiration giv'n,
That burns in Shakespear's or in Milton's page,
  The pomp and prodigality of heav'n.   20
As when conspiring in the diamond's blaze,
  The meaner gems, that singly charm the sight,
Together dart their intermingled rays,
  And dazzle with a luxury of light.
Enough for me, if to some feeling breast   25
  My lines a secret sympathy *impart*;
And as their pleasing influence *flows confest*,
  A sigh of soft reflection *heave the heart*.

STANZAS TO MR. BENTLEY. First published in *M*, i. 227–8. There is also a copy by Mason, omitting the italicized words in ll. 26–28, in *CB*, iii. [1107]. The text of *M* is followed here.

26–28. A corner of the only manuscript copy, which Mr. Gray left . . ., is unfortunately torn; and . . . I have endeavoured to supply the chasm. . . . I print my additions in italics. . . . [*M, i.* 228 *n.*] *Mitford thought that Gray was echoing Dryden's 'Epistle to Kneller' and suggested substituting for Mason's reconstruction the following terminal words*: . . . convey; / . . . is exprest, / . . . dies away.

SONG [1].

1

Midst Beauty & Pleasures gay triumphs to languish
And droop without knowing the source of my anguish
To start from short slumbers & look for the morning—
Yet close my dull eyes when I see it returning.

2

Sighs sudden & frequent, Looks ever dejected,   5
Sounds that steal from my tongue by no meaning connected.
Ah say Fellow-swains how these symptoms befell me.
They smile, but reply not. sure Delia will tell me.

[SONG (2).]

Thyrsis, when we parted, swore,
E'er the spring he would return.
Ah, what means yon violet-flower,
And the buds, that deck the thorn?
'Twas the lark, that upward sprung!   5
'Twas the nightingale, that sung!

SONG 1. First published in Warton's edition of Pope's *Works*, London, 1797, ii. 285 n., in a version given by Miss Speed to the Rev. Mr. Leman (1780), who gave them to Joseph Warton, and reprinted by Mitford (*WMt*). The text followed here is the copy made from 'an interlined & corrected Copy' by Mason in *CB*, iii. [1105]. The editors have provided terminal punctuation for ll. 3, 5, 6, 7.

Title: Song in CB, but entitled Amatory Lines *by Mitford and later editors.*

1 With beauty, with pleasure surrounded, to languish—*WMt.*   2 And droop] To weep *WMt.*   source] cause *WMt.*   3 look] wish *WMt.*   4 Yet] To *WMt.* 6 Sounds] Words *WMt.*   8 Delia] delia *CB.*

SONG 2. First published in the *European Magazine*, xix (Feb. 1791), 152. The only holograph MS. (*PM*) is the one in the Pierpont Morgan Library, New York, the text followed here. Several copies were made by others: (1) Mason in *CB*, iii. 1106 (*CBM* with a list of 'First Expressions' [*CBMF*]); (2) Mitford in his Note-book, vol. iii, f. 73 (*Mt*) with a list of variants (*MtV*); and (3) Walpole in a letter to the Countess of Ailesbury, 28 Nov. 1761 (*W*). Gray did not give the poem a title. 'Song' is provided by Mason. Terminal punctuation has been supplied by the editors for ll. 8 and 12.
  Texts collated: *CBM, CBMF, Mt, MtV, W.*

Idle notes, untimely green,
Why such unavailing haste?
Western gales, & skies serene
Prove not always Winter past.   10
Cease my doubts, my fears to move;
Spare the honour of my Love.

ODE

On the Pleasure arising from Vicissitude.

Now the golden Morn aloft
Waves her dew-bespangled wing,
With vermil cheek, and whisper soft
She wooes the tardy Spring:
Till April starts, and calls around   5
The sleeping fragrance from the ground;
And lightly o'er the living scene
Scatters his freshest, tenderest green.

---

7 green] bloom (*del*) *PM*; bloom *with* green *in margin*, *Mt*.   8 *In PM this line is in slightly smaller letters as if it had been inserted as an afterthought between ll. 7 and 9.*
such] this *W*.   9 Western] W̶a̶r̶m̶e̶r̶ ^estern *PM*; Warmer *CBMF, also Mt with* Western *in margin*.   10 C̶a̶n̶-̶n̶o̶t̶ prove, t̶h̶a̶t̶ ^ye Winter'$ not always past? *PM*; cannot prove that winters past *CBMF, also Mt but revised to* Can ye prove not always Winters past *with* Can you *for* Can ye *in MtV*; Speak not always . . . *W*.   past.] past? *PM, CBM*.   12 Dare not to reproach my Love *PM crossed out, CBMF, Mt*; Dare you to reproach your love *MtV*.

ODE ON THE PLEASURE ARISING FROM VICISSITUDE. First printed in *M* in two versions: (1) ll. 1–16, 25–56 in i. 236–7 (*M1*), and (2) the text followed here with Mason's additions in italics in ii. 78–81 (*M2*). A copy in Mason's hand appears in *CB*, iii. [1097], [1099], 1100 (*CBM*), accompanied by a list of variations which Mason found 'in the first copy' (*CBMV*).
    Texts collated: *M1, CBM, CBMV*.

Title: Fragment of an Ode found amongst Mr. Grays papers after his decease and here transcribed from the corrected Copy. *CBM*.

New-born flocks, in rustic dance,
Frisking ply their feeble feet;   10
Forgetful of their wintry trance
The birds his presence greet:
But chief, the Sky-Lark warbles high
His trembling thrilling extacy;
And, lessening from the dazzled sight,   15
Melts into air and liquid light.

Rise, my Soul! on wings of fire,
Rise the rapt'rous Choir among;
Hark! 'tis Nature strikes the Lyre,
And leads the general song: 20
Warm let the lyric transport flow,
Warm, as the ray that bids it glow;
And animates the vernal grove
With health, with harmony, and love.

Yesterday the sullen year   25
Saw the snowy whirlwind fly;
Mute was the music of the air,
The herd stood drooping by:
Their raptures now that wildly flow,
No yesterday, nor morrow know;   30
'Tis Man alone that joy descries
With forward, and reverted eyes.

Smiles on past Misfortune's brow
Soft Reflection's hand can trace;
And o'er the cheek of Sorrow throw   35
A melancholy grace;

10 Frisking] quaintly *CBMV*.   11 Rousd from their long & wintry trance
CBMV.   15 And, lessening] And towering *CBMV*.
17–20 *(See expl. notes.) Omitted from CBM, CBMV, M1, but added in M2; Mason also*
transcribed the lines from Gray's Pocket-Book of 1754 on p. 1110 in the following form:

> Rise my Soul on wings of fire
> Rise the raptu[r]ous Choir among
> Hark tis Nature strikes the Lyre
> And leads the general Song.

25 sullen] darkend *CBMV*.   26 snowy whirlwind] scowling tempest *and another*
variant: snow in whirlwind *CBMV*.   33 past] black *CBMV*.

While Hope prolongs our happier hour,
Or deepest shades, that dimly lower
And blacken round our weary way,
Gilds with a gleam of distant day.   40

Still, where rosy Pleasure leads,
See a kindred Grief pursue;
Behind the steps that Misery treads
Approaching Comfort view:
The hues of bliss more brightly glow,   45
Chastis'd by sabler tints of woe;
And blended form, with artful strife,
The strength and harmony of life.

See the Wretch, that long has tost
On the thorny bed of pain,   50
At length repair his vigour lost,
And breathe, and walk again:
The meanest floweret of the vale,
The simplest note that swells the gale,
The common sun, the air, the skies,   55
To Him are opening Paradise.

Humble Quiet builds her cell,
Near the source whence Pleasure flows;
She eyes the clear crystalline well,
And tastes it as it goes.   60
While far below the *madding* Croud
Rush headlong to the dangerous flood,
Where broad and turbulent it sweeps,
And perish in the boundless deeps.

Mark where Indolence, and Pride,   65
Sooth'd by Flattery's tinkling sound,
Go, softly rolling, side by side,
Their dull, but daily round:

55 the air, the skies,] the air & skies *CBM.*   57–58 *Reversed in CBM but correct
order indicated by numbers.*   57–68 *Omitted from CBM but written on opposite leaf
with ll. 61–64 replaced by the following fragments from which Mason constructed M2:*

       Far below   the crowd.
       Broad & turbulent it grows
             with resistless sweep
        They perish in the boundless deep

To these, if Hebe's self should bring
The purest cup from Pleasure's spring,   70
Say, can they taste the flavour high
Of sober, simple, genuine Joy?

Mark Ambition's march sublime
Up to Power's meridian height;
While pale-ey'd Envy sees him climb,   75
And sickens at the sight.
Phantoms of Danger, Death, and Dread,
Float hourly round Ambition's head;
While Spleen, within his rival's breast,
Sits brooding on her scorpion nest.   80

Happier he, the Peasant, far,
From the pangs of Passion free,
That breathes the keen yet wholesome air
Of rugged Penury.
He, when his morning task is done,   85
Can slumber in the noontide sun;
And hie him home, at evening's close,
To sweet repast, and calm repose.

He, unconscious whence the bliss,
Feels, and owns in carols rude,   90
That all the circling joys are his,
Of dear Vicissitude.
From toil he wins his spirits light,
From busy day, the peaceful night;
Rich, from the very want of wealth,   95
In Heav'n's best treasures, Peace and Health.

[EPITAPH ON A CHILD.]

Here free'd from pain, secure from misery, lies
A Child the Darling of his Parent's eyes:
A gentler Lamb ne'er sported on the plain,
A fairer Flower will never bloom again!
Few were the days allotted to his breath;   5
Here let him sleep in peace his night of death.

[EPITAPH ON SIR WILLIAM WILLIAMS.]

Here foremost in the dang'rous paths of fame
Young Williams fought for England's fair renown:
His mind each Muse, each Grace adorn'd his frame,
Nor Envy dared to view him with a frown.

EPITAPH ON A CHILD. First published in 1884 by Gosse (*Go*) from a copy made by Alexander Dyce (now in the Dyce Collection, South Kensington). There are two other copies in the Brit. Mus. in Mitford's Note-book, vol. iii, ff. 74 (*Mt-1*), 121 (*Mt-2*). The text followed here is the holograph MS. (*PM*) in the Pierpont Morgan Library, New York.
    Texts collated: *Go, Mt-1, Mt-2*.

Title: *None in PM*; Epitaph on a Child. *Mt-1, Mt-2, Go*.

1 free'd] free *Mt-2*.   2 Parent's] Parents' *Mt-1, Mt-2, Go*.   6 Here] Now *Go*.
his] the *Mt-2*.   *Below the copy in Mt-1 Mitford has written, evidently as an indication that the text was taken from a Gray holograph*: N.B. in Grays writing.

EPITAPH ON SIR WILLIAM WILLIAMS. First published in *M*, ii. 62. There is a holograph copy, the text followed here, in Gray's letter (T & W no. 339) to Mason, Aug. 1761 (*G*), and a transcript by Mason (*CBM*) has been made in *CB*, iii. 1108, with several variations (*CBMV*). A few variations are recorded by Mitford (*Mt*) in his Note-book, f. 119, with a copy of the poem.
    Texts collated: *CBM, CBMV, Mt, M*.

At Aix uncall'd his maiden-sword he drew 5
(There first in blood his infant-glory seal'd)
From fortune, pleasure, science, love, he flew,
And scorn'd repose, when Britain took the field.

With eyes of flame & cool intrepid breast
Victor he stood on Bellisle's rocky steeps: 10
Ah gallant Youth!—this marble tells the rest,
Where melancholy Friendship bends, & weeps.

[EPITAPH ON MRS. MASON.]

Tell them, tho 'tis an awful thing to die
('Twas ev'n to thee) yet the dread path once trod,
Heav'n lifts its everlasting portals high
And bids "the pure in heart behold their God."

5 uncall'd his maiden-] his voluntary *CBM, M.*   6 infant-] maiden *Mt.*   -glory]
honour *CBM, M.*   8 And scorn'd] nor brooked *CBMV.*   9 intrepid]
undaunted *CBM, M.*
12 *Two variants in CBMV:*

> When bleeding Friendship oer her altar weeps
> When Montagu & bleeding Friendship weep

At the end of CBMV appears: Rejected Stanza

> Warrior, that readst the melancholly line
> × × × × × ×
> Oh be his Genius be his spirit thine
> And share his Virtues with a happier fate

EPITAPH ON MRS. MASON. First printed in *The New Foundling Hospital for Wit*, new
ed., London, 1784, vi. 45. The lines are also recorded by Norton Nicholls in his
Reminiscences. The text (*BC*) followed here, with a few modifications of punctuation,
has been transcribed by the editors from the monument in Bristol Cathedral and
checked by the Vice-Dean, the Rev. A. R. Millbourn. The inscription is cut entirely
in capitals, which the editors have reduced to lower-case letters when necessary, and
is headed: MARY THE DAUGHTER OF WILLIAM SHERMAN OF KINGSTON
UPON HULL ESQ. AND WIFE OF THE REV.D WILLIAM MASON DIED
MARCH THE XXVII MDCCLXVII AGED XXVIII.

2 yet] yet. *BC.*

[COUPLET ABOUT BIRDS.]

There pipes the wood-lark, & the song thrush there
Scatters his loose notes in the waste of air.

COUPLET ABOUT BIRDS. First published by Mathias in his edition of Gray's *Works*, 1814, ii. 596. The text followed here is that of Nicholls's *Reminiscences*, which is the only source. See T & W, Appendix Z, p. 1290.

LATIN POETRY

TRANSLATED BY

J. R. HENDRICKSON

INTRODUCTION TO THE LATIN POEMS

The present edition is the first to include all Gray's Latin poems. Hitherto they have appeared in selections compiled according to the personal judgements of individual editors, some of whom did not have access to material now available. The Latin poems, which comprise the greater part of his early work, are essential to an understanding of Gray's development both as a writer and as a person. Yet they have been accorded relatively little editorial attention; the text of many has become corrupt, and manifestly inaccurate readings (see, for example, textual note to *Latin Verses at Eton*, l. 52) have been reproduced in edition after edition. The convenience of having all the Latin poems in a single work, with texts carefully restored to their original state, is obvious.

The editors have provided prose translations of the poems because verse translations, while superficially more pleasing, inevitably entail a greater intrusion of the translator's ideas. For example, a particularly attractive translation of *O Lachrymarum Fons* reads as follows:

> O Spring of tears, that, from a heart by grace
> Made tender, their divine procession trace!
> Happy, who from his bosom drawing deep
> That influence, dear Angel, learns to weep.

Pleasing though these lines are, they alter the spirit of the poem from pagan to Christian: the notion of 'grace' is not in Gray's poem at all, and the pagan Nymph appears as an 'Angel'; moreover, the latter transformation weakens the original unity of the poem, for Gray, in keeping with Roman ideas, made the nymph and the fountain a single entity.

Occasionally to indicate formal invocations or emotional intensity, *thou* (with related forms) has been used in a poem in which *you* (and related forms) has also been employed for less intense passages.

ORDER OF THE POEMS

The Latin poems have been arranged as nearly in chronological order as the uncertainty of dating permits, except for two of doubtful authenticity which appear in a separate section with the English poems of the same class. Since only fourteen of the twenty-six authentic poems can be dated with any precision, some rather arbitrary choices had to be made in the placing of individual poems. However, the present arrangement enables the reader to compare Gray's earlier and later work with reasonable assurance that the poems are correctly placed in the broad divisions of work done before, during, and after his student days at Cambridge. Only one or two poems (the *Orders of Insects* and possibly the translations from the Greek Anthology) were written after 1742, and probably none before 1730.

EXPLANATORY NOTES

Previous editions have supplied relatively little explanatory material for the Latin poems: Mitford devotes his notes largely to a citation of parallel passages from Greek and Latin authors and to a discussion of a few questions of Latin usage; Bradshaw, although his texts are excellent, has explanatory notes on only two of the Latin poems, one of which consists largely of an excerpt from a letter of Gray that refers to a different poem (see explanatory notes to the *Alcaic Ode*).

Gray quotes from Greek and Latin authors in some notes and marginal glosses, often with only a partial indication of the source or even with none at all. Except for a few which could not be traced, the editors have supplied exact citations for these passages.

Especially in his earlier works, Gray often incorporates whole phrases from Latin authors with little or no change. In general, the editors have confined their citation of parallel passages to those which have not previously been cited in major editions and to those from which Gray has borrowed a complete phrase; there is, however, some duplication, particularly with the notes to Mitford's edition, in which such parallels abound. When a parallel is exactly or almost exactly the same as Gray's text, the editors have not followed their general policy of providing translations of non-English material. The reader will note that exact parallels are fewer in the later poems; perhaps as Gray became more fluent in Latin, he grew more independent in his usage and therefore incorporated fewer phrases verbatim. Unfortunately, the texts of some Greek and Latin authors have variant readings and line numbers in different editions. In the present work the citations are usually according to the texts of the Loeb Library editions, since these are the most readily available to a majority of readers; a few are according to the text of some other standard edition. Readers who wish to consult the original works should be able to find all the passages cited with a minimum of confusion and trouble.

NOTE ON ACCENTS

In many Latin texts of the eighteenth century, both printed and manuscripts, accents are used, but there is wide variation in practice. Not only do different individuals employ different systems, but the same individual is often inconsistent, even in a single work.

About all that can safely be assumed from the presence of an accent is that the circumflex usually indicates a long vowel and that an acute or grave may do so. On the other hand, many long vowels are not marked at all, and even the same word in the same metrical position in the same work will sometimes be accented and sometimes not (for example, in *Luna Habitabilis*, *hìc* in l. 19, but *hic* in l. 54).

In view of the situation indicated above, the editors seriously considered omitting the accents entirely. However, tradition triumphed, and it was decided to reproduce the accents of the particular text being used as a standard, but not to list the variants when a number of texts were collated.

TEXT AND TEXTUAL NOTES

In general, the same system is employed in the notes to the Latin poems as in those to the English, with the following exceptions and additions:

1. Gray usually, but not invariably, writes 'q̲' for *-que* and '&' for *et*. Since he seems to attach no significance to the variation, all his abbreviations of these words have been expanded in the present text without a specific textual note for each one. It should perhaps be remarked that his abbreviation for *-que* was printed as 'q;' in early editions; this has caused some rather peculiar punctuation to appear in later editions based on earlier printed texts.

2. The initial letter of each sentence has been capitalized without specific comment, even though Gray may have followed his frequent practice of beginning with a lower-case letter.

3. As stated in the comment on accents above, variations in accents have not been indicated, except in a few passages where the presence of a circumflex might mislead the reader.

[LATIN EXERCISE FROM THE *TATLER*.]

> . . . pluviæque loquaces
> Descendêre jugis, et garrulus ingruit imber.

LATIN EXERCISE FROM THE *TATLER*.

. . . the babbling rain waters flowed down from the heights, and a shower of words fell thick and fast.

[PARAPHRASE OF PSALM LXXXIV.]

> Oh! Tecta, mentis dulcis amor meæ!
> Oh! Summa Sancti Relligio loci!
> Quæ me laborantem perurit
>   Sacra fames, et amœnus ardor?
>
> Præceps volentem quo rapit impetus!　　　　5
> Ad limen altum tendo avidas Manus.
> Dum Lingua frustratur precantem,
>   Cor tacitum mihi clamat intus.
>
> Illic loquacem composuit Domum,
> Laresque parvos Numinis in fidem　　　　10
> Præsentioris credit Ales
>   Veris amans, vetus Hospes aræ:

LATIN EXERCISE FROM THE *TATLER*. The text followed here is that given by Norton Nicholls in his *Reminiscences* of Gray (see T & W, Appendix Z, p. 1290). The lines are also quoted by Jacob Bryant (1715–1804), who was at Eton with Gray, in a letter which Mitford published in his edition of Gray's *Works* (1847).

PARAPHRASE OF PSALM LXXXIV. Five stanzas (ll. 1–20) were published in *The Gentleman's Magazine*, N.S. xxxii (Oct. 1849), 343 (*GM*). First complete publication in Tovey, *Gray and His Friends*, pp. 300–1 ((*TGF*).

　Text used: Mitford's transcription in his Note-book, vol. iii, ff. 67–69 (*Mt*). Texts collated: GM, TGF.

Title: None in *Mt*, but see last entry below.
2 Summa] summi *GM*.　loci!] loci *TGF*.　　4 amœnus] amicus *TGF*.　　5 rapit] rupit *GM*.　　6 avidas] avidus *GM*.

Beatus Ales! sed magis incola
Quem vidit ædes ante [*Focos Dei*]
   Cultu ministrantem perenni   15
      Quique sacrâ requievit umbrâ.

Bis terque felix qui melius Deo
Templum sub imo Pectore consecrat;
   Huic vivida affulget voluptas
      Et liquidi sine Nube Soles.   20

Integriori fonte fluentia
Mentem piorum gaudia recreant,
   Quod si datur lugere, quiddam
      Dulce ferens venit ipse luctus.

Virtute virtus, firmior evenit   25
Nascente semper, semper amabili,
   Æterna crescit, seque in horas
      Subjiciit per aperta Cæli.

Me, dedicatum qui Genus, et tuæ
Judææ habenas tempero, Regio   30
   Madens Olivo, dexter audi
      Nec libeat repulisse Regem.

Lux una Sanctis quæ foribus dedit
Hærere amatæ Limine Januæ,
   Lux inter extremas Columnas   35
      Candidius mihi ridet una,

Quam Seculorum Secula Barbaros
Inter Penates sub trabe gemmea
   Fastus Tyrannorum, brevesque
      Delicias, et amœna Regni: 40

14 Focos Dei *is Tovey's conjecture; Mt seems to have* Focos *with a line drawn through the first three letters, but the text is barely legible; GM has* focos.   28 subjiciit] subjiciet *TGF.*   30 Judææ] Judææ, *Mt. See expl. notes.*   tempero,] tempero. *Mt. At end, in Mitford's hand*: The above is the 84th Psalm. *Below this, also in Mitford's hand:* [N.B. The above Ode is written in Mr Grays [*sic*] Hand: but evidently when young, the hand being unformed, & like a Schoolboys [*sic*], tho' very plain & careful. The Leaf on which it is written, apparently torn from a Copy-book. Some of the expressions resemble those in the Gr. Chartreuse Ode.]

Feliciori flumine Copiam
Pronâque dextrâ Cælicolum Pater
Elargietur, porrigetque
Divitias diuturniores.

PARAPHRASE OF PSALM LXXXIV.

O dwellings, sweet love of my soul! O most high holy presence of the sacred place! What is this sacred hunger, this pleasant fire that consumes me in my affliction?

To what place does eager passion bear me in accordance with my desire! I stretch longing hands toward the lofty threshold; while my tongue mocks my efforts when I try to pray, my silent heart is shouting within.

There the bird that loves the springtime, the visitor to the altar for many years, has built his chattering home and entrusted his little Lares to the protection of a more propitious god:

Blessed the bird, but more blessed he who dwells within, whom the temple sees before the altars of God, ministering with perpetual worship, and who passes his life within the holy shades.

Twice, yea three times happy he who has consecrated a better temple to God in the depths of his heart; upon him shall living pleasure shine, and clear suns without a cloud.

Joys flowing from a purer fountain shall refresh the souls of those who obey God; but if it is their lot to mourn, even grief itself comes bearing with it something sweet.

By strength does strength become more firmly fixed, always being born, always lovable; it increases for ever; every hour it soars higher through the clear tracts of heaven.

As for me, ruler of the consecrated race, he who holds the reins of Thy Judaea, anointed with the royal olive, hear me with favour and be not pleased to have rejected a king.

A single day which gives the privilege of lingering in the blessed doorways, on the threshold of the beloved door, a single day among the outermost columns, smiles more brightly for me than an eternity among the houses of the barbarians, beneath gem-studded beams, amid the arrogance of tyrants and the brief delights and pleasures of royalty:

From a happier stream the father of the heaven-dwellers will pour forth abundance with unstinting hand and will bestow more lasting riches.

[TRANSLATION OF ODE 'AWAY; LET NOUGHT TO LOVE DISPLEASING'.]

Vah, tenero quodcunque potest obsistere amori,
    Exulet ex animo et Delia cara, tuo;
Ne timor infelix, mala ne fastidia sancti
    Gaudia distineant, Delia cara tori.
Quid si nulla olim regalia munera nostras   5
    Ornarunt titulis divitiisque domos?
At nobis proprioque et honesto lumine claris
    Ex meretis ortum nobile nomen erit.
Dum tanto colimus virtutem ardore volabit
    Gloria dulce sonans nostra per ora virûm.   10
Interea nostram mirata superbia famam
    Tales splendoris tantum habuisse gemet.
Quid si Diva potens nummorum divitis auri
    Haud largo nostros proluit imbre lares?
At nobis erit ex humili bona copia censu;   15
    Vitaque non luxu splendida, læta tamen.
Sic horas per quisque suas revolubilis annus
    Nostra quod expleret vota precesque dabit.
Nam duce naturâ peragemus, Delia, vitam:
    Vita ea vitalis dicier una potest.   20
Et juvenes et amore senes florebimus æquo.
    Et vitæ unâ alacres conficiemus iter.
Nostros interea ornabit pax alma Penates,
    Iucundum pueri, pignora cara, torum.

TRANSLATION OF ODE. First published by Tovey in *Gray and His Friends*, pp. 298–300 (*TGF*), from the text in Mitford's Note-books, vol. iii, ff. 86–87 (*Mt*). The text followed here is that of the holograph MS. recently discovered bound in a copy of Boswell's *Life of Johnson*, from a photostat furnished by Mr. Charles W. Traylen (*Bos*).
    Texts collated: *Mt, TGF, Br*.

2 cara,] cara *Mt*; caro *TGF, Br. See expl. notes.*   tuo;] meo *TGF, Br. See expl. notes.*
10 sonans] sonans, *Mt.*   12 Tales] Talis *Mt, TGF, Br*; e *and* i *superimposed between* l *and* s *in Bos*.   gemet.] gemet *Br*.   14 nostros] nostras *Mt, TGF, Br. See expl. notes.*   15 censu;] Censu, *Mt*; sensu *TGF, Br. Semicolon very faint in Bos; perhaps Gray's pencil not inked over.*   16 tamen.] tamen, *TGF*; tamen *Br*.
17 annus] annus, *Mt, TGF*; ætas (*del*), annus *above, Mt*.   18 expleret] expleret, *Mt*; explerit *TGF, Br*.   dabit.] dabit *Br*.   19 vitam:] vitam *Mt, TGF, Br*.
21 juvenes] *dot over first* e *in Mt*.   florebimus] -or- *of the word blotted in Bos*.   æquo.] æquo *Mt, TGF, Br*.   22 iter.] iter *Br*.   23 Penates,] Penates *Mt, TGF, Br. Comma very faint in Bos; perhaps Gray's pencil not inked over.*   24 pueri,] Pueri *Mt, TGF, Br*.   cara,] Cara *Mt*; cara *TGF, Br*.

Oh quanta aspicerem lepidam dulcedine gentem   25
  Luderet ad patrium dum pia turba genu
Maternos vultu ridenti effingere vultus,
  Balbo maternos ore referre sonos.
Iamque senescentes cum nos inviderit ætas
  Nostraque se credet surripuisse bona,   30
In vestris tu rursus amabere pulchra puellis,
  Rursus ego in pueris, Delia, amabo meis.

TRANSLATION OF ODE.

Ah, let whatever has power to stand in the way of tender love be banished from your mind, beloved Delia. Let no ill-omened fear, no misguided pride, postpone the joys of the sacred marriage-bed, beloved Delia.

What does it matter if no ancestral offices of state have adorned our houses with statues and wealth? At least we shall shine with our own honourable light and shall have a name made noble by worthy deeds.

As long as we pursue virtue with all our might, our glory will fly with a sweet sound through the mouths of men; Arrogance, meanwhile, amazed at our fame, will groan because such as we have achieved so much eminence.

What does it matter if the goddess who controls coins of wealth-bestowing gold has sent no bountiful shower to drench our Lares? At least we shall have generous abundance in accordance with our humble wealth and a life which, though it may not be sumptuous by the standards of luxury, will none the less be filled with joy. Thus each year, as it rolls through its seasons, will give all we need to fulfil our vows and grant our prayers. For we will lead our life, Delia, with nature as our guide: such a life alone can be called a real life.

We shall abound in love just as much when we are old as when we are young, and together we shall complete the journey of life with

27 ridenti] *Word looks like* rudenti ('*roaring*') *in Bos, but meaning makes that impossible; perhaps a mental echo of* rubenti ('*rosy*') *caused the slip in writing.*   29 inviderit] insederit *TGF, Br. See expl. notes.*   30 credet] credat *TGF, Br. Second vowel blotted in Bos so that it looks like* a, *but* credet *is the only idiomatic reading possible.* 32 pueris,] pueris *Br.* Delia,] Delia. *Bos;* Delia *Mt, TGF, Br. In Mt the poem is noted as a* free translation of Gilbert Cooper's Ode Away let Nought to Love displeasing *published in 1726. See expl. notes.*

lively zest; as we journey on through life, fostering peace will bless our Penates, sons (beloved tokens) our joyful bed.

While the loving throng plays at the father's knee, with how much sweet delight would I behold the charming brood as they picture the mother's features in their own laughing faces and as they echo the sounds of the mother's voice with lisping mouths.

And when at last, as we begin to grow old, age has cast its evil eye upon us and thinks it has stolen our blessings, you will be loved once again in the person of your daughters, and I, my Delia, will love once more in the person of my sons.

[LATIN VERSES AT ETON.]

—Quem te Deus esse
Jussit et humanâ qua parte locatus es in re
Disce—[Persius, *Satires*, iii. 71–73.]

Pendet Homo incertus gemini ad confinia mundi
Cui parti accedat dubius; consurgere stellis
An socius velit, an terris ingloria moles
Reptare, ac muto se cum grege credere campis:
Inseruisse choro divûm hic se jactat, et audet   5
Telluremque vocare suam, fluctusque polumque,
Et quodcunque videt, proprios assumit in usus.
'Me propter jam vere expergefacta virescit
'Natura in flores, herbisque illudit, amatque
'Pingere telluris gremium, mihi vinea fœtu   10
'Purpureo turget, dulcique rubescit honore;
'Me rosa, me propter liquidos exhalat odores;
'Luna mihi pallet, mihi Olympum Phœbus inaurat,
'Sidera mî lucent, volvunturque æquora ponti.'

LATIN VERSES AT ETON. First published by Gosse (*Go*).
  Text used: *CB*, i. 50 (ll. 1–39)–51 (ll. 40–74). Texts collated: *Go*, *Br*.

Title: None at head of poem in CB, but Play-Exercise at Eton *in margin at end of poem and listed in index as* Knowledge of Himself, Latin Verses at Eton; PLAY EXERCISE AT ETON. *Go*; PLAY-EXERCISE AT ETON. *Br*.

4 campis:] campis; *Br*.   14 ponti.'] ponti. *CB*.

Sic secum insistit, tantumque hæc astra decores   15
Æstimat esse suæ sedis, convexaque cœli
Ingentes scenas, vastique aulæa theatri.

At tibi per deserta fremit, tibi tigris acerbuḿ
Succenset, nemorum fulmen, Gangeticus horror?
Te propter mare se tollit, surgitque tumultu?   20

Hic ubi rimari, atque impallescere libris
Perstitit, anne valet quâ vi connexa per ævum
Conspirent elementa sibi, serventque tenorem;
Sufficiant scatebræ unde mari, fontesque perennes
Jugis aquæ fluviis, unde æther sidera pascat,   25
Pandere? nequaquam: secreta per avia mundi
Debile carpit iter, vix, et sub luce malignâ
Pergit, et incertam tendit trepidare per umbram.
Fata obstant; metam Parcæ posuere sciendi,
Et dixere: veni huc, Doctrina, hic terminus esto.   30
Non super æthereas errare licentiuś auras
Humanum est, at scire hominem; breve limite votum
Exiguo claudat, nec se quæsiverit extrá.
Errat, qui cupit oppositos transcendere fines,
Extenditque manus ripæ ulterioris amore;   35
Illic gurges hiat laté, illic sæva vorago,
Et caligantes longis ambagibus umbræ.

Oceani fontes, et regna sonantia fluctu,
Machina stellantis cœli, terræque cavernæ
Nullis laxantur mortalibus, isque aperiret   40
Hæc qui arcana poli, magnumque recluderet æquor,
Frangeret æternos nexus, mundique catenam.

Plurimus (hic error, demensque libido lacessit)
In superos, cœlumque ruit, sedesque relinquit,
Quas natura dedit proprias, jussitque tueri.   45
Humani sortem generis pars altera luget
Invidet armento, et campi sibi vindicat herbam.
'Oh quis me in pecoris felicia transferet arva,
'In loca pastorum deserta, atque otia dia?
'Cur mihi non Lyncisve oculi, vel odora canum vis   50
'Additur, aut gressus cursu glomerare potestas?

---

17 vastique] vestique *Br.*   21 rimari] rimavi *Go.*   22 Perstitit] Perstetit *Go.*
26 nequaquam:] nequaquam; *Br.*   30 dixere:] dixere; *CB*; dixere, *Br, Go.*

'Aspice, ubi, tenues dum texit aranea casses,
'Funditur in telam et laté per stamina vivit!
'Quid mihi non tactûs eadem exquisita facultas,
'Taurorumve tori solidi, pennæve volucrum?'   55
 Pertæsos sortis doceant responsa silere.
Si tanto valeas contendere acumine visûs,
Et graciles penetrare atomos; non æthera possis
Suspicere, aut lati spatium comprendere ponti.
Vis si adsit major naris; quam, vane, doleres,   60
Extinctus fragranti aurâ, dulcique veneno!
Si tactûs, tremat hoc corpus, solidoque dolore
Ardeat in membris, nervoque laboret in omni;
Sive auris, fragor exanimet, cum rumpitur igne
Fulmineo cœlum, totusque admurmurat æther: 65
Quam demum humanas, priscasque requirere dotes
Attonitus nimium cuperes, nimiumque reverti
In solitam speciem, veterique senescere formâ.
 Nubila seu tentes, vetitumque per aëra surgas,
Sive rudes poscas sylvas, et lustra ferarum;   70
Falleris; in medio solium Sapientia fixit.
Desine sectari majora, minorave sorte,
Quam Deus, et rerum attribuit natura creatrix.

LATIN VERSES AT ETON.

[What God has ordered you to be and in what human
 role you have really been cast, learn.... Persius ...]

Man lingers uncertainly on the borders of two worlds, doubtful
which one he should draw near to; he knows not whether he should
wish to rise up and mingle with the stars or creep over the face of
the earth, an inglorious hulk, and entrust himself to the fields with
the dumb beasts.
 He boasts that he has joined the chorus of the gods and dares to

52 tenues] teneros *Br*, teneres *Go.*   53 vivit!] vivit? *Go.*   55 volucrum?']
volucrum? *CB*; volucrum.' *Br*; volucrum *Go.*   56 silere.] silere *Go.*   60 quam,]
quam *Br.*   64 auris] aurîs *CB.*   65 æther:] æther; *Br.*   66 dotes]
dotes? *Go.*

call the earth his own, and the seas thereof, and the vault of heaven; whatever he beholds, he appropriates for his own use. 'For my sake awakening Nature blossoms into flowers in the spring and puts forth plants in gay profusion, and loves to paint the lap of earth; for me the vine swells with purple buds and blushes with ripe fruit; for my sake, for my sake only, the rose breathes pure fragrance; for me the moon sheds her pale light; for me Phoebus floods the heavens with golden radiance; the stars gleam for me, and the waters of the deep roll.' So Man thinks to himself, and believes that these stars are merely the ornaments of his abode, and that the dome of the sky is an immense stage, the canopy of a vast theatre.

But is it for you that the tiger rages through the desert, is it for you that he blazes fiercely, the fell lightning-bolt of the forest, the terror of the Ganges? Is it for your sake that the sea towers aloft and heaves in tumult?

When Man devotes himself to the pursuit of knowledge and grows pale over his books, does he acquire the power to reveal the force by which the elements, once they have been linked together, continue their harmonious union throughout the ages and preserve their state without change? Can he reveal the source from which the bubbling springs fill up the sea and the everlasting fountains the rivers of fresh water, or how the ether feeds the stars?

By no means! He makes his feeble way along lonely by-paths of the universe, hardly advancing at all, and pushes on under scanty light, and strives to make his fearful way through the dim shadows. The decrees of fate stand in his way; the Fates have set a limit to knowledge and have said, 'Only so far you may advance, O Learning; let this be your limit.'

Man is not meant to roam too freely above the upper air, but to know Man; let him confine his limited desire within narrow bounds, and let him not seek to know what is outside himself. That man errs who wishes to transcend the limits placed in his way and who stretches out his hands with love of the farther shore. At this point the flood stretches wide; at this point a savage whirlpool yawns, and shadows wrapped in a mist of vast obscurities.

The fountains of the deep, the kingdom of the roaring waves, the working of the starry heavens, and the caverns of the earth are revealed to no mortal; that man who would uncover these secrets of the sky and unlock the mighty deep would break the eternal ties, the bond of the universe.

Many a man (this perversity and insane desire leads to destruction) tries to rush into heaven, the dwelling of the gods, and leave behind the dwellings that Nature has given him for his own, and bade him keep.

Another group laments the fortune of the human race, envies the beast, and lays claim to the grass of the field for Man. 'Oh, who will carry me off to the happy fields of the herd, to places abandoned by the shepherds and to quiet retreats under the open sky? Why was I not given the eyes of the lynx or the keen scent of dogs or the ability to prance and gallop?

'Behold, when something is caught in the spider's web, while she weaves her delicate snares, it sends a lively motion far along the strands! Why is not the same exquisite faculty of touch mine, or the massive brawn of bulls, or the wings of birds?'

Let the answers teach those who have been chafing at their lot to be silent. If you should be able to vie in such great keenness of vision and to see into tiny atoms, you would not be able to look up at the heavens nor to take in the sweep of the broad ocean. If you had a keener sense of smell, how greatly, vain man, would you suffer—killed by a perfumed breeze, a sweet poison! If a livelier sense of touch were yours, your body would tremble, it would burn with unremitting pain in all its parts, it would suffer affliction in every nerve. Or, if your sense of hearing were sharper, the crash of sound would knock you senseless, when the sky is split by the fire of lightning and all the air of heaven reverberates: in a word, you would be overwhelmed; how eagerly you would long to regain the human endowments that you had to begin with, to become again the kind of being that you once were, to grow old in your former shape.

Whether you try to reach the clouds, to fly through the forbidden reaches of the air, or whether you pray for savage forests and the dens of wild beasts, you will be in error. Wisdom has planted her throne in a middle ground. Cease striving for a lot either greater or less than the one that God and Nature, the creatrix of things, has assigned.

[HYMENEAL.]

IGNARAE nostrûm mentes, et inertia corda,
Dum curas regum, et Sortem miseramur iniquam,
Quae Solio affixit, vetuitque calescere flammâ
Dulci, quae dono Divûm, gratissima serpit
Viscera per, mollesque animis lenè implicat aestus;   5
Nec teneros sensus, Veneris nec praemia nôrunt,
Eloquiumve oculi, aut facunda silentia linguae:

Scilicet ignorant lacrymas, saevosque dolores,
Dura rudimenta, et violentae exordia flammae;
Scilicet ignorant, quae flumine tinxit amaro   10
Tela *Venus*, caecique armamentaria Divi,
Irasque, insidiasque, et tacitum sub pectore vulnus;
Namque sub ingressu, primoque in limine Amoris
Luctus et ultrices posuere cubilia Curae;
Intus habent dulces Risus, et Gratia sedem,   15
Et roseis resupina toris, roseo ore Voluptas:
Regibus huc faciles aditus; communia spernunt
Ostia, jamque expers duris custodibus istis
Panditur accessus, penetraliaque intima Templi.

Tuque Oh! *Angliacis*, Princeps, spes optima regnis,   20
Ne tantum, ne finge metum; quid imagine captus
Haeres, et mentem picturâ pascis inani?
Umbram miraris: nec longum tempus, et Ipsa
Ibit in amplexus, thalamosque ornabit ovantes.
Ille tamen tabulis inhians longum haurit amorem,   25
Affatu fruitur tacito, auscultatque tacentem
Immemor artificis calami, risumque, ruboremque
Aspicit in fucis, pictaeque in virginis ore:
Tanta *Venus* potuit; tantus tenet error amantes.

HYMENEAL. First published in *Gratulatio Academiae Cantabrigiensis Auspicatissimas Frederici Walliae Principis & Augustae Principissae Saxo-Gothae Nuptias Celebrantis* (Cantabrigiae: Typis Academicis, 1736), the sole authority for the text, which is here reproduced from the original edition. There are no page numbers in *Gratulatio*.

Title: There is none for the poem. West's designation, 'Hymenêal', has been used as a title in later editions.

At end of poem, Tho. Gray [*in italics*] Pet. Coll.

Nascere, magna Dies, qua sese AUGUSTA *Britanno*   30
Committat Pelago, patriamque relinquat amoenam;
Cujus in adventum jam nunc tria regna secundos
Attolli in plausus, dulcique accensa furore
Incipiunt agitare modos, et carmina dicunt:
Ipse animo sedenim juvenis comitatur euntem,   35
Explorat ventos, atque auribus aëra captat,
Atque auras, atque astra vocat crudelia; pectus
Intentum exultat, surgitque arrecta cupido;
Incusat spes aegra fretum, solitoque videtur
Latior effundi pontus, fluctusque morantes.   40

Nascere, Lux major, quâ sese AUGUSTA *Britanno*
Committat juveni totam, propriamque dicabit;
At citius (precor) Oh! cedas melioribus astris:
Nox finem pompae, finemque imponere curis
Possit, et in thalamos furtim deducere nuptam;   45
Sufficiat requiemque viris, et amantibus umbras:
Adsit *Hymen*, et subridens cum matre *Cupido*
Accedant, sternantque toros, ignemque ministrent;
Ilicet haud pictae incandescit imagine formae
Ulterius juvenis, verumque agnoscit amorem.   50

Sculptile sicut ebur, faciemque arsisse venustam
Pygmaliona canunt; ante hanc suspiria ducit,
Alloquiturque amens, flammamque et vulnera narrat;
Implorata *Venus* jussit cum vivere signum,
Foemineam inspirans animam; quae gaudia surgunt,   55
Audiit ut primae nascentia murmura linguae,
Luctari in vitam, et paulatim volvere ocellos
Sedulus, aspexitque novâ splendescere flammâ;
Corripit amplexu vivam, jamque oscula jungit
Acria confestim, recipitque rapitque; prioris   60
Immemor ardoris, Nymphaeque oblitus eburneae.

HYMENEAL.

Ignorant our minds and dull our hearts when we pity the cares of kings and the narrow lot that chains them to the throne and forbids them to glow with that sweet fire which, by the gift of the gods, most gratefully creeps through our vitals and softly entwines gentle warmth in our souls; they (we say) know neither tender sensations nor the joys of love, neither the eloquent language of the eye nor the eloquent silence of the tongue.

In reality they are ignorant only of tears and cruel pangs, the painful preliminaries and kindling of the raging flame; they know nothing of the shafts that Venus dyed in the bitter stream nor the weapons of the blind god, nor fits of anger and deceptions, nor the silent wound in the depths of the heart. For, as everyone knows, at the entrance of the temple of Love, on the outer threshold, Grief and avenging Cares have placed their couches. But within sweet Laughter and Harmony have their seat, and rose-lipped Pleasure reclining on beds of roses. It is easy for kings to enter here; they scorn the public doors, and instantly, with no hindrance from the implacable guards that bar the way of ordinary mortals, the entrance is thrown open for them—yea, even the inmost sanctuary of the temple.

And you, O Prince, best hope of the British realms, should not even think of fear. Why do you linger, the captive of a portrait, and feed your passion on a lifeless picture? Now you gaze in wonder and awe at the shadow; soon the flesh-and-blood woman will enter your embrace and will adorn the joyous marriage chamber. But for the moment the prince, gazing in a rapture of desire, drains a long draught of love from the canvas, enjoys a wordless conversation, and, forgetting the artist's brush, hears her even though she is silent—hears her laugh and sees the blush on her cheeks and the red in the lips of the pictured maiden. Such great power has Venus; so great is the delusion that holds lovers.

Dawn, great Day, on which Augusta will entrust herself to the British sea and leave her pleasant home-land. Against her arrival three realms have already begun to rouse themselves to joyous applause, and, on fire with sweet madness, to recite verses and chant songs. But the prince himself accompanies her in spirit as she draws near; he tests the winds and strains his ears for every breath of air, and calls the breezes and the stars cruel; his eagerly waiting heart rejoices and burning desire leaps up; sick with longing he rails at the deep, and the sea seems to stretch out wider than it has ever been, and the waves that keep her from him.

Dawn, greater Day, when Augusta will entrust herself wholly to the British prince, and will declare herself all his. But Oh! (I pray) may you give way with all speed to the stars, for they are even better; let Night have power to put an end to the wedding festivities and an end to cares, and let her lead the bride sheltered in darkness into the marriage chamber; let her provide rest for men and shadows for lovers. May Hymen be present and may smiling Cupid with his mother approach and spread the couch and tend the fire. From this moment the prince will no longer be inflamed by a mere painted representation of beauty; he will know love in reality.

Thus, the poets sing, Pygmalion burned with love for the charming beauty of the sculptured ivory. He was standing before the statue, sighing and in his madness speaking to it and recounting the wounds caused by the flame of love, when Venus, responsive to his prayers, bade the statue live, breathing into it a woman's soul. What joys awoke when he heard the quickening sounds of her first speech and raptly beheld her struggling into life and saw her eyes little by little begin to roll and glow with new-found fire. He sweeps the living woman into his arms and rains fierce kisses on her lips— again and again he takes and gives them, unmindful now of his former passion, completely forgetful of the nymph of ivory.

In D[iem]: 29^{am} Maii.

Bella per Angliacos plusquam civilia campos
Præteritæ videre dies: desævit Enyo,
Tempestasque jacet; circum vestigia flammæ
Delentur, pacisque iterum consurgit imago:
Littore, quo nuper Martis fremuere procellæ,   5
Alcyone tutum struit imperterrita nidum.

IN DIEM 29^{AM} MAII. First published in Gosse (*Go*), 'from a MS in the handwriting of the poet, signed *Gray*, lately found at Pembroke College.' The present text (*PM*) is from the MS. (Pembroke College MS. 74).

  Texts collated: *Go, Br.*

Reddita spes solii regno, regemque vagantem
Patria chara tenet, dictisque affatur amicis.
    Quas ego te terras, quot per discrimina vectum
Accipio, quantis jactatum, Nate, periclis?   10
Quam metui, nequid tibi Gallica regna nocerent,
Belgarumque plagæ, perjuraque Scotia patri!
Quam tremui, cum læva tuas Vigornia turmas
Fudit præcipites, hostemque remisit ovantem!
Tuque, Arbor, nostræ felix tutela coronæ,   15
Gloria camporum, et luci regina vocare:
Tota tibi sylva assurget, quæ fronde dedisti
Securas latebras, nemorosa palatia regi;
Sacra Jovi Latio quondam, nunc sacra Britanno.
Olim factus honos, illi velâsse capillos,   20
Qui leto civem abripuit, salvumque reduxit;
Jam potes ipsa tribus populis præstare salutem.

ON THE TWENTY-NINTH DAY OF MAY.

Bygone days have seen the bitterest of civil wars throughout the British fields; Enyo has ceased to vent her cruelty, the tempest is stilled; on all sides the scars left by the flame are being wiped out, and the image of peace once more arises; on the shore, where recently the storms of Mars raged, the Halcyon, free from fear, is building her nest in safety. The hope of the throne has been returned to the realm, and his beloved country possesses her wandering king, and speaks with loving words.

My Son, at last I can welcome you home, after you have travelled through so many lands, and endured so many crises, and survived the many perils that assailed you. How I feared that the Gallic kingdoms would work you some harm, and the lands of the Belgians, and Scotland, traitor to your father! How I trembled when the accursed field of Worcester hurled your squadrons into headlong rout and sent the enemy back triumphant!

Be Thou, O Tree, hailed as the auspicious guardian of our crown, the glory of the plains, the queen of the grove; the whole forest shall

18 regi;] regi? *Go.*
At end of poem in PM, Gray.

rise in homage to you, who afforded a safe hiding-place with your
foliage, a leafy palace for a king! In ancient times you were sacred
to Jove in Latium; now you will be held sacred in Britain. In olden
days the honour was paid of placing a crown upon the head of the
man who had rescued a single citizen from death and brought him
safely home; now you alone can (claim to) be the saviour of three
nations.

In 5ᵗᵃᵐ Novembris.

Lis anceps, multosque diú protracta per annos,
    judice nec facile dissoluënda fuit;
Cui tribuenda modó sceleratæ premia palmæ?
    quem meritó tantus nobilitaret honos?
Multa sibi Romæ sævi ascivere tyranni,   5
    multa sibi primus, posteriorque Nero:
Qui retulit prædam nostro de litore Conchas:
    quem dedit ex purâ Flavia stirpe domus:
Multa sibi Phalaris petiit, Trinacria pestis;
    diraque causa tui, magna Diana, rogi: 10
Quæque referre mora est, portenta replentia famæ
    invitæ annales, crimine nota suo.
At demum innumeris belli Anglia clara triumphis
    militis ostentat parta tropæa manu;
Nec satis est, geminâ palma insignita nitere   15
    artibus et bellis, orbis et esse decus;
Accedat nactæ sceleris nisi gloria famæ,
    et laudis numeros impleat illa suæ:
Ex natis surgit mens aspernata priores,
    et tentare novas ingeniosa vias,   20
Quæ cæcis novit Martem sepelire latebris,
    tectosque a visu Solis habere dolos;
Scilicet, ut fallat, non ire in viscera terræ,
    non dubitat simili clade vel ipse mori.

IN 5 ᵀᴬᴹ NOVEMBRIS. First printed by Gosse (*Go*), 'from a MS in the handwriting
of the poet, signed *Gray*, lately found at Pembroke College'. The present text (*PM*)
is from the MS. (Pembroke College MS. 74).
  Texts collated: *Go, Br.*

    2 facile] facili *Go, Br.*   7 nostro] nostra *Br.*

Jamque incepit opus: careat successibus, opto;   25
et vetet inceptum Fors, precor, istud opus:
Nec frustra; effulget subitó lux aurea cæli,
(aspice) rimanti dum domus atra patet;
Reclusamque vides fraudem, letique labores,
antraque miraris sulphure fœta suo: 30
Quod si venturi hæc armamentaria fati
panderat haud sacri gratia dia poli;
Jure scelus se jactaret, procerumque ruinâ
tantum unâ gentem perdomuisse manu.

ON THE FIFTH OF NOVEMBER.

There has been a dispute, undecided and prolonged for many years, one not to be resolved easily by a judge: to whom is the prize for pre-eminence in evil now to be awarded? What man is so great an honour to ennoble as he deserves?

In Rome, cruel tyrants made many claims for themselves: the first one many for himself, and the later one, Nero, many for himself; he who brought sea-shells back as booty from our shore and the scion of the noble Flavian line did the same.

Phalaris made many an effort for himself, that bane of Sicily, and the dire cause of your funeral pyre, O great Diana.

It would take too long to recount one by one the monstrous deeds that fill up the annals of reluctant fame, each notorious for its own crime. But at last England, bright with the fame of countless triumphs won in war, proudly displays the trophies won by the soldier's hand; and yet it is not enough for her to shine distinguished by the twofold palm, in the arts and in war, and to be the glory of the world, if the glory of fame won by crime is not added and does not fill up the measure of her praise. From her sons arises a mind that scorns all those that came before, ingenious to try new paths, which knows how to entomb Mars in hidden coverts and to lurk in cunning ambushes hidden from the sight of the sun.

Verily, in order that he may go undetected, he does not hesitate to burrow into the bowels of the earth nor even to die in the same catastrophe. Already he has begun the work. It is my wish that it

25 careat] caveat *Go.*   26 Fors] Sors *Go, Br.*   *At end of poem in PM*, Gray.

lack success; let Fortune, I pray, forbid (the completion of) that task, even though it has been started. Nor are my prayers in vain: suddenly the golden light of heaven blazes forth (behold!), until the black dwelling is revealed to the searching light. You see the ambush revealed, the labours of death, and gaze in wonder at caves filled with their own sulphur.

But if the divine grace of sacred heaven had not revealed this arsenal of impending death, he would now have a right to boast of his crime, that with his unaided hand he had overthrown a nation by destroying the leaders.

Luna habitabilis.

DUM Nox rorantes non incomitata per auras
Urget equos, tacitoque inducit sidera lapsu;
Ultima, sed nulli soror inficianda sororum,
Huc mihi, Musa: tibi patet alti janua cœli,
Astra vides, nec te numeri, nec nomina fallunt.   5
Huc mihi, Diva veni: dulce est per aperta serena
Vere frui liquido, campoque errare silenti;
Vere frui dulce est; modo tu dignata petentem
Sis comes, et mecum gelidâ spatiere sub umbrâ.

   Scilicèt hos orbes, cœli hæc decora alta putandum est,   10
Noctis opes, nobis tantum lucere; virûmque
Ostentari oculis, nostræ laquearia terræ,
Ingentes scenas, vastique aulæa theatri?
Oh! quis me pennis æthræ super ardua sistet
Mirantem, propiusque dabit convexa tueri;   15
Teque adeo, undè fluens reficit lux mollior arva,
Pallidiorque dies, tristes solata tenebras?

   Sic ego, subridens Dea sic ingressa vicissim:
Non pennis opus hìc, supera ut simul illa petamus:
Disce Puer potiùs cœlo deducere Lunam;   20
Neu crede ad magicas te invitum accingier artes,

LUNA HABITABILIS. Republished in *ME* (*Musae Etonenses*, London, 1755), ii. 107–12, the sole authority for the text. See explanatory notes.

21 accingier] accingere *ME; see expl. notes.*

Thessalicosve modos: ipsam descendere Phœben
Conspicies novus Endymion; seque offeret ultrò
Visa tibi ante oculos, et notâ major imago.
  Quin tete admoveas (tumuli super aggere spectas,   25
Compositum) tubulo; simul imum invade canalem
Sic intentâ acie, cœli simul alta patescent
Atria; jamque, ausus Lunaria visere regna,
Ingrediêre solo, et caput inter nubila condes.
  Ecce autem! vitri se in vertice sistere Phœben   30
Cernis, et Oceanum, et crebris Freta consita terris;
Panditur *ille* atram faciem caligine condens
Sublustri, refugitque oculos, fallitque tuentem;
Integram Solis lucem quippè haurit aperto
Fluctu avidus radiorum, et longos imbibit ignes: 35
Verum *his*, quæ, maculis variata nitentibus, auro
Cærula discernunt, celso sese insula dorso
Plurima protrudit, prætentaque littora saxis;
Liberior datur his quoniàm natura, minusque
Lumen depascunt liquidum; sed tela diei   40
Detorquent, retròque docent se vertere flammas.
  Hinc longos videas tractus, terrasque jacentes
Ordine candenti, et claros se attollere montes;
Montes queîs Rhodope assurgat, quibus Ossa nivali
Vertice: tum scopulis infrà pendentibus antra   45
Nigrescunt clivorum umbrâ, nemorumque tenebris.
Non rores illî, aut desunt sua nubila mundo;
Non frigus gelidum, atque herbis gratissimus imber:
His quoque nota ardet picto Thaumantias arcu,
Os roseum Auroræ, propriique crepuscula cœli.   50
  Et dubitas tantum certis cultoribus orbem
Destitui? exercent agros, sua mœnia condunt
Hi quoque, vel Martem invadunt, curantque triumphos
Victores: sunt hic etiam sua præmia laudi;
His metus, atque amor, et mentem mortalia tangunt.   55
  Quin, uti nos oculis jam nunc juvat ire per arva,
Lucentesque plagas Lunæ, pontumque profundum:
Idem illos etiàm ardor agit, cum se aureus effert
Sub sudum globus, et Terrarum ingentior orbis;
Scilicet omne æquor tum lustrant, scilicet omnem   60

44 Ossa] ossa *ME* (*clearly a misprint*).

Tellurem, gentesque polo sub utroque jacentes:
Et quidam æstivi indefessus ad ætheris ignes
Pervigilat, noctem exercens, cœlumque fatigat;
Jam Galli apparent, jam se Germania latè
Tollit, et albescens pater Apenninus ad auras: 65
Jam tandem in Borean, en! parvulus Anglia nævus
(Quanquàm aliis longè fulgentior) extulit oras:
Formosum extemplò lumen, maculamque nitentem
Invisunt crebri Proceres, serùmque tuendo
Hærent, certatimque suo cognomine signant: 70
Forsitan et Lunæ longinquus in orbe Tyrannus
Se dominum vocat, et nostrâ se jactat in aulâ.

   Terras possim alias propiori Sole calentes
Narrare; atque alias, jubaris queîs parcior usus,
Lunarum chorus, et tenuis penuria Phœbi: 75
Nî, meditans eadem hæc audaci evolvere cantu,
Jam pulset citharam Soror, et præludia tentet.

   Non tamen has proprias laudes, nec facta silebo
Jampridèm in fatis, patriæque oracula famæ.
Tempus erit, sursùm totos contendere cœtus   80
Quo cernes longo excursu, primosque colonos
Migrare in lunam, et notos mutare Penates:
Dum stupet obtutu tacito vetus incola, longèque
Insolitas explorat aves, classemque volantem.

   Ut quondàm ignotum marmor, camposque natantes   85
Tranavit Zephyros visens, nova regna, Columbus;
Litora mirantur circùm, mirantur et undæ
Inclusas acies ferro, turmasque biformes,
Monstraque fœta armis, et non imitabile fulmen.
Fœdera mox icta, et gemini commercia mundi,   90
Agminaque assueto glomerata sub æthere cerno.
Anglia, quæ pelagi jamdudum torquet habenas,
Exercetque frequens ventos, atque imperat undæ;
Aëris attollet fasces, veteresque triumphos
Hùc etiam feret, et victis dominabitur auris.   95

73 propiori] propriori *ME* (*clearly a misprint*).   80 sursùm] *First* u *printed
upside down in ME.*

THE MOON IS INHABITED.

While Night, not without her retinue, urges her steeds on through the dewy air and moves the stars in their silent circle, be, O Muse, my aid—the youngest, but not to be disowned by any of your sisters. For you the portals of the lofty sky are open; you behold the stars, and neither their numbers nor their names are unknown to you. Come hither to my aid, Goddess; sweet it is to enjoy the liquid Spring under cloudless skies and to wander over the silent plain. Rather say it would be sweet to enjoy the Spring if only you, acquiescent to my prayer, would be my companion and stroll with me in the cool darkness.

Surely it is not to be imagined that these orbs, these lofty ornaments of the firmament, the jewels of the night, shine only for us and reveal themselves only to the eyes of men—mere ornamented ceilings of our world, giant stage-settings, the curtains of a vast theatre. Oh, who will give me wings to mount in wonder above the steeps of the upper air, who will grant me the privilege of beholding the vaulted arch from nearer by—at least as far as you, from whom a softer light flows and reveals the fields, a paler day, lightening gloomy shadows?

So I; in reply the smiling goddess thus began: No need of wings is here to enable us to seek those lofty realms together; rather, my son, learn how to draw the moon down from heaven. And do not believe that you must have recourse to magic arts or Thessalian incantations; a new Endymion, you shall behold Phoebe's self descending; of her own free will she shall present herself to you— seen before your very eyes, and larger than you have ever known her.

Just apply yourself to the little tube (you have reached a good position and are looking aloft from a hillock); as soon as you enter the bottom of the tube with gaze thus sharpened, the lofty mansions of the sky will be revealed. Instantly, when you have ventured to gaze upon the realms of the moon, you will walk upon the earth but place your head among the clouds.

Now look! You see Phoebe taking her place in the circle of glass, and an ocean and straits thickly sown with many lands. The ocean is revealed, although it hides its dark surface in a dimly-lit mist; it shrinks away and tries to conceal itself from the eyes of anyone who looks at it; indeed, it absorbs all the light of the sun on the open sea, thirsting for his beams and drinking in long streamers of fire. But from the straits, which, variegated with shining spots, interweave the dark blue reaches with gold, many an island protrudes, with lofty spine and beaches lying in front of rocks; for, you see, a freer nature is given to them, and they do not so completely absorb the clear light; rather, they twist aside the shafts of day and teach the flames to turn back.

From your vantage point you can see long tracts, lands lying in a gleaming row, and shining mountains rearing their heights aloft—mountains such as Rhodope looks up to and even Ossa with its snow-clad summit. Then, down below, caves fashioned out of beetling crags look black, because of the shade of the cliffs and the shadows cast by groves of trees.

That world does not lack dew, nor its own kind of clouds, nor congealing cold, nor rain welcome to plants. In these lands too the fabled daughter of Thaumas glows with painted bow, and the rosy face of Aurora, and its own twilight glows in its sky.

Can you believe that a world so vast lacks some kind of inhabitants? These beings till their fields and found cities of their own. No doubt, too, they wage war, and when they are victorious celebrate triumphs: here too glory has its fit reward. Fear and love and mortal chances affect the minds of these creatures. Moreover, just as at this very moment it pleases us to let our eyes traverse the fields and shining lands of the moon, and its deep, dark sea; so likewise must ardent excitement move them when the golden orb, our greater earth, presents itself in a cloudless sky. Surely then they must observe every sea, the whole body of the earth, and the nations that live under either pole; and some tireless creature watches through the night, gazing at the fires of the summer sky, and wearies the heavens with his searching. Presently the Gauls appear, then wide-spreading Germany rises into view, and white-topped father Apenninus towers aloft; finally, behold! Look to the north! tiny England, no bigger than a beauty spot (although brighter far than all other lands), offers its shores to view. Straightway throngs of princes come to see this lovely radiance, this shining dot, and continue looking far into the night; and each one vies eagerly to distinguish it with his name. It may well be, too, that some far-distant tyrant in the world of the moon calls himself master, and swaggers in our palace.

I could tell of other lands warmed by the nearer sun, and of still others where the warmth of the sun is feeble; although they have a thronging chorus of moons, they have a dearth of the light of Phoebus, even in his weakened state. And I would do so, if my sister, who is planning to reveal these same things in adventurous song, were not already striking her lyre and beginning her prelude.

Nevertheless I will not keep silent about those words of praise that are justly mine, nor about the deeds long since inscribed in the book of fate, prophecies of the fame of our native land. The time will come when you will see great throngs hastening into the sky in a long procession and the first colonists emigrating to the moon and leaving behind their familiar household gods: while this goes on, the ancient inhabitant will gaze in stunned silence and from afar will spy upon birds such as he has never seen, the fleet of flying ships.

As happened once upon a time when Columbus sailed across the watery plains of an unknown sea, seeking the lands of Zephyr, new kingdoms; the circling shores and the waters gaze in wonder at the troops encased in steel, the centaur-like squadrons, the ominous monsters filled with armed men, and the inimitable lightning.

Soon I see the conclusion of treaties and commerce between the two worlds and columns of men assembled under a sky with which they have become familiar.

England, which has already long ruled the sea, and, sending out her mariners in great numbers, has harnessed the wind and spread her empire over the waves, will raise her conquering standards over the air; here, too, she will celebrate the triumphs that have been her habit, and will be queen of the subjugated realms of air.

[GRATIA MAGNA.]

Gratia magna tuæ fraudi quod Pectore, Nice
Non gerit hoc ultrà regna superba Venus:
Respirare licet tandem misero mihi; tandem
Appensa in sacro pariete vincla vides.

GRATIA MAGNA. First published by Tovey in *Gray and His Friends*, pp. 296–8 (*TGF*).
Text used: Mitford's transcription (*Mt*), Note-book, vol. iii, ff. 83–85. Texts collated: *TGF*, *Br*.

4 vides.] vides *Mt*, *TGF*, *Br*.

Nunquam . . . uror; liber sum: crede doloso   5
     Suppositus Cineri non latet ullus amor:
Præsto non ira est, cujus se celet amictu;
     Sera, sed et rediit vix mihi nota quies,
Nec nomen si forte tuum pervenit ad aures,
     Pallor, et alternus surgit in ore rubor,   10
Corda nec incerto trepidant salientia pulsu
     Irrigat aut furtim lacryma fusa genas.
Non tua per somnos crebra obversatur imago
     Non animo ante omnes tu mihi mane redis.
Te loquor; at tener ille silet sub pectore sensus,   15
     Nec, quod ades, lætor; nec quod abes, doleo.
Rivalem tacitus patior; securus eburnea
     Quin ego colla simul laudo, manusque tuas.
Longa nec indignans refero perjuria: prodis
     Obvia, mens certâ sede colorque manet.   20
Quin faciles risus, vultusque assume superbos:
     Spernentem sperno, nec cupio facilem.
Nescit ocellorum, ut quondam, penetrabile fulgur
     ah! nimium molles pectoris ire vias;
Non tam dulce rubent illi, mea cura, labelli   25
     juris ut immemores, imperiique sui.
Lætari possum, possum et mærere; sed à te
     gaudia nec veniunt, nec veniunt lacrymæ.
Tecum etiam nimii Soles, et frigora lædunt
     Vere suo sine te prata nemusque placent.   30
Pulcra quidem facies, sed non tua sola videtur,
     (forsitan offendam rusticitate meâ)
Sed quiddam invenio culpandum, quâ mihi nuper
     parte est præcipuè visus inesse lepos.
Cum primum evulsi fatale ex volnere telum   35
     Credebam, ut fatear, viscera et ipsa trahi.
Luctanti rupere (pudor) suspiria pectus,
     tinxit et invitas plurima gutta genas.
Aspera difficilem vicit Medicina furorem;

---

8 quies,] quies *Mt*; quies. *TGF, Br.*   9 pervenit] prevenit *Br.*   12 genas.]
genas *Mt.*   14 redis.] redis *Mt.*   16 doleo.] doleo *Mt.*   20 *Faint dot after*
sede *Mt.*   manet.] manet *Mt.*   21 superbos:] superbos *Mt.*   25 Non] Nec
TGF, Br.   30 *Faint dot after* prata *Mt.*   31 videtur,] videtur. *Mt*; videtur
TGF, Br.   33 invenio] invenies *TGF, Br*   34 est] est, *Mt.*

ille dolor sævus, sed magis asper amor.   40
Aucupis insidiis, et arundine capta tenaci
    sic multo nisu vincula rupit avis:
Plumarum laceros reparat breve tempus honores,
    Nec cadit in similes cautior inde dolos.
Tu tamen usque illam tibi fingis vivere flammam,   45
    Et malè me veteres dissimulare faces,
Quod libertatem ostento, fractamque Catenam,
    tantus et insolitæ pacis in ore sonus.
Præteritos meminisse jubet natura dolores;
    quæ quisque est passus, dulce pericla loqui: 50
Enumerat Miles sua vulnera; navita ventos
    Narrat, et incautæ saxa inimica rati.
Sic ego Servitium durum, et tua regna. Laborant
    Nice, nullam a te quærere dicta fidem;
Nil nimium hæc Mandata student tibi velle placere,   55
    Nec rogito, quali perlegis ore notas.

MANY THANKS.

Much gratitude to your deceit, Nice, because haughty Venus no longer holds dominion in my heart: I, who used to be so wretched, can breathe at last; at last you can see my chains hung on the temple wall. No longer am I on fire; I am free: believe me, not a single spark of love lurks buried in the deceptive ashes: here is no anger for love to use as a cloak to hide itself; it has come late, but even the peace of mind that I used to know has returned, although with difficulty, and, if perchance your name reaches my ears, neither pallor nor its opposite, blushing redness, rises in my face; my pounding heart does not tremble with unsteady beats, nor does the flowing tear furtively furrow my cheeks. Your image no longer keeps floating through my dreams, nor are you any longer the first to come into my mind in the morning.

I speak of you; but the tender emotion that I once felt is silent in my heart, and I no longer rejoice because you are with me, nor do I grieve because you are not. Without complaint I endure the

40 amor.] Amor *TGF, Br.*   46 faces,] faces. *Mt, TGF, Br.*   48 sonus.] sonus, *TGF, Br.*

fact that another has taken my place; why, I can even praise your ivory neck and your hands with complete detachment.

I do not rehearse with anger the long list of broken vows: when you cross my path, my mind remains firmly fixed in its seat, nor does my colour change. For all I care, you may smile invitingly or put on a look of disdain: when you scorn me, I scorn you, but I do not desire you even when you are in a yielding mood. The penetrating lightning of your eyes cannot, as once it did, travel the pathways—too easily open, alas!—of my breast. Your lips are not so red and sweet, my dear, that they can make me forget your imperious rule.

I can rejoice and I can be sorrowful; but my joys do not come from you, nor do my tears. With you, moreover, too-hot suns and wintry chills alike were always causing pain; without you, it is spring, and fields and grove are pleasing.

To be sure, your face seems beautiful, but not yours alone (perchance I may give offence with my blunt country speech), but I find something unpleasing in the very part where only a while ago a special charm seemed to dwell.

When I first tore the deadly shaft from the wound, I thought, to confess the truth, that I was pulling out my very bowels with it. As I struggled (I am ashamed to say) sighs tore my heart, and many a tear stained my reluctant cheeks. The medicine was bitter that cured my deep-seated madness; the pain was cruel, but love was more cruel. Thus a bird, caught by the traps and sticky reed of a fowler, breaks its bonds with a mighty effort: in a little while it repairs the damaged beauty of its feathers, and, made more cautious by its experience, it does not fall into similar traps.

You, however, imagine that the old flame is still burning and that I am making a clumsy effort to conceal the old passions, because I am making such a show of my freedom and my broken chain, and so loud a sound of unaccustomed peace is on my lips.

Nature loves to remember pains that have passed away; everyone takes pleasure in telling of the dangers that he has undergone: the soldier recounts his wounds; the sailor speaks of winds and rocks deadly to a careless ship. So I my cruel bondage and the power you once had. My words, Nice, make no effort to seek belief from you; these verses that I have sent have no particular wish to please you, nor do I care how you look when you read about your disgraceful acts.

Ad C: Favonium Aristium.

Barbaras ædes aditure mecum,
Quas Eris sempér fovet inquieta,
Lis ubi laté sonat, et togatum
   Æstuat agmen!

Dulcius quanto, patulis sub ulmi   5
Hospitæ ramis temeré jacentem
Sic libris horas, tenuique inertes
   Fallere Musâ?

Sæpe enim curis vagor expeditâ
Mente; dum, blandam meditans Camœnam, 10
Vix malo rori, meminive seræ
   Cedere nocti;

Et, pedes quó me rapiunt, in omni
Colle Parnassum videor videre
Fertilem sylvæ, gelidamque in omni   15
   Fonte Aganippen.

Risit et Ver me, facilesque Nymphæ
Nare captantem, nec ineleganti,
Mané quicquid de violis eundo
   Surripit aura: 20

Me reclinatum teneram per herbam;
Quâ leves cursus aqua cunque ducit,
Et moras dulci strepitu lapillo
   Nectit in omni.

Hæ novo nostrum feré pectus anno   25
Simplices curæ tenuere, cælum
Quamdiú sudum explicuit Favonî
   Purior hora:

AD C: FAVONIUM ARISTIUM. First published in Mason, i. 30–32. The text followed here is that of the holograph MS. in *CB*, i. 53 (ll. 1–40) and 90 (ll. 41–52).
 Text collated: *M*. There are no significant variations.

Title: Mason gives none, but refers to the poem as a 'Sapphic Ode' in a footnote (see expl. notes).

Otia et campos nec adhúc relinquo,
Nec magiś Phœbo Clytie fidelis; 30
(Ingruant venti licet, et senescat
                    Mollior æstas).

Namque, seu, lætos hominum labores
Prataque et montes recreante curru,
Purpurâ tractus oriens Eoos 35
                    Vestit, et auro;

Sedulus servo, veneratus orbem
Prodigum splendoris: amœniori
Sive dilectam meditatur igne
                    Pingere Calpen; 40

Usque dum, fulgore magiś, magiś jam
Languido circuḿ, variata nubes
Labitur furtiḿ, viridisque in umbras
                    Scena recessit.

O ego felix, vice si (nec unquam 45
Surgerem rursus) simili cadentem
Parca me lenis sineret quieto
                    Fallere letho!

Multá flagranti, radiisque cincto
Integris ah! quaḿ nihil inviderem, 50
Cum Dei ardentes medius quadrigas
                    Sentit Olympus?

TO GAIUS FAVONIUS ARISTIUS.

O thou about to go with me to the barbaric temple which restless
Eris always haunts, where legal strife resounds on every side and the
toga-clad army swarms!

How much sweeter it would be to forget business and stretch at
ease beneath the spreading branches of a sheltering elm and while
away the idle hours with books and the humble Muse?

32 aestas).] aestas) *CB*.   *At end in CB, in Gray's hand*: Cambridge, June 1738[.]

For now I often wander with care-free mind, while, as I meditate the soft Italian Muse, I scarce remember to heed the sickly dew or the lateness of the night; and, wherever my feet take me, I seem to see in every hill a forest-clad Parnassus and in every spring a cool Aganippe.

Spring smiles on me, and gracious nymphs; my fastidious nose makes mine whatever the passing breeze of morning has stolen from the violets, as I lie at ease on the tender grass, wheresoever a brook traces its light course and hesitates with sweet clashings at every pebble.

About the time of the year's renewal these simple cares engrossed my heart, as long as the brighter season of Favonius afforded cloudless skies: nor yet have I abandoned leisure and the fields, nor is Clytie more faithful to Phoebus (though the winds are rising and the softer summer is fading).

For I am his diligent and faithful slave, a worshipper of the orb that sheds splendour so lavishly, whether, as his car brings new life to the joyful labours of men, to meadow and mountain, he is rising and clothing the lands of the East in purple and gold, or whether he is about to paint his beloved Calpe with a more tempered fire: aye, to the very moment when, as the splendour grows dimmer and dimmer, the many-coloured cloud slips away like a thief and the scene fades into green shadows.

Oh, how blessed would I think myself (though I could never rise again), if kindly fate would permit me, sinking low in like fashion, to hide myself in peaceful death!

Ah, how little would I envy the god, blazing with many fires and crowned with unclouded rays, when the middle of heaven feels his flaming chariot!

[ALCAIC FRAGMENT.]

O lachrymarum Fons, tenero sacros
Ducentium ortus ex animo; quater
Felix! in imo qui scatentem
Pectore te, pia Nympha, sensit!

ALCAIC FRAGMENT. First published in Mason, i. 33, at the end of the letter to West dated June 1738 (T & W no. 53).

Text used: *CB*, i. 90. Text collated: *M*.

Title: Gray listed as 'Tears, Alcaic fragment on them' in Index of *CB*.

ALCAIC FRAGMENT.

O fountain of tears which have their sacred sources in the sensitive soul! Four times blessed he who has felt thee, holy Nymph, bubbling up from the depths of his heart!

FROM PETRARCH. LIB: I: SONETT: 170.

Lasso ch' i ardo, & [ed] altri non me 'l crede, &c:
['Alas because I am aflame, and some one does not believe it of me. . . .']

Uror io! veros at nemo credidit ignes:
    quin credunt omnes; dura sed illa negat.
Illa negat, solî volumus cui posse probare:
    quin videt, et visos improba dissimulat.
Ah durissima mî, sed et ah pulcherrima rerum!   5
    nonne animam in miserâ, Cynthia, fronte vides?
Omnibus illa pia est, et, si non fata vetassent,
    tam longas mentem flecteret ad lachrymas.
Sed tamen has lachrymas, hunc tu, quem spreveris, ignem,
    carminaque auctori non benè culta suo   10
Turba futurorum non ignorabit amantûm:
    nos duo, cumque erimus parvus uterque cinis,
Jamque faces, eheu! oculorum, et frigida lingua
    hæ sine luce jacent, immemor illa loqui:
Infelix Musa æternos spirabit amores,   15
    ardebitque urnâ multa favilla meâ.

FROM PETRARCH. First published by Mathias, 1814, ii. 93 (*Ma*).
    Text used: *CB*, i. 139. Text collated: *Ma*.

Title: 170] 169 *underlined*, 170 *in parentheses*, CB. *The original is Sonnet 170 (poem 203 of the* Canzoniere).

6 Cynthia,] Cynthia; *CB*.   8 lachrymas.] lachrymas *CB*.

FROM PETRARCH.

Ah, I am on fire! but no one has believed that the fires are real: rather, everyone (else) believes, but she, cruel she, says they are not—she it is who will not believe, and yet she is the only one that I would convince. Worse, she even sees them, and then, perverse wench, pretends that she hasn't seen them at all. Ah, lady most cruel to me! But, for all your cruelty, fairest of women! Can you not see my soul, Cynthia, in my downcast face?

Kind she is to all; and surely, if the Fates had not forbidden, she would ere this have softened her heart in response to the tears that have been flowing for so long.

But at least the future throng of lovers will not be ignorant of these tears, this fire that you scorn, and the songs ill suited to their author; as for us two, when we shall some day each have become a handful of ashes—then, alas, the fires of my eyes will lie devoid of light and my cold tongue will forget how to speak: but the ill-fated Muse will still breathe eternal loves, and many a spark will glow in my urn.

[FROM GENOA.]

Horridos tractus, Boreæque linquens
Regna Taurini fera, molliorem
Advehor brumam, Genuæque amantes
　　Litora soles.

FROM GENOA.

Leaving those regions that tremble with cold and the savage realms ruled by Boreas of the Taurini, I am journeying to a milder winter and the sunny days that caress the shores of Genoa.

FROM GENOA. The sole authority for the text is Mason's transcription of Gray's letter to West, Genoa, 21 Nov. 1739 (T & W no. 75; *M*, p. 68).

Title: Mason gives none.

[ELEGIAC VERSES.]

Quà Trebiæ glaucas salices intersecat unda,
　Arvaque Romanis nobilitata malis.
Visus adhuc amnis veteri de clade rubere,
　Et suspirantes ducere mæstus aquas;
Maurorumque ala, et nigræ increbrescere turmæ,　　　5
　Et pulsa Ausonidum ripa sonare fugâ.

ELEGIAC VERSES.

Gray's letter (T & W no. 78) mixes English and Latin in the
same sentence. The sentence begins, 'Secondly, how we passed the
famous plains . . .', and then continues with the Latin verse, as
follows:
. . . where the water of the Trebia cuts through the grey-green
willows and the fields ennobled by Roman disasters. The stream
seemed even yet to run red with blood from the ancient slaughter
and to sigh in lamentation as it flowed. The cavalry squadron of
Moors, black bands of horsemen, seemed still to exult in triumph,
and the trampled bank to resound with the flight of the sons of
Ausonia.

ELEGIAC VERSES. The sole authority for the text is Mason's transcription of Gray's
letter to West, Florence, 15 Jan. 1740 (T & W no. 78; *M*, i. 75).

Title: Mason gives none. Usually headed 'Elegiac Verses' by subsequent editors.

1 Trebiæ] Trebie, *M. The editors have adopted the suggestion of T & W that* Trebie
(and undâ) *are errors in Mason's transcription. There is no authority in either ancient
'Trebia' or modern 'Trebbia' for the use of 'Trebie' as nominative.* unda] undâ, *M.
The change from* undâ (*abl.*) *to* unda (*nom.*) *follows from the error noted above.*

Ad C: Favonium Zephyrinum.

Mater rosarum, cui teneræ vigent
Auræ Favonî, cui Venus it comes
    Lasciva, Nympharum choreis
    Et volucrum celebrata cantu!
Dic, non inertem fallere quâ diem   5
Amat sub umbra, seu sinit aureum
    Dormire plectrum, seu retentat
    Pierio Zephyrinus antro,
Furore dulci plenus, et immemor
Reptantis inter frigora Tusculi   10
    Umbrosa, vel colles amici
    Palladiæ superantis Albæ.
Dilecta Fauno, et capripedum choris
Pineta, testor vos, Anio minax
    Quæcunque per clivos volutus   15
    Præcipiti tremefecit amne,
Illius altum Tibur, et Æsulæ
Audîsse sylvas nomen amabiles,
    Illius et gratas Latinis
    Naiasin ingeminâsse rupes.   20
Nam me Latinæ Naiades uvidâ
Vidêre ripâ, quà niveas levi
    Tam sæpe lavit rore plumas
    Dulce canens Venusinus ales:
Mirum! canenti conticuit nemus,   25
Sacrique fontes, et retinent adhuc
    (Sic Musa jussit) saxa molles
    Docta modos, veteresque lauri.

AD C: FAVONIUM ZEPHYRINUM. First published in Mason, i. 87–88. There are two
holograph MSS.: *CB*, i. 128, the text followed here; and *Wal* (Pembroke College MS.
L.C. 2. 123, no. 107).
    Texts collated: *Wal, M*.

Title: Alcaïca *Wal; none in M*.
The fourth line of each stanza is indented to the same depth as the third in Wal.

8 *In Wal, not in Gray's hand, a cross before* Zephyrinus *and* Rich'd West *in margin.*
20 Naiasin] *So also in Wal and M. See expl. notes.*   21 Naiades] *So also in Wal and*
M. See expl. notes.   22 levi] lavit *Wal.*   23 lavit rore plumas] plumas rore
puro *Wal.*   24 Dulce canens] Et gelido *Wal.*

Mirare nec tu me citharæ rudem
Claudis laborantem numeris: loca   30
Amœna, jucundumque ver in-
    Compositum docuere carmen.
Hærent sub omni nam folio nigri
Phœbea lucî (credite) somnia;
    Argutiusque et lympha, et auræ   35
Nescio quid solito loquuntur.

TO GAIUS FAVONIUS ZEPHYRINUS.

Mother of roses, for whom the gentle breezes of the West Wind swell, to whom sportive Venus lends her company, attended by choruses of nymphs and the song of birds!

Tell me, beneath what shade does Zephyrinus love to while away the busy day? Perhaps he permits the golden lyre to sleep; perhaps, full of sweet rage, he wakes it again to song in the Pierian grotto, forgetful of his friend strolling amid the cool shades of Tusculum or among the hills of lofty Alba, sacred to Pallas.

O Pine forests beloved by Faunus and the goat-footed chorus, I call you to witness, which of you soever the brawling Anio, rolling down the cliffs, causes to tremble with his headlong stream, that lofty Tibur has heard the name of Favonius, as have also the enchanting groves of Aesula, and that the cliffs dear to the Latin Naiads have re-echoed it: for the Latin Naiads have seen me on the moist bank where the sweet-singing bird of Venusia so often bathed his snowy plumes in limpid dew. Then a miracle! To hear him as he sang, the grove became silent, and the sacred springs; and to this very day (for so the Muse commanded), the rocks, taught to sing, and the ancient laurels, keep repeating the soft strains.

Do not, then, be astonished that I, a novice of the lyre, struggle with limping numbers: lovely places and joyful spring have taught the song, badly composed though it be; for (be sure) under every leaf in the dark grove cling dreams inspired by Phoebus, and stream and breezes speak more melodiously than any virtuoso.

32 *A hyphen before* Compositum *CB, Wal, M.*   *At end in CB, in Gray's hand,* Wrote at Rome, the latter end of the Spring, 1740 after a journey to Frescati [*sic*], & the cascades of Tivoli. *At end in Wal, not in Gray's hand,* by T. Gray, from Tivoli.

[THE GAURUS.]

Nec procul infelix se tollit in æthera Gaurus,
Prospiciens vitreum lugenti vertice pontum.
Tristior ille diù, et veteri desuetus olivâ
Gaurus, pampineæque eheu jam nescius umbræ:
Horrendi tam sæva premit vicinia montis,   5
Attonitumque urget latus, exuritque ferentem.
   Nam fama est, olim, mediâ dum rura silebant
Nocte deo victa, et molli perfusa quiete;
Infremuisse æquor ponti, auditamque per omnes
Laté tellurem surduḿ immugire cavernas: 10
Quo sonitu nemora alta tremunt, tremit excita tuto
Parthenopæa sinu, flammantisque ora Vesevi.
At subitó se aperire solum, vastosque recessus
Pandere sub pedibus, nigrâque voragine fauces:
Tum piceas cinerum glomerare sub æthere nubes   15
Vorticibus rapidis, ardentique imbre procellam.
Præcipites fugere feræ, perque avia longé
Silvarum fugit pastor, juga per deserta,
Ah, miser! increpitans sæpe altâ voce per umbram
Nequicquam natos, creditque audire sequentes: 20
Atque ille excelso rupis de vertice solus
Respectans notasque domos, et dulcia regna,
Nil usquam videt infelix præter mare tristi
Lumine percussum, et pallentes sulphure campos,
Fumumque, flammasque, rotataque turbine saxa.   25
   Quin ubi detonuit fragor, et lux reddita cœlo:
Mæstos confluere agricolas, passuque videres
Tandem iterum timido deserta requirere tecta;
Sperantes, si forté oculis, si forté darentur
Uxorum cineres, miserorumve ossa parentum   30

THE GAURUS. First published in Mason, i. 105-8. There are two holograph MSS.:
CB, i. 115 (ll. 1–52), and 128 (ll. 53–61), the text followed here; and *Wal* (Pembroke
College MS. L.C. 2. 123, no. 108).
   Texts collated: *Wal*, *M*.

Title: None given by Gray, who refers to it in his letter to West (T & W no. 94) as
'a piece of a poem' and a fragment.

7 Nam fama est, olim] Nam fama est; oliḿ *Wal*.   10 Laté tellurem] Tellurem late
Wal.   immugire] mugire *Wal*.   15 Tum] Et *Wal*.

(Tenuia, sed tanti saltem solatia luctûs)
Uná colligere, et justâ componere in urnâ.
Uxorum nusquam cineres, nusquam ossa parentum
(Spem miseram) assuetosve Lares, aut rura videbunt;
Quippe ubi planities campi diffusa jacebat,   35
Mons novus: ille supercilium, frontemque favillâ
Incanum ostentans, ambustis cautibus, æquor
Subjectum, stragemque suam, mæsta arva, minaci
Despicit imperio, soloque in littore regnat.

Hinc infame loci nomen, multosque per annos   40
Immemor antiquæ laudis nescire labores
Vomeris, et nullo tellus revirescere cultu:
Non avium colles, non carmine matutino
Pastorum resonare; adeó undique dirus habebat
Informes laté horror agros, saltusque vacantes.   45
Sæpius et longé detorquens navita proram
Monstrabat digito littus, sævæque revolvens
Funera narrabat noctis, veteremque ruinam.

Montis adhuć facies manet hirta atque aspera saxis
Sed furor extinctus jamdudum, et flamma quievit,   50
Quæ nascenti aderat; seu forté bituminis atri
Defluxere olim rivi, atque effœta lacuna
Pabula sufficere ardori, viresque recusat:
Sive in visceribus meditans incendia jam nunc,
Horrendum! arcanis glomerat genti esse futuræ   55
Exitio, sparsos tacitusque recolligit ignes.

Raro per clivos haud secius ordine vidi
Canescentem oleam. Longum post tempus amicti
Vite virent tumuli, patriamque revisere gaudens
Bacchus in assuetis tenerum caput exerit arvis   60
Vix tandem, infidoque audet se credere cœlo.

44 adeó undique] informes tam *Wal. But the verse does not scan with text of Wal.*
45 Informes laté horror agros] Horror agros laté circum *Wal.*   46 et] hoc *Wal.*
54 meditans] meditata *Wal.*   57 Raro per clivos haud] Per clivos raro nec *Wal.*
59 *Word, probably* colles, *del. after* virent *Wal.*   60 exerit] exserit *Wal. A variant
spelling only.*   At end in *CB,* Rome—July, 1740 just return'd from Naples. *At end
of Wal,* Rome. . June 1740. *The latter is perhaps more accurate, since Gray left Rome
on 4 July 1740.*

THE GAURUS.

And not far away the ill-fated Gaurus lifts its heights into the upper air, looking forth from its grieving summit at a sea of glass: Famous Gaurus, sad for a long time and no longer accustomed to the ancient olive tree, now, alas, ignorant of the shade of vines: so cruelly the frightful neighbouring mountain assails it and over-whelms its blasted side and has burnt (the vegetation that) it bore.

For the story is that once, while the fields lay silent in the middle of the night, overcome by the god and drenched in soft slumber, the waters of the deep roared and the mute earth was heard to bellow far and wide through all its caverns. At the sound the lofty forests tremble, and Parthenope, roused from sleep, trembles in her snug harbour, as did the shore of flaming Vesuvius. Suddenly the earth gaped and beneath the feet opened vast chasms and the yawning jaws of a black whirlpool. Then pitch-black clouds of ashes gathered in the air in swift whirling masses and there was a gale-driven rain of fire.

The wild animals fled headlong, and the herdsman fled far through the pathless forest and along the deserted ridges, often calling loudly through the darkness to his children, in the belief that they hear him and are following him; but he was wasting his breath, unhappy man. At last, all alone, looking back from the lofty summit of a cliff to see the familiar homes and sweet countryside, he descries not a thing, ill-starred man, except the sea suffused with gloomy light and fields whitened by sulphur, and smoke and flames and rocks tossed about by the whirlwind.

Even worse, when the thundering crashes had ceased and the light of day had returned to the sky, you could see the grieving farmers assembling and seeking out with fearful steps their desolated homes. They hope, if by any chance they should find the ashes of their wives or the bones of their unfortunate parents (slight solaces, but at least some comfort for their great sorrow), to gather them up and inter them decently in a proper urn. But no ashes of their wives were they fated to see, nor bones of parents (sad hope!), nor familiar Lares, nor even their farms. Indeed, where the level surface of the plain used to lie in a broad sweep, a new mountain rose. Flaunting a face and crest white with still-warm ashes and covered with fire-scorched rocks, it looks down like a menacing tyrant upon the sea lying at its feet, upon the destruction it has wrought, upon the sorrowing fields, and lords it over the desolate shore.

Hence the evil name of the place, and for many years, forgetful of its ancient glory, the land has not known the labours of the plough nor responded to cultivation with fresh green. The slopes have not echoed to the morning song of birds or of shepherds. Everywhere, indeed, ominous horror broods over the distorted fields and lifeless swamps. Many a time some sailor, turning his ship far out from the coast, would point at the shore with his finger and recall and tell the deaths of that savage night and the destruction of long ago.

To this day the face of the mountain remains shaggy and bristling with rocks, but the fury has been calmed for a long time now, and the flame which aided the birth of the mountain has subsided. Perhaps the streams of black asphalt have long since dried up and the exhausted crater refuses to furnish fuel and strength for the fire; perhaps (horrible thought) it is biding its time and is even now amassing fires in its secret bowels to be the destruction of some future race, and is silently gathering up its scattered fires once more.

However, I have seen hoary olive trees in a sparse line along the slopes; after a long time the vine-clad mounds are green; glad to see his home again, Bacchus is at last, with difficulty, raising his tender head in the familiar fields and daring to entrust himself to the sky that once betrayed him.

[FAREWELL TO FLORENCE.]

> . . . oh Fæsulæ amœna
> Frigoribus juga, nec nimiuṁ spirantibus auris!
> Alma quibus Tusci Pallas decus Apennini
> Esse dedit, glaucâque suâ canescere sylvâ.
> Non ego vos posthac Arni de valle videbo   5
> Porticibus circum, et candenti cincta coronâ
> Villarum longe nitido consurgere dorso,
> Antiquamve ædem, et veteres præferre cupressus
> Mirabor, tectisque super pendentia tecta.

FAREWELL TO FLORENCE. First published in Mason, i. 115.
    Text used: *CB*, i. 139. Text collated: *M*.
Title: None in *CB* or *M*.

1 Fæsulæ] Fæsulæ, *CB*. *See expl. notes.*   *At end in CB, a blurred date, apparently* 1740. *If this is the reading, it is probably wrong (see expl. notes).*

FAREWELL TO FLORENCE.

O lovely hills of Fiesole, cooled by breezes that never blow too hard! To whom fostering Pallas gave the privilege of being the spot of greatest beauty and charm in the Tuscan Apennines and of being hoary with groves of her silver-green tree. Never again shall I see you in the distance from the valley of the Arno, girt all around with porticoes and a chaplet of gleaming white villas, as you soar aloft on the shining ridge; never again shall I gaze in wonder at the ancient temple with its screen of aged cypress and the roofs hanging over roofs.

Imitated [from Buondelmonti].

Lusit amicitiæ interdum velatus amictu,
   et bené compositâ veste fefellit Amor.
Mox iræ assumsit cultus, faciemque minantem,
   inque odium versus, versus et in lacrymas:
Ludentem fuge, nec lacrymanti, aut crede furenti: 5
   idem est dissimili semper in ore Deus.

IMITATED FROM BUONDELMONTI.

Sometimes Cupid sports veiled in the cloak of friendship and disguises his presence under garments all in decent array. Presently he puts on a cloak of anger and assumes a threatening expression; then his look of hatred swiftly melts into tears. Fly from him when he is in a sportive mood, neither put any trust in him, whether he weeps or rages: his face may change, but he is always the same god.

IMITATED FROM BUONDELMONTI. First published in Mason, i. 115, where the text of the Italian poem is also printed. There are no significant textual variations; however, Mason does have the correct grave accents in the Italian, but this is probably an accidental result of the fact that he always uses grave instead of acute accents.
   Text used: *CB*, i. 139. Text collated: *M*.

Title: None in *M*.

5 furenti:] furenti *CB*.   *At end in CB, a blurred date, 174?. See expl. notes.*

[ALCAIC ODE.]

In the Book at the Grande Chartreuse among
the Mountains of Dauphiné.

O Tu, severi relligio loci,
Quocunque gaudes nomine (non leve
   Nativa nam certé fluenta
     Numen habet, veteresque sylvas;
Præsentiorem et conspicimus Deum   5
Per invias rupes, fera per juga,
   Clivosque præruptos, sonantes
     Inter aquas, nemorumque noctem;
Quam si repôstus sub trabe citreâ
Fulgeret auro, et Phidiacâ manu)   10
   Salve vocanti rité, fesso et
     Da placidam juveni quietem.
Quod si invidendis sedibus, et frui
Fortuna sacrâ lege silentii
   Vetat volentem, me resorbens   15
     In medios violenta fluctus:
Saltem remoto des, Pater, angulo
Horas senectæ ducere liberas;
   Tutumque vulgari tumultu
     Surripias, hominumque curis.   20

ALCAIC ODE.

  O Thou, Holy Spirit of this stern place, what name soever
pleases Thee (for surely it is no insignificant divinity that holds
sway over untamed streams and ancient forests; and surely, too, we
behold God nearer to us, a living presence, amid pathless steeps,
wild mountain ridges and precipitous cliffs, and among roaring
torrents and the nocturnal gloom of sacred groves than if He were

ALCAIC ODE. First published in Mason, i. 117-18.
  Text used: *CB*, i. 129. Text collated: *M*.

Title: Ode. *M*. *Listed as* Alcaic Ode *in Northup and Starr*.
At end in CB, August—1741.

confined under beams of citron and gleaming with gold wrought by the hand of Phidias)—hail to Thee! And if I invoke Thy name aright, grant to a youth already weary calm and peaceful rest.

But if Fortune now forbids me to enjoy this enviable dwelling and the sacred rule of silence, despite my wish, sucking me back with violence into the midst of the waves, at least, Father, grant that I may spend the hours of my old age free of care in some secluded corner; carry me off in safety from the tumult of the mob and the anxieties of men.

[OH UBI COLLES.]

Oh ubi colles, ubi Fæsularum,
Palladis curæ, plaga, Formiæque
Prodigæ florum, Genuæque amantes
    Littora soles?

Abstulit campos oculis amœnos   5
Montium quantus, nemorumque tractus?
Quot natant eheu! medii profundo
    Marmore fluctus?

OH UBI COLLES.

Oh, where are the hills, where the region of Fiesole, which Pallas loves and protects, and Formiae rich in flowers, and the suns that caress the shores of Genoa?

How vast a tract of mountains and forests has taken the pleasing fields from my sight? How many waves, alas, roll in the shining deep between?

OH UBI COLLES. First published by Tovey in *Gray and His Friends*, p. 296 (*TGF*). Text used: *CB*, i. 381. Text collated: *TGF*.

Title: None given by Gray.

6 *Between* Montium *and* quantus *in CB, a word obliterated with a heavy pen-stroke.*

[SOPHONISBA MASINISSAE.
EPISTOLA.]

Egregium accipio promissi Munus amoris,
    Inque manu mortem jam fruitura fero:
Atque utinam citius mandasses, luce vel unâ;
    Transieram Stygios non inhonesta lacus.
Victoris nec passa toros, nova nupta, mariti,   5
    Nec fueram fastus, Roma superba, tuos.
Scilicet hæc partem tibi, Masinissa, triumphi
    Detractam, hæc pompæ jura minora suæ
Imputat, atque uxor quòd non tua pressa catenis,
    Objecta et sævæ plausibus urbis eo: 10
Quin tu pro tantis cepisti præmia factis,
    Magnum Romanæ pignus amicitiæ!
Scipiadæ excuses, oro, si tardius utar
    Munere. Non nimiùm vivere, crede, velim.
Parva mora est, breve sed tempus mea fama requirit: 15
    Detinet hæc animam cura suprema meam.
Quæ patriæ prodesse meæ Regina ferebar,
    Inter Elisæas gloria prima nurus,
Ne videar flammæ nimis indulsisse secundæ,
    Vel nimis hostiles extimuisse manus.   20
Fortunam atque annos liceat revocare priores,
    Gaudiaque heu! quantis nostra repensa malis.
Primitiasne tuas meministi atque arma Syphacis
    Fusa, et per Tyrias ducta trophæa vias?
(Laudis at antiquæ forsan meminisse pigebit,   25
    Quodque decus quondam causa ruboris erit.)
Tempus ego certe meminì, felicia Pœnis
    Quo te non puduit solvere vota deis;
Mœniaque intrantem vidi: longo agmine duxit
    Turba salutantum, purpureique patres.   30

SOPHONISBA MASINISSAE. EPISTOLA. The sole authority for the text is Mason, i.
153–5, the text followed here, with exceptions noted below (M).
    Texts collated: Mt, Br.

Title: SOPHONISBA MASSINISSAE / EPISTOLA. *M.* PART OF AN HEROIC
EPISTLE / from Sophonisba to Masinissa. *Mt.* Sophonisba ad Masinissam. *Br.*

7 Masinissa] Massinissa *M.*   10 urbis] orbis *Mt, Br.*   27 Pœnis] Pænis *M.*
29 Mœnia] Mænia *M.*

Fœminea ante omnes longe admiratur euntem
    Hæret et aspectu tota caterva tuo.
Jam flexi, regale decus, per colla capilli,
    Jam decet ardenti fuscus in ore color!
Commendat frontis generosa modestia formam,   35
    Seque cupit laudi surripuisse suæ.
Prima genas tenui signat vix flore juventas,
    Et dextræ soli credimus esse virum.
Dum faciles gradiens oculos per singula jactas,
    (Seu rexit casus lumina, sive Venus)   40
In me (vel certè visum est) conversa morari
    Sensi; virgineus perculit ora pudor.
Nescio quid vultum molle spirare tuendo,
    Credideramque tuos lentius ire pedes.
Quærebam, juxta æqualis si dignior esset,   45
    Quæ poterat visus detinuisse tuos:
Nulla fuit circum æqualis quæ dignior esset,
    Asseruitque decus conscia forma suum.
Pompæ finis erat. Totâ vix nocte quievi:
    Sin premat invitæ lumina victa sopor,   50
Somnus habet pompas, eademque recursat imago;
    Atque iterum hesterno munere victor ades.

     *   *   *   *   *   *

SOPHONISBA TO MASINISSA. AN EPISTLE.

    Distinguished is this gift that I now receive, the reward of plighted love; and as I prepare to enjoy it, I hold death in my hand. Ah, would that you had given it to me just one day sooner: then surely I would have crossed the Stygian waters with my honour unsullied: I would neither have allowed myself, a bride fresh from the altar, to share the bed of the conqueror who became my husband, nor would I have suffered your arrogance, haughty Rome. No doubt Rome will charge it to your account, Masinissa, that a portion of triumph has been snatched away, that the prerogatives of her triumphal parade have been lessened because I, your wife, am not going to march laden with chains and exposed to the exultant howls of the savage city: what rewards you have received for so many

31 Fœminea] Fæminea *M*.   52 munere] numere *Br*.

great deeds! A magnificent token of Roman friendship! Beg the
pardon of Scipio, I pray, if I use your gift too slowly; I assure you,
I would not wish to live too long. The delay will be short, but my
reputation demands a brief time: concern for this, the last concern
I shall ever feel, is all that keeps my soul from departing.

I should not wish that I, who used to be considered of some worth
to my native land when I was queen, the foremost glory of the
daughters of Elisa, should seem to have indulged too eagerly in a
second passion or to have been overmuch terrified by the violence
of my enemies. Let me recall the good fortune of past years and my
joys, purchased (alas!) at the cost of so much misfortune.

Do you remember your first victory and the rout of Syphax's
troops and the trophies of victory borne through Tyrian streets?
(But perhaps you will be ashamed to remember your former praise,
and what was once a glorious distinction will become a cause for
blushing.) As for me, I clearly remember the time when you were
not ashamed to fulfil the vows you made to the gods of Carthage,
when your prayers had been granted. I saw you as you entered the
city: the multitude of those who came to hail you stretched in a long
line, and the purple-clad elders were there. As you strode along,
a noisy throng of women gazed at you with far more admiration
than all the others, and every one of them kept her eyes fixed upon
you. How becoming your hair flowing to your shoulders, a royal
badge of honour; how becoming the dark colour of your glowing
face! Well-bred modesty heightens the beauty of your person, and
wants to slip unobtrusively away from the praise it has itself aroused.
The beginning of young manhood just barely adorns your cheeks
with a slight bloom, and we believe that you are a man solely because
of what your hand has wrought. As you advanced, glancing quickly
at each sight in turn, (whether accident or Venus took control of
your eyes) I sensed (or so at least it surely seemed to me) that your
eyes lingered when you turned them on me; a blush of virgin
modesty suffused my face. I was sure that your expression softened
a little as you gazed and that your feet advanced more slowly. I
asked myself if there was any other woman near me who might have
been more worthy of attracting and holding your gaze; there was
not one who might be more worthy around me, and consciousness
of beauty declared that the attention was its own.

The triumphal procession came to an end. All night I found
hardly any rest: even if sleep overcame me and closed my eyes

against my will, the procession would continue in my dreams, and the same sight would come back; once more you were with me as a conqueror, acting just as you had the day before.

De Principiis Cogitandi.
Liber Primus. Ad Favonium.

Unde Animus scire incipiat: quibus inchoet orsa
Principiis seriem rerum, tenuemque catenam
Mnemosyne: Ratio unde rudi sub pectore tardum
Augeat imperium; et primum mortalibus ægris
Ira, Dolor, Metus, et Curæ nascantur inanes,   5
Hinc canere aggredior. Nec dedignare canentem,
Oh decus! Angliacæ certe oh lux altera gentis!
Si quâ primus iter monstras, vestigia conor
Signare incerta, tremulâque insistere plantâ.
Quin potiús duc ipse (potes namque omnia) sanctum   10
Ad limen, (si rité adeo, si pectore puro,)
Obscuræ reserans Naturæ ingentia claustra.
Tu cæcas rerum causas, fontemque severum
Pande, Pater; tibi enim, tibi, veri magne Sacerdos,
Corda patent hominum, atque altæ penetralia Mentis.   15
   Tuque aures adhibe vacuas, facilesque, Favonî,
(Quód tibi crescit opus) simplex nec despice carmen,

DE PRINCIPIIS COGITANDI, LIBER PRIMUS. First published by Mason, i. 160–7. The text followed here is that of the holograph MS. in *CB*, i. 129 (ll. 1–27), 138 (ll. 28–79), 289 (ll. 80–151), 438 (ll. 152–207).

   In the lower left corner of p. 289 is written, in Mason's hand, 'V[ide]: 380.' This is the usual method of referring to the next portion of a work written on more than one page of *CB*; however, this cross-reference appears to be a slip, for p. 380 is blank except for the following: (1) 'V: 289,' and (2) a short paragraph on Cato. 'V: 289' also appears at the top of p. 381, which contains *Ode on the Death of a Favourite Cat* and *Oh Ubi Colles*. The text of *De Principiis Cogitandi* is resumed on p. 438, to which there is also a cross-reference on p. 289.

   Text collated: *M*.

   Gray has captions in the margin of *CB* which Mason published as footnotes. These captions are given in the present edition in the textual notes, separated by a colon from the line number and word which immediately follows Mason's footnote number.

In margin of CB, i. 129: Begun at Florence in 1740.
Title: There are no significant variations.

1 Unde: Plan of the Poem   6 Nec: Invocation to Mr. Lock   17 simplex:
Use & Extent of the Subject

Nec vatem: non illa leves primordia motus,
Quanquam parva, dabunt. Lætum vel amabile quicquid
Usquam oritur, trahit hinc ortum; nec surgit ad auras,   20
Quin ea conspirent simul, eventusque secundent:
Hinc variæ vitaï artes, ac mollior usus,
Dulce et amicitiæ vinclum: Sapientia dia
Hinc roseum accendit lumen, vultuque sereno
Humanas aperit mentes, nova gaudia monstrans,   25
Deformesque fugat curas, vanosque timores:
Scilicet et rerum crescit pulcherrima Virtus.
Illa etiam, quæ te (mirum) noctesque diesque
Assidué fovet inspirans, linguamque sequentem
Temperat in numeros, atque horas mulcet inertes;   30
Aurea non aliâ se jactat origine Musa.
    Principio, ut magnum fœdus Natura creatrix
Firmavit, tardis jussitque inolescere membris
Sublimes animas; tenebroso in carcere partem
Noluit æthaeream longo torpere veterno: 35
Nec per se proprium passa exercere vigorem est,
Ne sociæ molis conjunctos sperneret artus,
Ponderis oblita, et cœlestis conscia flammæ.
Idcircó innumero ductu tremere undique fibras
Nervorum instituit: tum toto corpore miscens   40
Implicuit laté ramos, et sensile textum,
Implevitque humore suo (seu lympha vocanda,
Sive aura est; tenuis certé), atque levissima quædam
Vis versatur agens, parvosque infusa canales
Perfluit; assiduè externis quæ concita plagis,   45
Mobilis, incussique fidelis nuntia motûs,
Hinc indé accensâ contage relabitur usque
Ad superas hominis sedes, arcemque cerebri.
Namque illic posuit solium, et sua templa sacravit
Mens animi: hanc circum coëunt, densoque feruntur   50
Agmine notitiæ, simulacraque tenuia rerum:
Ecce autem naturæ ingens aperitur imago
Immensæ, variique patent commercia mundi.

---

32 Principio: Union of the Soul & Body   38 cœlestis] cœlestîs *CB. See expl. notes.*
39 innumero: Office of the nervous System   43 Sive aura est; tenuis certé),] Sive
aura est) tenuis certé, *CB, M.*   44 versatur agens] *in margin of CB,* agitat late
in text, both underlined.   50 Mens: Sensation, the Origin of our Ideas

Ac uti longinquis descendunt montibus amnes
Velivolus Tamisis, flaventisque Indus arenæ,   55
Euphratesque, Tagusque, et opimo flumine Ganges;
Undas quisque suas volvens, cursuque sonoro
In mare prorumpunt: hos magno acclinis in antro
Excipit Oceanus, natorumque ordine longo
Dona recognoscit venientum, ultróque serenat   60
Cæruleam faciem, et diffuso marmore ridet.
Haud aliter species properant se inferre novellæ
Certatim menti, atque aditus quino agmine complent.
  Primas tactus agit partes, primusque minutæ
Laxat iter cæcum turbæ, recipitque ruentem.   65
Non idem huic modus est, qui fratribus: amplius ille
Imperium affectat senior, penitusque medullis,
Visceribusque habitat totis, pellisque recentem
Funditur in telam, et laté per stamina vivit.
Necdum etiam matris puer eluctatus ab alvo   70
Multiplices solvit tunicas, et vincula rupit;
Sopitus molli somno, tepidoque liquore
Circumfusus adhúc: tactûs tamen aura lacessit
Jamdudum levior sensus, animamque reclusit.
Idque magis simul ac solitum blandumque calorem   75
Frigore mutavit cæli, quod verberat acri
Impete inassuetos artus: tum sævior adstat,
Humanæque comes vitæ Dolor excipit; ille
Cunctantem frustrá, et tremulo multa ore querentem
Corripit invadens, ferreisque amplectitur ulnis.   80
Tum species primum patefacta est candida Lucis
(Usque vices adeó Natura bonique, malique,
Exæquat, justâque manu sua damna rependit)
Tum primum, ignotosque bibunt nova lumina soles.

---

58 magno . . . antro] *in text of CB,* magna . . . urna *with* -na *and* urna *underlined; in margin,* -no antro *also underlined.*   61 *In margin of CB, written vertically,*

ποντίων τέ [*sic*] κυμάτων
Ἀνήριθμον γέλασμα
                                        —Prometheus ap. Aeschylum

[and the countless smiles of the waves of the sea—Aeschylus, *Prometheus Bound,* 89–90].
64 Primas: The Touch, our first & most extensive Sense   68 pellisque] pellisque
CB, M. *See expl. notes.*   74 levior] teneros *in text of CB,* levior *in margin, both*
underlined.   75 simul ac] simul, ac CB. *See expl. note.*   81 Tum: Sight, our
second Sense

Carmine quo, Dea, te dicam, gratissima cœli   85
Progenies, ortumque tuum; gemmantia rore
Ut per prata levi lustras, et floribus halans
Purpureum Veris gremium, scenamque virentem
Pingis, et umbriferos colles, et cærula regna?
Gratia te, Venerisque Lepos, et mille Colorum,   90
Formarumque chorus sequitur, Motusque decentes.
At caput invisum Stygiis Nox atra tenebris
Abdidit, horrendæque simul Formidinis ora,
Pervigilesque æstus Curarum, atque anxius Angor:
Undique Lætitiâ florent mortalia corda,   95
Purus et arridet largis fulgoribus Æther.
   Omnia nec tu ideó invalidæ se pandere Menti
(Quippe nimis teneros posset vis tanta diei
Perturbare, et inexpertos confundere visus)
Nec capere infantes animos, neu cernere credas   100
Tam variam molem, et miræ spectacula Lucis:
Nescio quâ tamen hæc oculos dulcedine parvos
Splendida percussit novitas, traxitque sequentes;
Nonne videmus enim, latis inserta fenestris
Sicubi se Phœbi dispergant aurea tela,   105
Sive lucernarum rutilus colluxerit ardor,
Extemplo huć obverti aciem, quæ fixa repertos
Haurit inexpletum radios, fruiturque tuendo.
   Altior huic veró sensu, majorque videtur
Addita, Judicioque arcté connexa potestas,   110
Quod simul atque ætas volventibus auxerit annis,
Hæc simul, assiduo depascens omnia visu,
Perspiciet, vis quanta loci, quid polleat ordo,
Juncturæ quis honos, ut res accendere rebus
Lumina conjurant inter se, et mutua fulgent.   115
   Nec minor in geminis viget auribus insita virtus,
Nec tantum in curvis quæ pervigil excubet antris
Hinc atque hinc (ubi Vox tremefecerit ostia pulsu
Aëriis invecta rotis) longeque recurset:
Scilicet Eloquio hæc sonitus, hæc fulminis alas,   120

85 Carmine: Digression on Light   96 largis fulgoribus] *In margin of CB.*
Original text obliterated.   102 Nescio: Sight, imperfect at first, gradually improves
108 tuendo.] tuendo? *seems required by* nonne *of l. 104, but, with some reservation,*
Gray's punctuation retained.   112 Hæc: Ideas of Beauty, Proportion & Order
116 in: Hearing, also improveable by the Judgement

Et mulcere dedit dictis et tollere corda,
Verbaque metiri numeris, versuque ligare
Repperit, et quicquid discant Libethrides undæ,
Calliope quotiés, quoties Pater ipse canendi
Evolvat liquidum carmen, calamove loquenti   125
Inspiret dulces animas, digitisque figuret.

At medias fauces, et linguæ humentia templa
Gustus habet, quá se insinuet jucunda saporum
Luxuries, dona Autumni, Bacchique voluptas.

Naribus interea consedit odora hominum vis,   130
Docta leves captare auras, Panchaïa quales
Vere novo exhalat, Floræve quod oscula fragrant
Roscida, cum Zephyri furtiḿ sub vesperis horâ
Respondet votis, mollemque aspirat amorem.

Tot portas altæ capitis circumdedit arci   135
Alma Parens, sensûsque vias per membra reclusit;
Haud solas: namque intus agit vivata facultas,
Quâ sese explorat, contemplatusque repenté
Ipse suas animus vires, momentaque cernit.

Quid velit, aut possit, capiat, fugiatve, vicissim   140
Percipit imperio gaudens; neque corpora fallunt
Morigera ad celeres actus, ac numina mentis.

Qualis Hamadryadum quondam si forté sororuḿ
Una, novos peragrans saltus, et devia rura;
(Atque illam in viridi suadet procumbere ripâ   145
Fontis pura quies, et opaci frigoris umbra)
Dum prona in Latices speculi de margine pendet,
Mirata est subitam venienti occurrere Nympham:
Mox eosdem, quos ipsa, artus, eadem ora gerentem
Uná inferre gradus, uná succedere sylvæ   150
Aspicit alludens; seseque agnoscit in undis.
Sic sensu interno rerum simulacra suarum
Mens ciet, et proprios observat conscia vultus.
Nec veró simplex ratio, aut jus omnibus unum
Constat imaginibus. Sunt quæ bina ostia nôrunt;   155
Hæ privos servant aditus; sine legibus illæ

---

127 At: Taste   130 Naribus: Smell   135 Tot: Reflection, the other Source
of our Ideas   137 intus] *Faint blur over* u *which might be accent in CB.*   140 capiat]
cupiat *M. See expl. notes.*   151 *This line numbered* 150 *by Gray, but correct number-*
ing resumed at l. 160.   154 Nec: Ideas approach the Soul, some by single Avenues,
some by two, others by every Sense

Passiṁ, quá data porta, ruunt, animoque propinquant.
Respice, cui a cunis tristes extinxit ocellos,
Sæva et in æternas mersit natura tenebras:
Illî ignota dies lucet, vernusque colorum   160
Offusus nitor est, et vivæ gratia formæ.
Corporis at filum, et motus, spatiumque, locique
Intervalla datur certo dignoscere tactu:
Quandoquidem his iter ambiguum est, et janua duplex,
Exclusæque oculis species irrumpere tendunt   165
Per digitos. Atqui solis concessa potestas
Luminibus blandæ est radios immittere lucis.
      Undique proporró sociis, quácunque patescit
Notitiæ campus, mistæ lasciva feruntur
Turba voluptatis comites, formæque dolorum   170
Terribiles visu, et portâ glomerantur in omni.
Nec vario minús introïtu magnum ingruit Illud,
Quo facere et fungi, quo res existere circuṁ
Quamque sibi proprio cum corpore scimus, et ire
Ordine, perpetuoque per ævum flumine labi.   175
      Nunc age quo valeat pacto, quâ sensilis arte
Affectare viam, atque animi tentare latebras
Materies (dictis aures adverte faventes)
Exsequar. Inprimiś spatii quaṁ multa per aequor
Millia multigenis pandant se corpora seclis,   180
Expende. Haud unum invenies, quod mente licebit
Amplecti, nedum propriús deprendere sensu,
Molis egens certæ, aut solido sine robore, cujus
Denique mobilitas linquit, texturave partes,
Ulla nec orarum circumcæsura coërcet.   185
Hæc conjuncta adeó totâ compage fatetur
Mundus, et extremo clamant in limine rerum,
(Si rebus datur Extremum) primordia. Firmat
Hæc eadem tactus (tactum quis dicere falsum
Audeat?) hæc oculi nec lucidus arguit orbis.   190
      Inde potestatum enasci densissima proles
Nam quodcunque ferit visum, tangive laborat

158 Respice: Illustration—Light, an Example of the first   162 Corporis: Figure,
Motion, Extension, of the second   168 Undique: Pleasure, Pain, of yᵉ 3ᵈ
172 Nec: Also Power, Existence, Unity, Succession, Duration   177 Affectare:
Primary Qualities of Bodies   183 Molis: Magnitude, Solidity, Mobility, Texture,
Figure

Quicquid nare bibis, vel concava concipit auris,
Quicquid lingua sapit, credas hoc omne, necesse est
Ponderibus, textu, discursu, mole, figurâ   195
Particulas præstare leves, et semina rerum.
Nunc oculos igitur pascunt, et luce ministrâ
Fulgere cuncta vides, spargique coloribus orbem
Dum de sole trahunt alias, aliasque superné
Detorquent, retróque docent se vertere flammas.   200
Nunc trepido inter se fervent corpuscula pulsu,
Ut tremor æthera per magnum, latéque natantes
Aurarum fluctus avidi vibrantia claustra
Auditûs queat allabi, sonitumque propaget.
Cominus interdum non ullo interprete per se   205
Nervorum invadunt teneras quatientia fibras,
Sensiferumque urgent ultró per viscera motum.

ON THE ELEMENTS OF THOUGHT, BOOK I.

From what source the Mind begins to have knowledge; from what
beginnings Memory arises and begins to arrange events in order and
to weave its slender chain; from what centre Reason extends its
slow-maturing empire in the uncultivated breast; and how, in sick
men at first, there come to birth Anger, Grief and Pain, Fears and
baseless Anxieties: of these questions I begin to sing. And thou, O
glory, O second sun of the English race, scorn not the singer. If thou
first showest the way, no matter where, I will attempt to mark the
faint traces and to follow, though with timorous tread. Better still,
lead me thyself (for unto thee are all things possible) to the holy
threshold (if I approach with due reverence and a pure heart) and
throw wide the mighty doors of secret Nature. O Father, reveal the
hidden causes of things and their awful source, for unto thee, great
Priest of Truth, the hearts of men are open, and the secret places
of the lofty Mind.

Do you also, Favonius, lend attentive ears and favourable (since
it is for you that the work advances) and do not scorn the simple
song, nor the singer: these first-beginnings, although small, will
give rise to no slight activities. Whenever anything joyful and
lovable is conceived, it owes its origin to these first-beginnings; nor

does it soar into the light of day unless they work together in harmony and favour the result. From this source [arise] the varied arts
of life and milder practice, and the sweet bond of friendship; divine
Wisdom lights her rosy torch from this source and with serene
countenance enlarges the minds of men, shows the way to new joys,
and scatters into flight monstrous cares and unsubstantial terrors:
and thus, in truth, Virtue, fairest of all things, waxes strong. She,
moreover, who constantly (wondrous deed) fosters you night and
day with her inspiration, trains the obedient tongue to numbers and
charms idle hours, the golden Muse, proudly affirms that she has
no other origin.

In the beginning, when Nature, the law-giver of creation, established the great covenant and bade lofty souls grow in sluggish
bodies, she did not wish the ethereal part to grow torpid through
long inaction in a dark prison; neither did she permit it to exercise
its special vigour unchecked, lest it spurn the linked joints of the
united mass, forgetful of weight and conscious of celestial fire. For
this reason she caused fibres of nerves to vibrate in numberless
ducts from all parts; then, distributing them throughout the body,
she wove branches everywhere, a sensitive network, and filled the
ducts with their own peculiar fluid (it is uncertain whether it should
be called lymph or air; at any rate, it is very rarefied); some very
slight force drives it along and circulates it; after it has been instilled,
it flows through tiny canals.

When this fluid is stirred by external impulses, being easily
moved and a faithful messenger of the movement imparted to it by
the impulses, it flows back from the point of the impact to the
upper regions of the man, to the citadel of the skull. For there the
mind, the rational element of the soul, has placed its throne and
dedicated its temples; around the mind the sensations, ethereal
images of things, come together and are swept along in a dense
crowd. Then, lo! a full representation of boundless nature is
revealed and the comings and goings of the varied universe are
unfolded.

And just as rivers flow down from distant mountains—the
Thames studded with sails, the Indus full of yellow sand, and the
Euphrates and the Tagus, and the Ganges with its fruitful stream:
each one rolling its own waters—and burst with resounding flood
into the sea; and welcoming Ocean receives them in its great basin
and recognizes as its own the gifts of its children coming in a long

line and keeps its blue face calm and laughs in scattered ripples:
not otherwise do sensations vie with each other in their haste to
pour themselves into the fresh mind, and they crowd around the
entrances in a fivefold procession.

The sense of touch plays the leading role; it goes first, widening
the dark path for the lesser crowd, and restrains its headlong rush.
This sense is not subject to the same restrictions that its brothers
are: since it is the first-born, it asserts a wider sway, and has its
dwelling deep in the marrow of the bones and throughout the
viscera, and is widely diffused and has its being in the warp and
woof of the skin. Indeed, even the child that has not yet struggled
forth from its mother's womb dissolves the many layers of covering
and bursts the chains; although it is as yet wrapped in soft slumber
and bathed in warm fluid, nevertheless a very slight breeze has
already been stimulating the sense of touch and opening the way
for the breath of life. This activity is intensified the moment the
child has exchanged the soothing warmth to which it has grown
accustomed for the chill of the outer air, which assails its untried
limbs with savage fury. Then a more excruciating sense of touch
begins to function, and Pain, the constant companion of human life,
takes possession. Striking home inexorably, Pain seizes the infant,
despite his vain attempts to delay and the many wails of complaint
from his quivering lips, and folds him in an iron embrace.

Then for the first time the shining vision of light is made manifest
(so true is it that Nature balances the alternations of good and of
evil, and with a just hand makes amends for the damage that she
has caused); then, as I say, for the first time the new eyes drink in
the light of the sun that up to now has been unknown.

With what song, Goddess, shall I speak of you, most pleasing
child of heaven, and of your origin; of how you pass in divine progress over meadows bejewelled with light dew and fill the purple
lap of spring with flower-scented breath; of how you paint the green
landscape and the shady hills and the realms of deepest blue? The
grace and charm of Venus attend you, and a chorus of a thousand
colours and shapes of loveliness, and comely motions. But black
Night hides her hated head in Stygian shadows: so too the face of
horrible Fear and raging hordes of sleep-destroying Cares and
carking Anguish. How different when an unclouded sky smiles with
abundant shafts of radiance! Then the hearts of mortals blossom
with joy.

And yet you do not reveal yourself in full splendour to the mind in the weakness of infancy (perhaps because so great a flood of daylight might dazzle eyes still too tender and confuse them before they have grown accustomed to use) for the reason that you have no confidence that infant souls can take in and perceive such a varied host of visions revealed by miraculous light: nevertheless the shining novelty strikes the eyes of infants with some sort of charm and draws them along so that they follow; for have we not seen their gaze turn instantly to any place where the golden shafts of Phoebus shine through a broad window or the golden glow of lamps shines forth, and remain fixed, drinking in with insatiable appetite the beams that they have spied and taking delight in gazing?

In truth, another power, firmly bound up with Judgement, one that is deeper and greater, seems to have been added to this sense. As soon as age, in the course of the circling years, shall have increased Judgement, this power, nourishing itself on all things with uninterrupted gaze, will perceive how great the force of place is, what strength order confers, and what the reward of combination, as the eyes conspire with each other to illuminate things with things and shine with united effort.

And no less a power, planted in the two ears, grows and increases; keeping constant vigil, it not only stands like a sentinel in the curved hollows on either side (where Voice, borne on a chariot of air, makes the doors tremble at its knock), but also runs far back: in truth, this faculty gives to eloquence the sounds and speed of the thunderbolt and to speech the power to calm the hearts of men or to arouse them; it has found out how to accommodate words to rhythms and to bind them together in a verse; it has revealed what the waters of Libethra learn, whenever Calliope, or the Father of Music himself, chants a clear-voiced song or breathes sweet airs into the vocal reed and patterns the sounds with his fingers.

The sense of taste has its seat in the midst of the jaws, the moist expanses of the tongue, whereby the delightful riot of savours finds its way in, the gifts of Autumn and the pleasure that Bacchus affords.

Meanwhile the sense of smell has its seat in the noses of men; it has learned how to seize upon light airs, such as Panchaia breathes forth in early spring, or the fragrances that the dewy kisses of Flora impart when, at the hour of twilight, she shyly responds to the prayers of Zephyr and sighs with gentle love.

This number of gates the gracious mother has placed around the lofty citadel of the head, and she has hidden avenues of sense throughout our bodies; but not these only, for a lively faculty works within, by means of which the mind examines itself, and having made the examination instantly perceives its own powers and movements. What it wishes, what it can do, what it should seize hold of and what it should fly from—all these it surveys one by one, rejoicing in its power of command. And neither bodies obedient to swift actions nor the notions of the mind escape unnoticed.

One might, perhaps, liken it to one of the Hamadryads in the old story, who was wandering through strange mountain valleys and pathless tracts (and the unbroken silence and the cool darkness of the shade persuaded her to lie down on the green bank of a spring). While she was lying prone and hanging over the bank looking into the liquid mirror, she was amazed to see a nymph coming to meet her suddenly as she leaned toward the water: presently, playfully advancing and retreating, she realized that the nymph had the same limbs as herself, and the same features, that they advanced from and went back into the forest at the same instant. She recognized herself in the waters.

In the same way, the mind, by an internal sense, arouses images of its own actions and consciously observes its own features. But no uniform pattern has been established, nor does a single law always govern all images. There are some that know two entrances: some confine themselves to particular entrances; others, without fixed laws, rush in helter-skelter, wherever a door opens up, and draw near the soul.

Take for example the man whose unhappy eyes cruel nature has extinguished in the cradle and sunk in everlasting darkness; for him the light of day gleams unknown and on him the spring-time splendour of colours is lavished in vain, and the grace of living beauty. But the power is granted to him to distinguish with a sure sense of touch the shape of a body, and motions, and space, and the intervals between places: for, you see, these sensations have a twofold pathway, a double entrance door, and when they have been locked out by the eyes, they hasten to burst in through the fingers. And yet the power of admitting beams of pleasing light has been granted to the eyes alone.

Moreover, from every direction, wherever the field of conception stretches, a sportive band, companions of pleasure mingled with their friends, is borne along, and so also shapes of pain terrifying to behold, and they crowd around every entrance. And by entrances no less varied that power breaks in by means of which we know that we do and suffer and that things around us exist, each with its own characteristic form, and proceed in order and glide along through time in an uninterrupted stream.

Come now! I shall explain by what means and by what art matter endowed with sensation is able to aim at and penetrate into the inner recesses of the mind (lend favouring ears to my words). In the first place, consider how many bodies of every sort are diffused through space. You will not find one that can be grasped by the mind, let alone be apprehended and accurately reported by the senses, that lacks definite mass and is without any firm solidity, whose parts are devoid of mobility or texture and that some outline of form does not define. In all its frame the universe testifies to the binding together of these bodies, and, as first-beginnings, they clamour on the outermost threshold of things (if any final limit can be assigned to things). The sense of touch proves that these things exist (who would dare to say that the sense of touch lies?), and the bright orb of the eye does not disprove that they exist.

Hence a very thick crowd of powers arises: for if you believe what strikes the sense of sight or struggles to be felt, the sensations that enter through the nose or what the hollow ear takes in, what the tongue tastes—if you believe all this, you must believe that light particles, the seeds of things, are responsible for weight, texture, motion, mass, and shape. Now, therefore, they feed the eyes and with the aid of light you see all things gleaming brightly and the world splashed with colours, while they draw some fires from the sun and twist others from above aside and teach the flames to turn themselves back. Again, tiny bodies seethe and boil among themselves with vibrating pulsation, with the result that the vibration throughout the vast expanse of ether—waves of air flowing freely in all directions—is able to slip through the vibrating doors of the eager sense of hearing and begets sound. Meanwhile, in close array, vibrating bodies, with no intermediary, directly invade the delicate fibres of the nerves and, unassisted, set up a motion that produces sensation throughout the vitals.

Liber Secundus.
De Principiis Cogitandi.

Hactenus haud segnis Naturæ arcana retexi
Musarum interpres, primusque Britanna per arva
Romano liquidum deduxi flumine rivum.
    Cum Tu opere in medio, spes tanti et causa laboris,
Linquis, et æternam fati te condis in umbram!   5
Vidi egomet duro graviter concussa dolore
Pectora, in alterius non unquam lenta dolorem;
Et languere oculos vidi, et pallescere amantem
Vultum, quo nunquam Pietas nisi rara, Fidesque,
Altus amor Veri, et purum spirabat Honestum.   10
Visa tamen tardi demum inclementia morbi
Cessare est, reducemque iterum roseo ore Salutem
Speravi, atque una tecum, dilecte Favoni!
Credulus heu longos, ut quondaṁ, fallere Soles:
Heu spes nequicquam dulces, atque irrita vota!   15
Heu mæstos Soles, sine te quos ducere flendo
Per desideria, et questus jam cogor inanes!
    At Tu, sancta anima, et nostri non indiga luctûs,
Stellanti templo, sincerique ætheris igne,
Unde orta es, fruere; atque oh si secura, nec ultra   20
Mortalis, notos oliṁ miserata labores
Respectes, tenuesque vacet cognoscere curas;
Humanam si forté altâ de sede procellam
Contemplere, metus stimulosque cupidinis acres,
Gaudiaque et gemitus, parvoque in corde tumultum   25

DE PRINCIPIIS COGITANDI, LIBER SECUNDUS. First published in Mason, i. 168-9.
There are two holograph MSS.: *CB*, i. 286, the text followed here; and *Wal*, a letter
to Walpole of 8 Feb. 1747 (T & W no. 131), Pembroke College MS. L.C. 2. 90.
    Texts collated: *Wal, M*.

Title: In *CB* the title is *Liber Secundus De Principiis Cogitandi*, but Gray refers to the
poem in his letter to Walpole as 'the fourth Book', which is the designation adopted in
Mason and subsequent editions. However, since there is no other trace of additional
books, the *CB* title has been restored.

3 flumine] flumina *Wal*.   13 Favoni!] Favonî, *Wal*.   22 tenuesque] parvasque
in text of CB, tenues *in margin*; tenues *and* parvas *underlined*.   23 *In margin of
CB* ὁ τῆς ψυχῆς χειμών [the tempest of the soul] Epicurus ad Menoeceum [Sec. 128,
l. 6 in Cyril Bailey's *Epicurus, the Extant Remains* (Oxford: Clarendon Press, 1926)].

Irarum ingentem, et sævos sub pectore fluctus:
Respice et has lacrymas, memori quas ictus amore
Fundo; quod possum, juxtá lugere sepulchrum
Dum juvat, et mutæ vana hæc jactare favillæ.

. . . .

ON THE ELEMENTS OF THOUGHT.
BOOK II.

So far had I advanced in my zeal to uncover the secrets of Nature, and, the vocal instrument of the Muses, had been the first to lead a clear brook from the Roman river through British fields, when thou, the hope and inspiration of so great a task, didst leave in the midst of the labour and conceal thyself in the eternal shadow of death! With my own eyes I had seen thy breast gravely smitten with cruel pain, a breast never insensitive to another's pain; I had seen thine eyes languish and thy loving face grow pale, whence naught but extraordinary Devotion, and Trust, and deep love of Truth, and uncorrupted Honour used to breathe. At length, however, the merciless cruelty of lingering sickness seemed to be departing, and I hoped for the restoration of rosy-cheeked Health, and thee along with it, beloved Favonius! Fondly trusting, alas, that we would while away the long sunny days as before: alas, the vain sweet hopes, the unavailing prayers and vows! Alas, the sunny days, now filled with grief! Deprived of thee, I must pass them in longing and vain complaints, weeping all the while.

But thou, blessed spirit, hast no need of my lamentations; thou enjoyest the starry region and the fire of the pure aether from whence thou wert born. But Oh! if thou art free from care yet not completely beyond the reach of mortal concerns, and if thou dost look back with compassion upon the labours that once were so familiar and hast leisure to think of trifling cares; if, perchance, thou dost contemplate from thy lofty seat the human storm, the fears, the sharp goads of desire, the joys and griefs, the tumult of anger that seems so immense in the tiny heart of man and the savage waves that surge in the human breast: then look back also on these tears

28 juxtá] propter *Wal.*   *In margin of CB* Begun at Stoke, June, 1742.

of mine, which, stricken as I am with love, I am shedding in memory of thee; I can do no more, so long as my only desire is to lament here beside thy tomb and to address these vain words to thy silent ashes.

.   .   .   .

[TRANSLATIONS FROM THE GREEK ANTHOLOGY.]

[I]

From the Greek.

Fertur Aristophanis fatorum arcana rogatum,
    tempore sementis, rusticus îsse domum;
(Sideris an felix tempestas, messis an esset
    magna, vel agricolam falleret ustus ager.)
Ille supercilio adducto multâ anxius arte   5
    disposuit sortes, consuluitque Deos;
Tum responsa dedit: vernus suffecerit imber
    si modo, nec fruges læserit herba nocens;
Si mala robîgo, si grando pepercerit arvis,
    attulerit subitum pigra nec aura gelu;   10
Caprea si nulla, aut culmos attriverit hædus;
    nec fuerit cælum, nec tibi terra gravis:
Largas polliceor segetes, atque horrea plena.
    tu tamen, ut veniat sera locusta, cave.

TRANSLATIONS FROM THE GREEK ANTHOLOGY. The thirteen 'imitations' (more precisely, translations) in this section follow the order as well as the text of the holograph MS. in *CB*, i. 287–8.

    Eleven were first published in Mathias, ii. 94–97 (*Math*), in a slightly different order; no. 1 and no. 12 were first published by Tovey in *Gray and His Friends*, p. 295 (*TGF*). First published complete and in Gray's order by Bradshaw, pp. 168–72 (*Br*).

    Texts collated: *Math*, *Br*, *TGF*.

Titles: Those at the head of the Latin texts are Gray's from *CB*; in no. 12 and no. 13, Gray's mark of ellipsis (four periods) has been expanded.

I
FROM THE GREEK.

The story is told that a farmer went to the home of Aristophanes at planting time to ask what the fates had secretly decreed (whether the moon was in a lucky phase, whether the harvest would be plentiful or whether the parched field would disappoint the farmer).

Aristophanes, with wrinkled brow, solicitously arranged the lots with a great show of skill, and consulted the gods. Then he gave the following oracular response: If there shall have been just enough rain in the spring, and if weeds shall not have harmed the crops and if a numbing wind shall not have brought unexpected cold; if baleful blight and hail shall have spared the fields; if some nanny-goat and her kid shall not have chewed up the grain; if neither sky nor earth shall have been unfriendly to you—then I promise you bountiful crops and a full granary. However, you must be sure that no locusts arrive late in the summer.

[II]

From the Greek of Antiphilus Byzantius
In Medeæ Imaginem, Nobile Timomachi Opus.

En ubi Medeæ varius dolor æstuat ore,
  jamque animum nati, jamque maritus, habent!
Succenset; miseret; medio exardescit amore
  dum furor, inque oculo gutta minante tremit.
Cernis adhuc dubiam: quid enim? licet impia matris   5
  Colchidos, at non sit dextera Timomachi.

II

ON A REPRESENTATION OF MEDEA,
THE NOBLE WORK OF TIMOMACHUS.

See how the painful conflict seethes in the face of Medea, and her sons are still living, and her husband! She is enraged; she feels pity; furious anger blazes even in the midst of love, and a tear glistens in her threatening eye. You see her as yet irresolute: do you wonder why? Though the hand of the Colchian mother was wicked, that of Timomachus would not depict wickedness.

[III]
Imitation of the Greek; of Paul Silentiarius.
In Bacchæ Furentis Statuam.

Credite, non viva est Mænas; non spirat imago.
  artificis rabiem miscuit ære manus.

III
ON A STATUE OF A FRENZIED BACCHANTE.

Rest assured, the Maenad is not alive, the statue is not breathing. The hand of the artist mixed madness with the bronze.

[IV]
From the Greek, of Posidippus.
In Alexandrum, Ære Effictum.

Quantum audet, Lysippe, manus tua! surgit in ære
  spiritus, atque oculis bellicus ignis adest.
Spectate hos vultus, miserisque ignoscite Persis:
  quid mirum, imbelles si leo sparsit oves?

IV
ON ALEXANDER, PORTRAYED IN BRONZE.

How bold was your hand, Lysippus! The breath of life seems to surge in the bronze, and warlike fire glows in the eyes; behold these features, and forgive the unfortunate Persians. What wonder if a lion scattered peaceful sheep?

[V]

From the Greek. [Anonymous.]
In Niobes Statuam.

Fecerat é vivâ lapidem me Jupiter: at me
Praxiteles vivam reddidit é lapide.

V

ON A STATUE OF NIOBE.

From a living woman, Jupiter turned me into stone; Praxiteles
has turned me from stone into a living woman.

[VI]

From the Greek, of Lucian, offering
a Statue of herself to Venus.

En tibi te, Cytherea, fero: formosius ipsâ
cum tibi, quod ferrem, te, Dea, nil habui.

VI

FROM THE GREEK OF LUCIAN, OFFERING
A STATUE OF HERSELF TO VENUS.

Lo, Cytherea, to thee I offer thyself; for I had nothing to offer
thee, goddess, more lovely than thyself.

VI

Title: See expl. note.

1 En tibi te, Cytherea, fero] Te tibi, sancta, fero nudam *in text of CB, present reading
in margin, both underlined. Both Math and Br print the rejected reading, Br with revised
reading in footnote.*

[VII]

From the Greek of Statyllius Flaccus.
In Amorem dormientem.

Docte Puer vigiles mortalibus addere curas!
  anne potest in te somnus habere locum?
Laxi juxtá arcus, et fax suspensa quiescit,
  dormit et in pharetrâ clausa sagitta suâ:
Longé mater abest, longe Cythereïa turba.   5
  verum ausint alii te prope ferre pedem;
Non ego: nam metuo valdé; mihi, perfide, quiddam
  forsan et in somnis ne meditere mali.

VII
TO CUPID, AS HE SLEEPS.

Oh learned Boy—learned, that is, in the skill of imposing sleep-destroying cares on mortals—can it be that sleep has found a home in you? Your unstrung bow lies quietly near by, your unlighted torch has been hung up, and, locked in the quiver, your arrow sleeps: your mother is far away, far away too the throng of Cytherea's train. Others, no doubt, may have the courage to venture near you, but not I; for I am mightily afraid, treacherous boy, that even in your sleep you may be hatching some trick to play on me.

[VIII]

From a Fragment of Plato.

Itur in Idalios tractus, felicia regna,
  fundit ubi densam myrtea sylva comam:
Intus Amor teneram visus spirare quietem,
  dum roseo roseos imprimit ore toros.

VII
7 metuo] metui *Math, Br.*

Sublimem procul a ramis pendere pharetram,   5
et de languidulâ spicula lapsa manu
Vidimus, et risu molli diducta labella,
murmure quæ assiduo pervolitabat apes.

VIII

FROM A FRAGMENT OF PLATO.

I went to the regions of Idalium, happy realms, where a forest of myrtle spreads its thick foliage in rich profusion: within, I saw Cupid breathing softly in sleep, pressing his rosy cheek into a couch of roses. A little way off, I saw his quiver hung aloft in the branches, and the barbed shafts that had slipped from his languid hand; a soft smile parted his lips, about which a bee kept flying with a never-ending murmur.

[IX]

From the Greek of Marianus.

In Fontem aquæ calidæ.

Sub platanis puer Idalius prope fluminis undam
dormiit, in ripâ deposuitque facem.
Tempus adest, sociæ! Nympharum audentior una,
tempus adest: ultra quid dubitamus? ait.
Ilicet incurrit, pestem ut divûmque, hominumque,   5
lampada collectis exanimaret aquis.
Demens! nam nequit sævam restinguere flammam
Nympha, sed ipsa ignes traxit, et inde calet.

IX

ON A SPRING OF HOT WATER.

The Idalian boy was sleeping under the plane-trees near the water of a stream and had laid his torch on the bank. 'Now is the

VIII
8 apes] apis *Br.*
IX
2 facem.] facem *CB.*   7 nequit] nequiit *Math, Br.*

time, comrades!' said one of the nymphs, bolder than the rest. 'Now surely the time has come. Why do we hesitate any longer?' At the words, she rushed forward, intending to extinguish in the pool the torch that is the bane of gods and men. Surely she was bereft of reason; for the nymph could not extinguish the flame, but the water instead caught fire and to this day is still hot.

[X]
From Lucillius.

Irrepsisse suas murem videt Argus in ædes,
    atque ait, heus! a me numquid, amice, velis?
Ille autem ridens, metuas nihil; inquit, apud te,
    oh bone, non epulas, hospitium petimus.

X
FROM LUCILIUS.

Argus saw that a mouse had crept into his house and said, 'Ho, there, friend! What do you want from me?' Then with a smile the mouse said, 'Have no fear; at your house, my good fellow, I am not seeking a banquet—just a place to sleep.'

[XI]
Imitated from the Greek of Posidippus.
Ad Amorem.

Paulisper vigiles, oro, compesce dolores,
    respue nec Musæ supplicis aure preces:
Oro brevem lacrymis veniam, requiemque furori.
    ah, ego non possum vulnera tanta pati!
Intima flamma; vides, miseros depascitur artus,   5
    surgit et extremis spiritus in labiis.
Quod si tam tenuem cordi est exolvere vitam;
    stabit in opprobrium sculpta querela tuum:

(Juro perque faces istas, arcumque sonantem,
    spiculaque hoc unum figere docta jecur)   10
Heu fuge crudelem puerum, sævasque sagittas!
    huic fuit exitii causa, viator, amor.

XI
TO LOVE.

A little while, I pray, restrain the wakeful torments and do not
turn a deaf ear to the prayers of the suppliant Muse: I beg a brief
reprieve from tears, a moment of rest from madness. Ah, I cannot
endure wounds so great! An inner flame, you see, feeds upon my
wretched limbs, and my soul is poised for flight at the very edge of
my lips. But if your heart is set on cutting the thread of life that is
already so thin, my complaint will remain engraved in stone, a
monument to your eternal shame (I swear by that celebrated torch
of yours, and the twanging bow, and the darts that have been taught
to transfix my heart alone): Alas, passer-by, flee from the cruel boy
and his savage arrows! Love caused the death of him who lies
buried here.

[XII]
[Imitated from the Greek] of Bassus.

Non ego, cum malus urit amor, Iovis induor arma.
    Nil mihi cum plumis, nil mihi cum corio:
Non ego per tegulas mittor liquefactus in aurum.
    Promo duos obolos: sponte venit Danaë.

XII
IMITATED FROM THE GREEK OF BASSUS.

As for me, when I burn with wicked love, I do not put on the
trappings of Jove. I have no truck with feathers nor yet with the
hides of bulls; I do not pour myself over the roof-tiles in golden rain.
I just jingle a couple of coins: Danaë comes running to me.

[XIII]
[Imitated from the Greek] of Rufinus.

Hanc tibi Rufinus mittit, Rodoclea, coronam.
  has tibi decerpens texerat ipse rosas.
Est viola, est anemone, est suave-rubens hyacinthus,
  mistaque Narcisso lutea caltha suo.
Sume: sed aspiciens ah fidere desine formæ!   5
  qui pingit, brevis est, sertaque teque, color.

XIII
IMITATED FROM THE GREEK OF RUFINUS.

Rufinus sends you this crown, Rhodoclea. With his own hands
he has picked these flowers and woven them together. There are
violets and anemones and sweet-blushing hyacinths and yellow
marigold mingled with Narcissus, whom you are like. Accept it:
but as you look upon it, cease to have confidence in your beauty!
The colour is short-lived that paints the garland and you.

XIII

6 pingit] pinxit *Math.*

[ORDERS OF INSECTS.]

[I. COLEOPTERA.]

Alas loricâ tectas Coleoptera jactant.

*[Antennis clavatis.]

Serra pedum prodit Scarabæum et fissile cornu.
Dermesti antennæ circuḿ ambit lamina caulem,
Qui caput incurvum timidus sub corpore celat.
In pectus retrahens caput abdit claviger Hister.   5
Occiput Attelabi in posticum vergit acumen.
Curculio ingenti protendit cornua rostro.
Silpha leves peltæ atque elytrorum exporrigit oras.
Truncus apex clavæ, atque antennula Coccionellæ.

**[Antennis filiformibus.]

Cassida sub clypei totam se margine condit.   10
Chrys'mela inflexâ loricæ stringitur orâ.
Gibba caput Meloë incurvat, thorace rotundo.
Oblongus frontem et tenues clypei exerit oras
Tenebrio. Abdomen Mordellæ lamina vestit.
Curta elytra ostentat Staphylis, caudamque recurvam.   15

ORDERS OF INSECTS. First published by Mathias (1814), ii. 570–3 (*Math*). Published by Gosse (1884), i. 198–202 (*Go*), with the following prefatory note: 'Preserved at Pembroke College among the Stonehewer [*sic*] MSS. [*CB*]. Never before included in Gray's *Poetical Works*' (see explanatory notes).

The text of the present edition is taken from Gray's holograph MS. in his inter-leaved copy of *Linnaei Systema Naturae, Editio Decima Reformata* (Holmiae, 1758), from a photostat furnished by the Library of Harvard College, Cambridge, Mass. (*GL*). The names of the Orders are taken from Linnaeus's text, Gray having no headings in his MS. except Roman numbers at the beginning of all sections except the first and last; the subheadings under Coleoptera are also from Linnaeus's text, Gray having only asterisks in his MS. to indicate them.

Texts collated: *Math, Go, Br*.

Title: None in GL. Except for the variation Generick: Generic *and slight differences in type faces*, Math, Go, *and* Br *all have* GENERICK CHARACTERS OF THE ORDERS OF INSECTS, and of the Genera of the first six Orders, named Coleoptera, Hemiptera, Lepidoptera, Neuroptera, Hymenoptera, and Diptera; expressed in Technical Verses.

11 Chrys'mela] Chrysomela *Math, Go, Br. GL has* Chrysomela *with* o *crossed out.*

***[*Antennis setaceis.*]

Tubere cervicis valet, antennisque Cerambyx.
Pectore Leptura est tereti, corpusque coarctat.
Flexile Cantharidis tegmen, laterumque papillæ.
Ast Elater resilit sterni mucrone supinus.
Maxillâ exertâ est, oculoque Cicindela grandi.   20
Bupresti antennæ graciles, cervice retractâ.
Nec Dytiscus iners setosâ remige plantâ.
Effigiem cordis Carabus dat pectore trunco.
Necydalis curto ex elytro nudam explicat alam.
Curtum, at Forficulæ tegit hanc, cum forcipe caudæ.   25
Depressum Blattæ corpus, venterque bicornis.
Dente vorax Gryllus deflexis saltitat alis.

[HEMIPTERA.]

II. (Dimidiam rostrata gerunt Hemiptera crustam.
    Fœmina serpit humi interdum: volat æthere conjux.)

Rostro Nepa rapax pollet, chelisque. Cicada   30
Fastigio alarum et rostrato pectore saltat.
Tela Cimex inflexa gerit, cruce complicat alas.
Notonecta crucem quoque fert, remosque pedales;
Cornua Aphis caudæ et rostrum: sæpé erigit alas;
Deprimit has Chermes, dum saltat, pectore gibbo.   35
Coccus iners caudæ setas, volitante marito;
Thrips alas angusta gerit, caudamque recurvam.

[LEPIDOPTERA.]

III. (Squamam alæ, linguæ spiram Lepidoptera jactant.)

Papilio clavam et squamosas subrigit alas.
Prismaticas Sphinx antennas, medioque tumentes;   40
At conicas gravis extendit sub nocte Phalæna.

[NEUROPTERA.]

IV. (Rete alæ nudum, atque hamos Neuroptera caudæ.)

Dente alisque potens, secat æthera longa Libella.
Caudâ setigerâ, erectis stat Ephemera pennis.

---

31 Fastigio] Remigio *Math, Go, Br. See expl. note.*   32 alas.] alas *Go, Br.*

Phryganea elinguis rugosas deprimit alas; 45
Hemerinusque bidens: planas tamen explicat ille.
Et rostro longo et caudâ Panorpa minatur.
Raphidia extento collo setam trahit unam.

[HYMENOPTERA.]

V. (At vitreas alas, jaculumque Hymenoptera caudæ,
Fœmineo data tela gregi, maribusque negata.) 50

Telum abdit spirale Cynips, morsuque minatur.
Maxillas Tenthredo movet, serramque bivalvem;
Ichneumon gracili triplex abdomine telum.
Haurit Apis linguâ incurvâ, quod vindicat ense.
Sphex alam expandit lævem, gladiumque recondit. 55
Alæ ruga notat Vespam, caudæque venenum;
Squamula Formicam tergi, telumque pedestrem,
Dum minor alatâ volitat cum conjuge conjux.
Mutilla impennis, sed caudâ spicula vibrat.

[DIPTERA.]

VI. (Diptera sub geminis alis se pondere librant.) 60

Os Oestro nullum est, caudâque timetur inermi.
Longa caput Tipula est, labiisque et prædita palpis.
Palpis Musca caret, retrahitque proboscida labris;
Qua Tabanus gaudet pariter, palpis sub acutis.
Os Culicis molli é pharetrâ sua spicula vibrat; 65
Rostrum Empis durum et longum sub pectore curvat;
Porrigit articuli de cardine noxia Conops;
Porrigit (at rectum et conicum) sitibundus Asilus;
Longum et Bombylius, qui sugit mella volando.
Unguibus Hippobosca valet: vibrat breve telum. 70

[VII. APTERA.]

(Aptera se pedibus pennarum nescia jactant)

ORDERS OF INSECTS.

I. COLEOPTERA.

The Coleoptera boast wings covered with leather armour.

Those with club-shaped antennae.

A saw on the feet and a split horn distinguish the Scarabaeus.

A plate surrounds the stalk of the antenna of Dermestes, who timidly hides his head curved in below his body.

Club-bearing Hister hides his head, drawing it back into his breast.

The occiput of Attelabus narrows backward to a sharp point.

Curculio stretches horns from a huge beak.

Silpha stretches out slight margins of a moon-shaped shield and sheaths.

An undeveloped top of the club and a small antenna are characteristic of Coccionella.

Those with thread-like antennae.

Cassida hides herself completely under the rim of her shield.

Chrysomela is bound by the in-turned margin of her leather armour.

Humped Meloë has an inward-curving head and rounded thorax.

Long Tenebrio thrusts forward his brow and the thin edges of his shield.

A plate clothes the abdomen of Mordella.

Staphylis flaunts short sheaths and a tail curving backward.

Those with bristle-covered antennae.

Cerambyx shows strength in the thickness of his neck and in his antennae.

Leptura has a smooth round breast and constricts her body.

The covering of Cantharis is pliable, and there are nipple-like nodes on her sides.

Elater when supine leaps back up by means of the point of the breast.

Cicindela has an out-thrust jaw and a huge eye.

The antennae of Buprestis are graceful and the neck retracted.

Dytiscus is not motionless because of his rowing with his bristle-covered foot.

With shortened breast Carabus gives a representation of a heart.

Necydalis unfolds a bare wing from a short sheath.

The sheath of Forficula is also short, but it covers the wing and the forceps on the tail.

The body of Blatta is flattened, and her belly has two horns.

Gryllus, voracious of tooth, leaps with down-turned wings.

II. HEMIPTERA.

The beaked Hemiptera wear a shell divided into two equal parts. The female crawls on the ground at other times, but when mating she flies in the air.

Preying Nepa is strong with beak and crab-like claws.

Cicada leaps by means of the tip of her wings and beaked breast.

Cimex is armed with in-curved stings and folds her wings in a cross.

Notonecta also carries a cross and has oar-like feet.

Aphis has horns on her tail and a beak; often she raises her wings upright.

Chermes presses her wings down on her humped breast while she leaps.

Sluggish Coccus has bristles on his tail; the male flies when mating.

Slender Thrips has wings and a backward-curving tail.

III. LEPIDOPTERA.

The Lepidoptera boast scale of wing and coil of tongue.

Papilio raises a club and scale-covered wings upright.

Sphinx stretches forth antennae prism-shaped and swelling in the middle,

But heavy Phalaena cone-shaped ones by night.

IV. NEUROPTERA.

The Neuroptera have a bare net-like wing and hooks on the tail.

Powerful in tooth and wings, long Libella cleaves the air.

With bristle-bearing tail, Ephemera stands with wings erect.

Tongueless Phryganea lets wrinkled wings droop,

And so does two-toothed Hemerinus; but when he unfolds them, they become smooth.

Panorpa threatens with both long beak and tail.

With out-stretched neck Raphidia carries a single bristle.

V. HYMENOPTERA.

The Hymenoptera have glassy wings and a dart on the tail; to the females weapons are given, but denied to the males.

Cynips conceals a coiled weapon and threatens to bite.

Tenthredo moves jaws and a bivalve saw,

Ichneumon a three-fold shaft with slender abdomen.

Apis drinks with in-curved tongue what she wins with the sword.

Sphex spreads a smooth wing and hides a sword.

A wrinkle on the wing and poison in the tail distinguish Vespa;

A tiny scale on the back and a weapon [distinguish] Formica, which goes on foot except while the smaller husband flies with winged wife.

Mutilla is wingless, but vibrates darts with her tail.

VI. DIPTERA.

The Diptera balance themselves with a weight under their two wings.

Oestrus has no mouth and is feared because of his tail, although it is unarmed.

Tipula is long in the head and is furnished with lips and palpi.

Musca lacks palpi and draws a proboscis back into lips;

Tabanus likewise rejoices in a proboscis under sharp palpi.

The mouth of Culex brandishes its darts from a soft sheath;

Empis bends a long hard beak beneath her breast;

Noxious Conops stretches out [a beak] from the hinge of a joint,

And so does thirsty Asilus (but his is straight and cone-shaped),

And Bombylius a long one, who sucks honey in flight.

Hippobosca is strong by reason of talons; she brandishes a short weapon.

VII. APTERA.

The Aptera, knowing nothing of wings, move about on foot.

[ADDITIONAL LINES ON INSECTS.]

Palpos ore duos, triplexque Lepisma flagellum
Pone gerit: caudâ saltatque Podura bifurcâ.
Maxillis Termes, at linguâ pollet acutâ
Phthir laterumque lobis. Compresso abdomine Pulex
Inflexoque minax rostro salit.

ADDITIONAL LINES ON INSECTS.

Lepisma has two palpi on her mouth and a triple-branched whip-
like appendage behind;
Podura leaps by means of a forked tail.
Termes derives his power from his jaws, Phthir from a sharp-
pointed tongue and lobes on his sides.
Pulex, distinguished by a compressed abdomen and menacing
with inward-curving beak, leaps.

ADDITIONAL LINES ON INSECTS. These lines, in Gray's hand, are recorded by
W. P. Jones in *Thomas Gray Scholar* (p. 181) as found on a sheet in H. Paul's *Queen
Anne* (Asnières, 1906). They are here published for the first time, from a photostat of
the holograph MS. supplied by the Trustees of the Pierpont Morgan Library.

They are evidently a rough draft, only partially corrected and abandoned before
completion.

1 triplexque *above* caudæque *with latter del.*   flagellum *apparently first written* flagella
with um *in heavier ink,* u *superimposed on final* a.   2 gerit *above* trahit *del.*   bifurcâ.]
bifurcâ *in MS.*   3 Maxillis *originally* Maxillas *with* is *above* as *del.*   linguâ *originally*
linguam *with* m *del.*   pollet *above* vibrat *del.*   5 minax *above* salit *del. before* rostro.

GREEK POETRY

Inscription for a Wood in a Park.

Ἀζόμενος πολύθηρον ἐκηβόλου ἄλσος Ἀνάσσας,
  τᾶς δεινᾶς τεμένη λεῖπε, κυναγὲ, θεᾶς·
Μοῦνοι ἄρ' ἔνθα κύνων ζαθέων κλαγγεῦσιν ὑλαγμοὶ,
  ἀνταχεῖς Νυμφᾶν ἀγροτερᾶν κελάδῳ.

INSCRIPTION FOR A WOOD IN A PARK.

In reverent awe, hunter, leave the game-filled grove of the far-darting queen, the sacred precinct of the dread goddess; for there only the baying of the divine hounds should ring out, in answer to the cry of the huntress nymphs.

INSCRIPTION FOR A WOOD IN A PARK. First published in Mason, i. 152.
Text used: *CB*, i. 278. Texts collated: *M*, *Mt*, *Go*.

Title: None in M. GREEK EPIGRAM *Mt.*

1 Ἀζόμενος] Ἀζόμενος *Mt*, *Go*.   πολύθηρον] πολυθήρον *CB*.   ἐκηβόλου] ἐκηβόλου
Mt, *Go*.   2 λεῖπε] λείπε *CB*.   θεᾶς·] θεᾶς, *Mt*, *Go*; θεᾶς *M*.   3 ὑλαγμοὶ]
ὑλάγμοι *Mt*.   *At end in CB:* May: 1742.

POEMS OF DOUBTFUL
AUTHENTICITY

Martials Lib. 10. Epig. 13 [23]. paraphrased.

Th. 1

1

Reverend Antonius seated in his chair,
Full of experience, and grey hair,
But void of Anxious care
Reflecting on ye Acts of threescore year,
            life
Did even his own unblemist [age] arraign,   5
And years, slipt [?] safely by, were fetcht ag^n.
And e'ry day did answer at ye barr
              its
(Unto ye day sufficed not [y^e] former care.)

2

Here e'ry thing's to tryal bro't
He scanns each action, word ā tho't   10
And tho' herein himself concerned might be
And his self interest,
Might his own steddy Judgment wrest
Yett strictly he
Did censure all impartially,   15
On every thing he did just sentence pass,
And, 'spight of all his rigor, this it was.

3

In vain, said he, this hour of tryal's spent,
Of Nothing else can I repent,
For Openly I here declare   20
Not only every day, ānd year,
But every hour and minute were
Most innocent,
Even conscience y^eir accuser must decree y^m clear.

MARTIAL'S LIB. 10. EPIG. 13. [23] PARAPHRASED. The initial eight lines appeared in Sotheby's *Catalogue of . . . Printed Books . . . Letters and Manuscripts . . .* (Tuesday 6 Nov. 1951, p. 53, item no. 393), but the first printing of the entire poem is by H. W. Starr in *N & Q*, N.S. i (Oct. 1954), 435-6. The only known MS., which is not in Gray's hand, was in the collection of John Bowyer Buchanan Nichols and was sold at Sotheby's as a holograph MS. to Maggs Bros. and by Maggs to the Bibliothèque Martin Bodmer (Coligny, Genève) in 1951. The text followed here is the Bodmer MS. See expl. notes.

THE CHARACTERS OF THE
CHRIST-CROSS ROW,
BY A CRITIC, TO M^rs - - -.

*   *   *

Great D draws near—the Duchess sure is come,
Open the doors of the withdrawing-room;
Her daughters deck'd most daintily I see,
The Dowager grows a perfect double D.
E enters next, and with her Eve appears.   5
Not like yon Dowager deprest with years;
What Ease and Elegance her person grace,
Bright beaming, as the Evening-star, her face;
Queen Esther next—how fair e'en after death,
Then one faint glimpse of Queen Elizabeth;   10
No more, our Esthers now are nought but Hetties,
Elizabeths all dwindled into Betties;
In vain you think to find them under E,
They're all diverted into H and B.
F follows fast the fair—and in his rear,   15
See Folly, Fashion, Foppery, straight appear,
All with fantastic clews, fantastic clothes,
With Fans and Flounces, Fringe and Furbelows.
Here Grub-street Geese presume to joke and jeer,
All, all, but Grannam Osborne's Gazetteer.   20
High heaves his hugeness H, methinks we see,
Henry the Eighth's most monstrous majesty,
But why on such *mock* grandeur should we dwell,
H mounts to Heaven, and H descends to Hell.
As H the Hebrew found, so I the Jew,   25
See Isaac, Joseph, Jacob pass in view;
The walls of old Jerusalem appear,
See Israel, and all Judah thronging there.

*   *   *

THE CHARACTERS OF THE CHRIST-CROSS ROW. First printed by Mitford in his
Correspondence of . . . Gray and Nicholls . . . (London: Pickering, 1843), pp. 217-21,
the text followed here. There is no known MS. The asterisks apparently represent lines
deleted by Mitford, who said, 'a few omissions deemed necessary were made in printing
the poem', and added that 'Gray's MSS [*sic*] copy was destroyed'.

P pokes his head out, yet has not a pain;
Like Punch, he peeps, but soon pops in again;   30
Pleased with his Pranks, the Pisgys call him Puck,
Mortals he loves to prick, and pinch, and pluck;
Now a pert Prig, he perks upon your face,
Now peers, pores, ponders, with profound grimace,
Now a proud Prince, in pompous Purple drest,   35
And now a Player, a Peer, a Pimp, or Priest;
A Pea, a Pin, in a perpetual round,
Now seems a Penny, and now shews a Pound;
Like Perch or Pike, in Pond you see him come,
He in plantations hangs like Pear or Plum,   40
Pippin or Peach; then perches on the spray,
In form of Parrot, Pye, or Popinjay.
P, Proteus-like all tricks, all shapes can shew,
The Pleasantest Person in the Christ-Cross row.

*   *   *

As K a King, Q represents a Queen,   45
And seems small difference the sounds between;
K, as a man, with hoarser accent speaks,
In shriller notes Q like a female squeaks;
Behold K struts, as might a King become,
Q draws her train along the Drawing-room,   50
Slow follow all the quality of State,
Queer Queensbury only does refuse to wait.

*   *   *

Thus great R reigns in town, while different far,
Rests in Retirement, *little* Rural R;
Remote from cities lives in lone Retreat,   55
With Rooks and Rabbit-burrows round his seat—
S, sails the Swan slow down the Silver stream.

*   *   *

So big with Weddings, waddles W,
And brings all Womankind before your view;
A Wench, a Wife, a Widow, and a W[hor]e,   60
With Woe behind, and Wantonness before.

[VERSE FRAGMENTS.]

Gratitude
    The Joy that trembles in her eye
    She bows her meek & humble head
               in silent praise
        beyond the power of Sound.

(Mr Pope dead)
    and smart beneath the visionary scourge

    —'tis Ridicule & not reproach that wounds
    Their vanity & not their conscience feels'.

    a few shall
    The cadence of my song repeat
    & hail thee in my words.

[TRANSLATION OF PHILIPS' *SPLENDID SHILLING*, ll. 1–12.]

Oh! nimium felix! Cura et discordibus armis
Cui procul exigua non deficiente Crumenâ
Splendet adhuc Solidus. Non illum torquet egentem
Ostriferi Cantus, non allae dira Cupido.
Ille inter Socios gelido sub vespere notum   5
Tendit iter, genialis ubi se Curia pandit
Juniperive Lares: hic Nympham, si qua protervo
Lumine pertentat Sensus, uritque videndo
(Sive Chloe, seu Phillis amanti gratior audit)
Alternis recolit cyathis, tibi, virgo, salutem   10

VERSE FRAGMENTS. First published by Tovey in *Gray and His Friends*, pp. 269–70. The text followed here, the only known one, is Tovey's original, which was copied by Mason in *CB*, iii. 1110, from Gray's Pocketbook of 1754. See expl. notes.

TRANSLATION OF PHILIPS' *SPLENDID SHILLING*. First published by Tovey in *Gray and His Friends*, p. 298 (*TGF*).
    Text used: *Mt* (Mitford's transcription, Note-book, vol. iii, ff. 110-11). Texts collated: *TGF, Br*

4 Cupido.] Cupido *Mt*; Cupido. *TGF, Br.*

Lætitiamque optans, et amoris mutua vincla.
Nec minus interea fumique jocique benignus
Non lateri parcit, si quando argutior alter
Fabellam orditur lepidam, vel Scommata spargit
Ambiguosve Sales, festiva Crepundia vocum.   15

*   *   *   *

TRANSLATION OF PHILIPS' *SPLENDID SHILLING*.

Ah, fortunate indeed, and far removed from care and clashing arms, that man in whose slender but not-quite-empty purse a shilling gleams. Him (no starving wretch) the chant of the oyster-vendor tortures not, nor burning thirst for ale. That man, as cool evening draws near, makes his familiar way with his Companions to the place where the genial Town-Hall or the Lares of Juniper throw wide their doors: here, if some Nymph stirs his senses with a wanton eye, and he grows warm with gazing (whether Chloe or Phillis hears him with greater favour as he proclaims his love), he woos her with one cup after another, wishing thee, O virgin, health and joy and the mutual bonds of love. Meanwhile, mellowed also by tobacco and jokes, he does not spare his lungs, whenever some more clever companion spins a pleasant tale, or scatters taunts around or sallies of wit with double meanings—a jolly clatter of voices.

[IMITATION OF MARTIAL.]

Fulvia *formosa* est multis—mihi candida, longa
    Recta est; hoc ego sic singula confiteor:
Totum illud, *formosa*, nego: nam nulla venustas
    Nulla in tam magno corpore mica salis.
Caelia *formosa* est; quae cum pulcherrima tota est,   5
    Omnibus una omnes surripuit Veneres.

11 vincla.] vincla *TGF, Br.*

IMITATION OF MARTIAL. First and apparently only previous publication in *The Gentleman's Magazine*, lxxi (July 1801), 591.

Title: So given by Northup, no. 1193.

2 Recta est; hoc ego sic] Recta est, hoc ego: sic *GM.*

IMITATION OF MARTIAL.

To many Fulvia is beautiful—to me she is fair, tall, straight; this I concede, that, taken singly, her features are beautiful: it is in the whole effect that I say she is not beautiful; for there is not a bit of charm, not a spark of wit in that huge body, big as it is.

Celia is *beautiful*; not only is she very pretty in all her parts, but she has stolen from all women and united in herself every trait that makes women lovable.

EXPLANATORY NOTES

ODE ON THE SPRING

The poem was written for Richard West (Favonius) and sent to him in June 1742. According to Mitford, the chief source is Horace's ode (i. 4) *Ad Sestium*, but there are also obvious echoes of Milton and Matthew Green (1696–1737); for a detailed record of possible parallels see the notes of Mitford, Bradshaw, and Tovey. Mason (ii. 75) made the following speculation (the correctness of which Tovey doubts) concerning Gray's intent when writing the poem: 'The original ... title ... was NOONTIDE: probably he then meant to write two more, descriptive of Morning and Evening. His unfinished Ode [*Vicissitude*] ... opens with a fine description of the former: and his Elegy with as beautiful a picture of the latter, which perhaps he might, at that time, have meditated upon for the exordium of an Ode; but this is only conjecture.'

‡14.——a bank ...

> [Quite] O'ercanopied with luscious woodbine.
>
> > *Shakesp. Mids. Night's Dream.* [II. i. 249–51] *Gray.*

19–20. Mason (ii. 75) says of the earlier version: 'The author corrected it on account of the point of *little* and *great*. It certainly had too much the appearance of a Concetto, tho' it expressed his meaning better than the present reading.'

‡27. 'Nare per æstatem liquidam——' [To swim through cloudless summer] *Virgil. Georg. lib.* 4. [l. 59] *Gray.*

‡30.   ——sporting with quick glance
        Shew to the sun their waved coats drop'd with gold.
        Milton's Paradise Lost, book 7. [ll. 405–6] *Gray.*

‡31. While insects from the threshold preach, *&c.*

> M. GREEN, *in the Grotto.*
>
> > *Dodsley's Miscellanies, Vol. v, p.* 161. *Gray.*

Gray wrote to Walpole in Jan. or Feb. of 1748 (T & W no. 144, pp. 299–300): 'I send you a bit of a thing for two reasons: first, because it is one of your favourites, Mr. M. Green; and next, because I would do justice. The thought on which my second ode [*Spring*] turns is manifestly stole from hence:—not that I knew it at the time, but, having seen this many Years before, to be sure it imprinted itself on my Memory, & forgetting the Author, I took it for my own. the Subject was the Queen's Hermitage.' Gray then quotes a long passage from Green, ll. 57 ff., of which the most relevant part is as follows:

> While Insects from the Threshold preach,
> And Minds disposed to Musing teach;
> Proud of strong Limbs & painted Hues
> They perish by the slightest Bruise

Or Maladies begun within
Destroy more slow Life's frail Machine:
From Maggot-Youth thro' Change of State
They feel like us the Turns of Fate;
Some born to creep have lived to fly,
And changed Earth's Cells for Dwellings high:
And some, that did their six Wings keep,
Before they died, been forced to creep.
They Politicks, like ours, profess:
The greater prey upon the less.
Some strain on Foot huge Loads to bring,
Some toil incessant on the Wing:
Nor from their vigorous Schemes desist
Till Death; & then are never mist.
Some frolick, toil, marry, increase,
Are sick & well, have War & Peace,
And broke with Age in half a Day
Yield to Successors, & away.

ODE ON THE DEATH OF A FAVOURITE CAT

Walpole's cat was drowned at his home in Arlington Street, and Gray evidently wrote the poem shortly thereafter, early in 1747, for in a letter (T & W no. 133) to Walpole, 22 Feb. 1747, he made this comment: 'As one ought to be particularly careful to avoid blunders in a compliment of condolence, it would be a sensible satisfaction to me (before I testify my sorrow, and the sincere part I take in your misfortune) to know for certain, who it is I lament. I knew Zara and Selima [Gray actually wrote 'Zara I know & Selima I know', but Mason altered the phrasing because he disapproved of the scriptural parallel ('Jesus I know, and Paul I know', Acts xix. 15); see T & W no. 133, n. 1], (Selima, was it? or Fatima) or rather I knew them both together; for I cannot justly say which was which. Then as to your handsome Cat, the name you distinguish her by I am no less at a loss, as well knowing one's handsome cat is always the cat one likes best; or, if one be alive and the other dead, it is usually the latter that is the handsomest. Besides, if the point were never so clear, I hope you do not think me so ill-bred or so imprudent as to forfeit all my interest in the surviver: Oh no! I would rather seem to mistake, and imagine to be sure it must be the tabby one that had met with this sad accident. Till this affair is a little better determined, you will excuse me if I do not begin to cry:

> "Tempus inane peto, requiem, spatiumque doloris."

[The passage from the *Aeneid*, iv. 433–4, that Gray has in mind is one in which Dido is begging Anna to ask Aeneas to delay his sailing for a short time which will have no effect on his ultimate plans (*inane*) but which will give her a chance to adjust to her sorrow at losing him: Tempus inane peto, requiem spatiumque furori, / Dum mea me victam doceat fortuna dolere. (I ask only for a short time [that will be] meaningless [to him], an interval of rest from my madness until my fortune, now that I have been conquered, teaches me to bear my pain.)]

Which interval is the more convenient, as it gives time to rejoice with you on your new honors [Walpole's election to the Royal Society].' See also T & W nos. 134, 135. The remarks in this letter and Gray's references (ll. 4, 10) in the poem to both 'tabby' and 'tortoise' are rather confusing. Tovey gives this explanation: 'Yet it is clear, I think, that he believes that the deceased cat was not "the tabby"— but the other, presumably a tortoise-shell; but he wishes to be in the good graces of the survivor; and therefore he will pretend that it is the "tabby" whose death he is mourning; that the "tabby" may be charmed with the fine things which the poet has said about her, under the impression that she is no more. Therefore to please her he writes

> "Demurest of the *tabby* kind."

And, though he says also

> "Her coat, that with the *tortoise* vies,"

that, to the "tabby", will mean that she was quite as beautiful as her deceased rival. If, as Gray rather anticipates, the victim of "Malignant Fate" was the tortoise-shell, then "the tabby kind" is simply a synonym for "cats", and the other ambiguous line has its more obvious meaning. But this is the *exoteric* doctrine of the poem; the *esoteric* doctrine is for the private ear of the "tabby".' In any event, Walpole finally had a pedestal made for the tub and engraved on it the first stanza of the poem.

1–6. The exordium of this mock-heroic is in imitation of the opening lines of Dryden's *Alexander's Feast. Br.*

> 'Twas at the royal feast for Persia won
> By Philip's warlike son;
> Aloft in awful state
> The godlike hero sat
> On his imperial throne.

42. In one form or another this is an old saying. The best-known variant is the one in *Merchant of Venice* (II. vii. 65) which Gray is deliberately echoing here: 'All that glisters is not gold.' He may also have had in mind Dryden's 'All, as they say, that glitters is not gold' (*The Hind and the Panther*, 2nd ed. [Pt. II], l. 787).

ODE ON A DISTANT PROSPECT OF ETON COLLEGE

The poem was written about Aug. 1742; according to Mason (ii. 77), 'This was the first English production of Mr. Gray which appeared in print. It was published in folio by Dodsley in 1747; about the same time, at Mr. Walpole's request, Mr. Gray sat for his picture to Echart, in which, on a paper which he held in his hand, Mr. Walpole wrote the title of this Ode, and to intimate his own high and just opinion of it, as a first production, added this line of Lucan by way of motto.

> Nec licuit populis parvum te, Nile, videre. [Nor have the people been permitted to see thee, Nile, when thou art small.] *Phars[alia]. lib.* x. *l.* 296.'

Parallel to the margin, reading up from l. 55 to l. 41, in *CB* (i. 279) and immediately after the title in *M*, ii. [9], is the following motto from Menander:

ἄνθρωπος· ἱκανὴ πρόφασις εἰς τὸ δυστυχεῖν [I am a man, a sufficient excuse for being unhappy]. Liddell–Scott (7th ed.) lists this phrase, s.v. πρόφασις, as being from 'Menand., Incert. 263'. Mitford cites 'Menander. Incert. Frag. ver. 382'. The present editors have been unable to verify the citation from any text available to them of Menander; however, the above citations leave no room for doubt that the quotation is correctly given from a work attributed to him.

‡4. *Henry.* King Henry the Sixth, Founder of the College. *Gray.*

‡19. And bees their honey redolent of spring. *Dryden's Fable on the Pythag. System* [l. 110 of Dryden's translation of Ovid, *Metamorphoses*, xv]. *Gray.*

‡79. [And] Madness laughing in his ireful mood. *Dryden's Fable of Palamon and Arcite* [ii. 582]. *Gray.*

98. Mitford sees a parallel between this line and l. 554 of the *Ajax* of Sophocles. Mr. J. C. Maxwell has also pointed out to us that there is a parallel in thought between Sophocles, *Oedipus Coloneus*, ll. 1225–38, and this ode.

ODE, TO ADVERSITY

The poem was completed at Stoke Poges in Aug. 1742. For the Greek mottoes which Gray attached to it, see the textual notes. The most important sources appear to be Dionysius' *Ode to Nemesis* and Horace's *O Diva* (*Odes*, i. 35).

1. *Daughter.* Adversity has been identified by Mitford as Ate (Blind Folly) or, more probably, merely Affliction. However, the 'Daughter of Jove' *par excellence* is Athena, who bears the head of Medusa on her shield—hence 'Gorgon-terrors' of l. 35. Athena, daughter of Metis (wisest of gods) and Zeus (most powerful), represented the perfect blend of wisdom and power. The 'vengeful Band' (l. 36) must be the Eumenides (Erinyes, Furies), whose worship Athena instituted at Athens. Tovey (p. 99) also questions the identification with Ate. Perhaps, as Mitford suggests in his alternative, Gray was simply stressing that Adversity is sent by God to chasten and harden men, and here used a variety of appropriate attributes without having any one goddess in mind.

32. ἁ γλυκύδακρυς. Apparently Gray's indication of the precedent for 'sadly-pleasing'. The editors have not been able to identify the source of this phrase. We have found only three examples of the use of γλυκύδακρυς (*Pal. Anth.* v. 177; vii. 419; xii. 167); all passages are in poems by Meleager and in each the adjective modifies *Eros.* Since ἁ is feminine, Gray presumably had some other passage in mind.

THE PROGRESS OF POESY

Gray was working on the poem early in 1752 'by fits & starts at very distant intervals' (T & W nos. 169, 215), but probably completed it well before Dec. 1754 (T & W no. 194, n. 1), although, according to Mason (i. 145 n.), he at one time lost interest in the ode: 'I was . . . the innocent cause of his delaying to finish . . . the progress of Poetry. I told him . . . that "though I admired it greatly, and thought that it breathed the very spirit of Pindar, yet I suspected it would by no means hit the public taste". Finding afterwards that he did not proceed in finishing it, I often expostulated with him on the subject, but he always replied

"No, you have thrown cold water upon it". I mention this little anecdote, to shew how much the opinion of a friend, even when it did not convince his judgment, affected his inclination.'

In both the *Progress* and the *Bard* his aversion to the irregular Pindaric odes practised by Cowley caused him to attempt the rather difficult task of making a strict imitation of Pindar in English. (For an analysis of the metrics, see Starr, *Gray as a Literary Critic* [Philadelphia, 1941], Appendix, pp. 132–40.) Accordingly the editors have inserted in brackets the designations *Strophe*, *Antistrophe*, and *Epode*, which appear in the MSS.

Gray wrote to Walpole, July 1752 (T & W no. 169): '. . . I may send . . . a high Pindarick upon stilts, which one must be a better scholar than he [Dodsley] is to understand a line of, and the very best scholars will understand but a little matter here and there.' Despite this comment Gray was rather exasperated to learn that so many of his readers found *The Bard* and *The Progress of Poesy* obscure—hence when he finally decided to add explanatory notes to the 1768 editions, he prefixed to the poems the somewhat double-edged 'Advertisement'. For his comments on the reaction of the public and the parody by Colman and Lloyd see T & W nos. 247, 248, 249, 312, 367. In the first edition the motto was φωνᾶντα συνετοῖσιν [speaking clearly to the wise] (Pindar, *Olymp*. ii. 85); in the 1768 edition it was expanded to φωνᾶντα συνετοῖσιν· ἐς δὲ τὸ πᾶν ἑρμηνέων χατίζει [(shafts) that speak clearly to the wise; but for the generality they need interpreters].

‡1. Awake [up], my glory: awake, lute and harp. *David's Psalms* [Prayer Book version, lvii. 9]. *Gray*.

‡Pindar styles his own poetry with its musical accompanyments, Αἰοληῒς μολπή, Αἰολίδες χορδαί, Αἰολίδων πνοαὶ αὐλῶν, Æolian song, Æolian strings, the breath of the Æolian flute. *Gray*.

This note was inserted by Gray as a result of an error made by the reviewer in the *Critical Review*, iv (Aug. 1757), 167, who thought that by 'Æolian lyre' Gray meant an Æolian harp, an instrument which when hung in the open air produces notes as the wind strikes it. On 7 Sept. 1757 Gray wrote to Mason (T & W no. 248) concerning the review: 'even the Critical Review . . . that is rapt, & surprised, & shudders at me; yet mistakes the Æolian Lyre for the *Harp of Æolus*, wch indeed, as he observes, is a very bad instrument to dance to.'

‡3. The subject and simile, as usual with Pindar, are united. The various sources of poetry, which gives life and lustre to all it touches, are here described; its quiet majestic progress enriching every subject (otherwise dry and barren) with a pomp of diction and luxuriant harmony of numbers; and its more rapid and irresistible course, when swoln and hurried away by the conflict of tumultuous passions. *Gray*.

‡13. Power of harmony to calm the turbulent sallies of the soul. The thoughts are borrowed from the first Pythian of Pindar. *Gray*. See note to l. 20.

‡20. This is a weak imitation of some incomparable lines in the same Ode. *Gray*. A translation of Pythian Ode i. 1–12, is as follows:
'O golden lyre, joint possession of Apollo and the violet-tressed* Muses! The
violet-tressed. In Pindar, ἰοπλοκάμων. This epithet is an excellent illustration of

feet of the dancers heed thy first note, leader of the festive joys, and the singers obey thy signals to begin, whenever thy vibrating strings sound the first note of the preludes that precede the choral dance.

'Thou dost also dim the everlasting fire of the pointed thunderbolt. The eagle sleeps upon the sceptre of Zeus, with his swift wings drooping at his sides, the king of birds, when round his beaked head thou hast poured a dusky cloud, a sweet seal upon his eyelids; and as he sleeps, overcome by thy trembling notes, he arches his supple back.

'Nor is this the limit of thy power, for fierce Ares, leaving far away the deadly clash of arms, takes delight in deep slumber, and thy shafts cast a spell of enchanted sleep over the passions of demi-gods, by the skill of the son of Leto and the deep-breasted Muses.'

‡25. Power of harmony to produce all the graces of motion in the body. *Gray.*

‡35. Μαρμαρυγὰς θηεῖτο ποδῶν· θαύμαζε δὲ θυμῷ. [He (Odysseus) gazed at the quick twinkling of (the dancers') feet; and he wondered in his heart.] HOMER. Od[yssey] θ [viii. 265]. *Gray.*

38. *sublime.* In the physical sense of Latin *sublimis*, 'raised aloft'.

‡41. Λάμπει δ’ ἐπὶ πορφυρέῃσι/Παρείῃσι φῶς ἔρωτος. [And on his rose-red cheeks there gleams the light of love.] PHRYNICHUS, apud Athenæum [*Deipnosophistae*, xiii. 604a]. *Gray.* Modern texts give the line as follows:

λάμπει δ’ ἐπὶ πορφυρέαις παρῆσι φῶς ἔρωτος.

‡42. To compensate the real and imaginary ills of life, the Muse was given to Mankind by the same Providence that sends the Day by its chearful presence to dispel the gloom and terrors of the Night. *Gray.*

‡52. Or seen the Morning's well-appointed Star
Come marching up the eastern hillˢ afar.

Cowley [*Brutus, an Ode*, st. 4]. *Gray.*

What Cowley wrote was ' Or seen her well-appointed star / Come marching up the Eastern Hill afar'. See also *Alliance of Education and Government*, ll. 46–47; *Statius* (vi. 646–88), ll. 30–31; *Agrippina*, l. 94.

‡54. Extensive influence of poetic Genius over the remotest and most un-civilized nations: its connection with liberty, and the virtues that naturally attend on it. ⌈See the Erse, Norwegian, and Welch Fragments, the Lapland and American songs.⌋ *Gray.* Gray has in mind the 'translations' of Macpherson and the sources mentioned in the explanatory notes to *The Fatal Sisters* and *The Death of Hoël.*

solar road. "Extra anni solisque vias—" [Beyond the paths of the year and the sun—] *Virgil* [*Aeneid*, vi. 796]. *Gray.*
"Tutta lontana dal camin del sole." [Quite far from the road of the sun.] *Petrarch, Canzon* 2 [*Canzoniere*, 'Canzone II', l. 48]. *Gray.*

63. *track* is the object of *pursue*.

how inadequate and even misleading translations frequently are. The more common epithet would be ἰοστεφάνων, 'violet-crowned'; but Pindar avoids common expressions, and so he uses here a metaphor instead of a visual image.

64. *pursue*. In the sense of the Latin *prosequi*, 'to follow closely after' or 'accompany', not 'to chase'.

‡66. Progress of Poetry from Greece to Italy, and from Italy to England. Chaucer was not unacquainted with the writings of Dante or of Petrarch. The Earl of Surrey and Sir Tho. Wyatt had travelled in Italy, and formed their taste there; Spenser imitated the Italian writers; Milton improved on them: but this School expired soon after the Restoration, and a new one arose on the French model, which has subsisted ever since. *Gray.*

Delphi. There is a sketch and an extended description of Delphi in *CB*, i. 168–9.

69. *Mæander's amber waves*. The Mæander is a muddy (hence brown or amber), winding river in western Asia Minor.

‡84. *Nature's Darling*. Shakespear. *Gray.*

‡95. *He*. Milton. *Gray.*

‡98. '—flammantia mœnia mundi' [—the flaming ramparts of the world]. *Lucretius* [i. 74]. *Gray.*

‡99. For the spirit of the living creature was in the wheels—And above the firmament, that was over their heads, was the likeness of a throne, as the appearance of a saphire-stone.—This was the appearance [of the likeness] of the glory of the Lord. *Ezekiel* i. 20, 26, 28. *Gray.*

‡102. Ὀφθαλμῶν μὲν ἄμερσε·δίδου δ' ἡδεῖαν ἀοιδήν [(the Muse) took away (his) eyes, but she gave (him the gift of) sweet song]. HOMER. Od[yssey, viii. 64]. *Gray.*

104. Juvenal, i. 19–20;
．．． decurrere campo,
per quem magnus equos Auruncae flexit alumnus
[to traverse the field through which the great son of Arunca drove his horses].

‡105. Meant to express the stately march and sounding energy of Dryden's rhimes. *Gray.*

‡106. Hast thou cloathed his neck with thunder? *Job* [xxxix. 19]. *Gray.*

‡110. Words, that weep, and tears, that speak. *Cowley. Gray.* Gray is quoting 'The Prophet', l. 20, as it appears in the 1656 edition of *The Mistress*. See T & W no. 222, n. 15.

‡111. We have had in our language no other odes of the sublime kind, than that of Dryden on St. Cecilia's day: for Cowley (who had his merit) yet wanted judgment, style, and harmony, for such a task. That of Pope is not worthy of so great a man. Mr. Mason indeed of late days has touched the true chords, and with a masterly hand, in some of his Choruses,—above all in the last of Caractacus,

Hark! heard ye not yon footstep dread? *&c. Gray.*

112. *what daring Spirit*. Gray himself.

‡115. Διὸς πρὸς ὄρνιχα θεῖον [against the god-like bird of Zeus]. [Pindar] Olymp. 2 [88]. Pindar compares himself to that bird, and his enemies to ravens that croak and clamour in vain below, while it pursues its flight, regardless of their noise. *Gray.*

121–3. See the last four lines of the *Alcaic Ode*.

THE BARD

Gray evidently started the poem late in 1754 and worked on it, probably very intermittently, through August of 1755 (T & W no. 199). He then seems to have lost interest in it until May 1757, when he heard John Parry 'play on the Welch Harp at a concert at Cambridge . . . which he often declared inspired him with the conclusion' (Mason, ii. 92). On 24 or 31 May 1757 Gray wrote to Mason (T & W no. 238): ' . . . Mr Parry has been here, & scratch'd out such ravishing blind Harmony, such tunes of a thousand year old with names enough to choak you, as have set all this learned body a'dancing, & inspired them with due reverence for *Odikle* [*The Bard*], whenever it shall appear. Mr Parry (you must know) it was, that has put Odikle in motion again, & with much exercise it has got a *tender Tail* grown, like Scroddles [Mason], and here it is. if you don't like it, you may kiss it.' Gray continued to revise the poem until its publication in August (see textual notes to *Progress of Poesy*). Mason (ii. 91) writes:

I promised the reader . . . the original argument of this capital Ode, as its author had set it down on one of the pages of his commonplace book. It is as follows: 'The army of Edward I. as they march through a deep valley, are suddenly stopped by the appearance of a venerable figure seated on the summit of an inaccessible rock, who, with a voice more than human, reproaches the King with all the misery and desolation which he had brought on his country; foretells the misfortunes of the Norman race, and with prophetic spirit declares, that all his cruelty shall never extinguish the noble ardour of poetic genius in this island; and that men shall never be wanting to celebrate true virtue and valour in immortal strains, to expose vice and infamous pleasure, and boldly censure tyranny and oppression. His song ended, he precipitates himself from the mountain, and is swallowed up by the river that rolls at its foot.' Fine as the conclusion of this Ode is at present, I think it would have been still finer, if he could have executed it according to this plan: but unhappily for his purpose, instances of English Poets were wanting.

For the influence of Welsh rhythm and alliteration on *The Bard* see W. P. Jones, *Thomas Gray, Scholar* (Cambridge, Mass., 1937), pp. 92–94, and the notes in *CB*.

‡4. Mocking the air with colours idly spread. *Shakespear's King John* [v. i. 72]. *Gray.*

‡5. The Hauberk was a texture of steel ringlets, or rings interwoven, forming a coat of mail, that sate close to the body, and adapted itself to every motion. *Gray.*

‡9. [By] The crested adder's pride. *Dryden's Indian Queen* [III. i. 84]. *Gray.*

‡11. *Snowdon* was a name given by the Saxons to that mountainous tract, which the Welch themselves call *Craigian-eryri*: it included all the highlands of Caernarvonshire and Merionethshire, as far east as the river Conway. R. Hygden[,] speaking of the castle of Conway built by King Edward the first, says, 'Ad ortum amnis Conway ad clivum montis Erery [At the source of the River Conway on the slope of Mt. Erery];' and Matthew of Westminster, (ad ann. 1283,) 'Apud Aberconway ad pedes montis Snowdoniæ fecit erigi castrum forte. [Near (*or* at) Aberconway at the foot of Mt. Snowdon, he caused a fortified camp to be constructed.]' *Gray.*

‡13. Gilbert de Clare, surnamed the Red, Earl of Gloucester and Hertford, son-in-law to King Edward. *Gray.*

‡14. Edmond de Mortimer, Lord of Wigmore.
They both were *Lords-Marchers*, whose lands lay on the borders of Wales, and probably accompanied the King in this expedition. *Gray.*

18. *haggard*. '. . . *haggard*, wᶜʰ conveys to you the Idea of a *Witch*, is indeed only a metaphor taken from an unreclaim'd Hawk, wᶜʰ is called a *Haggard*, & looks wild & *farouche* & jealous of its liberty.' *Gray* to Wharton, 21 Aug. 1755, T & W no. 205.

‡19. The image was taken from a well-known picture of Raphaël, representing the Supreme Being in the vision of Ezekiel: there are two of these paintings (both believed original), one at Florence, the other at Paris. *Gray.* Moses breaking the tables of the law, by Parmegiano, was a figure which Mr. Gray used to say came still nearer to his meaning than the picture of Raphael. *M*, ii. 93; see also T & W no. 222.

‡20. Shone, like a meteor, streaming to the wind. *Milton's Paradise Lost* [i. 537]. *Gray.*

‡35. The shores of Caernarvonshire opposite to the isle of Anglesey. *Gray.*

‡38. Cambden and others observe, that eagles used annually to build their aerie among the rocks of Snowdon, which from thence (as some think) were named by the Welch *Craigian-eryri*, or the crags of the eagles. At this day (I am told) the highest point of Snowdon is called *the eagle's nest*. That bird is certainly no stranger to this island, as the Scots, and the people of Cumberland, Westmoreland, *&c.* can testify: it even has built its nest in the Peak of Derbyshire. /See Willoughby's *Ornithol.* published by Ray./ *Gray.* John Ray (1627–1705) published (1676) and translated (London, 1678) the *Ornithologia* of his patron Francis Willughby (1635–72).

‡40–41.　　　　　　　As dear to me as are the ruddy drops,
　　　　　　　　　　　　That visit my sad heart—
　　　　　　　　　　　　　　Shakesp. Jul. Cæsar [ii. i. 289–90]. *Gray.*

‡47–48. See the Norwegian Ode, that follows [*Fatal Sisters*]. *Gray.* Gray is here pointing out that the idea of a web of destiny being woven appears in both poems. He felt that, under certain circumstances, it was perfectly proper to incorporate ideas from one mythology in another; he wrote to Mason, 13 Jan. 1758 (T & W no. 262): 'might we not be permitted (in that scarcity of Celtic Ideas we labour under) to adopt some of these foreign whimsies, dropping however all mention of Woden, & his Valkhyrian Virgins, &c. . . .'

49. The chorus of bards begins here and is indicated by Gray's double quotation marks; the remarks of the bard alone are enclosed in single quotation marks. Incidentally, despite Dr. Johnson's criticism, it is perfectly possible to 'weave the warp, and weave the woof', especially in the sense of 'interweave them'.

‡54–55. Edward the Second, cruelly butchered in Berkley-Castle [near the Severn River in western England]. *Gray.*

‡57. Isabel of France, Edward the Second's adulterous Queen. *Gray.*

‡59. Triumphs of Edward the Third in France. *Gray.*

‡64. Death of that King, abandoned by his Children, and even robbed in his last moments by his Courtiers and his Mistress [Alice Perrers]. *Gray.*

‡67. Edward, the Black Prince, dead some time before his Father. *Gray.*

‡71. Magnificence of Richard the Second's reign. See Froissard, and other contemporary Writers. *Gray.*

71–76. See textual notes for the deleted passage describing the death of Richard II at Pomfret (Pontefract) Castle.

75. See *Alliance of Education and Government*, l. 48.

‡77. Richard the Second, (as we are told by Archbishop Scroop and the confederate Lords in their manifesto, by Thomas of Walsingham, and all the older Writers,) was starved to death. The story of his assassination by Sir Piers of Exon, is of much later date. *Gray.*

‡83. Ruinous civil wars of York and Lancaster. *Gray.*

‡87. Henry the Sixth, George Duke of Clarence, Edward the Fifth, Richard Duke of York, &c. believed to be murthered secretly in the Tower of London. The oldest part of that structure is vulgarly attributed to Julius Cæsar. *Gray.*

‡89. *Consort.* Margaret of Anjou, a woman of heroic spirit, who struggled hard to save her Husband and her Crown. *Gray.*
Father. Henry the Fifth. *Gray.*

‡90. Henry the Sixth very near being canonized. The line of Lancaster had no right of inheritance to the Crown. *Gray.*

‡91. The white and red roses, devices of York and Lancaster [presumably woven above and below on the loom]. *Gray.*

‡93. The silver Boar was the badge of Richard the Third; whence he was usually known in his own time by the name of *the Boar*. *Gray.*

96. Gray seems to have in mind simultaneously three meanings of *stamp*: (1) to beat the woof thread firmly into the warp threads on a loom, (2) to imprint a picture or design on a coin, (3) to ratify a treaty or agreement by affixing a seal or some other official mark.

‡99. Eleanor of Castile died a few years after the conquest of Wales. The heroic proof she gave of her affection for her Lord [she is supposed to have sucked the poison from a wound Edward I received] is well known. The monuments of his regret, and sorrow for the loss of her, are still to be seen at Northampton, Geddington, Waltham, and other places. *Gray.*

102. See textual notes. Gray explained to Walpole, 11 July 1757 (T & W no. 240), that he had decided not to name the bard Caradoc: 'Caradoc I have private reasons against; and besides it is in reality Carādoc, and will not stand in the verse.' See the poem *Caradoc*, in which the accent clearly falls on the second syllable. Tovey speculated that the 'private reasons' were that Gray did not wish *The Bard* confused with Mason's *Caractacus*.

‡109. It was the common belief of the Welch nation, that King Arthur was still alive in Fairy-Land, and should return again to reign over Britain. *Gray.*

‡110. Both Merlin [Myrddin] and Taliessin had prophesied, that the Welch should regain their sovereignty over this island; which seemed to be accomplished in the House of Tudor. *Gray.* The prophecies attributed to these poets are actually of a far later date.

‡117. Speed, relating an audience given by Queen Elizabeth to Paul Dzialinski, Ambassadour of Poland, says, 'And thus she, lion-like rising, daunted the malapert Orator no less with her stately port and majestical deporture, than with the tartnesse of her princelie checkes.' *Gray.* John Speed (1552–1629) published his *History of Great Britaine . . . to . . . King James* in 1611.

‡121. Taliessin, Chief of the Bards, flourished in the VIth Century. His works are still preserved, and his memory held in high veneration among his Countrymen. *Gray.* His *Book* exists in only a thirteenth-century version and many of the poems in it may not be by Taliessin.

‡126. Fierce wars and faithful loves shall moralize my song. *Spenser's Proëme to the Fairy Queen* [l. 9]. *Gray.*

‡128. Shakespear. *Gray.*

‡131. Milton. *Gray.*

‡133. The succession of Poets after Milton's time. *Gray.*

THE FATAL SISTERS

The Fatal Sisters was written in 1761 and is a paraphrase of a poem (often attributed to the eleventh century) preserved in *Njáls Saga*, ch. 157, which is part of an account of the Battle of Clontarf; this battle was fought on 23 Apr. (Good Friday) 1014 (not 'Christmas-day . . . about the year 1029' as Gray incorrectly entered in *CB*). In *Njáls Saga* the vision is said to have been seen *in* Caithness by a man named Dorruðr (not 'by a Native of Caithness'; this phrase together with the unfortunate placing of 'in Scotland' in the preface might lead a reader to infer that the vision was seen near Clontarf).

The original poem has no title in any of the MSS.; the name *Darraðar Ljóð* was attached to it later, probably as a means of identification when it began to be reproduced separately, although the present editors have been unable to find by whom. Tovey has assumed that the title means 'Lay of Darts' (disregarding the fact that *Darraðar* is singular) and that the name of the man who saw the vision was a mythical one derived from the title. Since the man's name appears quite some time before the title, this theory is untenable. It is more likely that the name was taken from *vef darraðar* ('web of the dart', probably a kenning for 'battle') of strophes 4 and 5 (see below, ll. 30, 38, 46 of the English translation of the Latin version, where the phrase is incorrectly rendered 'web of Darrad') and that the title is just what it seems to be, 'The Song of Dorruðr'.

Apparently the coincidence of *darraðar* in the text and title misled Torfaeus, who rendered *vef darraðar* as *Telam Darradi* and *Telam Darradar* in ll. 30 and 38 respectively. It should be noted that Gray was not misled by these renderings, having written 'web of war' both times. Indeed, it seems to the present editors, whose knowledge of ON is also rather limited, that Gray did much better than he has usually been given credit for in avoiding the pitfalls of this poem.

This passage appears in Lockhart's *Life of Scott* (London: Millet, n.d.), iv. 223–4: 'A clergyman . . . while some remnants of the Norse were yet spoken in North Ronaldsha, . . . carried thither the translation [of *Darraðar Ljóð*] of Mr. Gray, then newly published, and read it to some of the old people as referring to the ancient history of their islands. But so soon as he had proceeded a little way, they exclaimed they knew it very well in the original . . . [as] *The Enchantresses.*'

To understand the basic imagery of the poem, the reader must have an idea of the looms employed in Iceland and the Scandinavian countries. The upright loom which the author of *Darraðar Ljóð* has in mind is constructed and functions essentially in the following manner, although the details are not definitely known. There is a more detailed account, with a cut, in Smith's *Dictionary of Greek and Roman Antiquities*, s.v. *tela*.

The problem in weaving is to pass a free thread (*weft* or *woof*, ON *veptr*) alternately under and over a series of relatively fixed parallel threads (the *warp*).

The warp threads were attached to a round bar (*warp-beam*, ON *rifr*) which was set in sockets near the top of two upright posts so that it could be turned and the finished cloth rolled around it. The lower ends of the warp threads, either singly or in bundles, were weighted with stones to keep them taut.

Near the middle of the uprights there was a device that ran horizontally across the loom to enable the weaver to pull a certain series of warp threads forward, thus leaving a space (the *shed*) between them and the rest of the warp. Through this space the weft thread, probably attached to a stick or bone instrument (the *shuttle*), was passed (*thrown* is the usual weaver's term). After each passage of the weft thread, it was tamped firmly into place (*beaten*) by means of a straight stick.

In the Scandinavian upright loom the beating was upward, so that the cloth seemed to rise on the loom as more was woven. After a time, there would be a solid web (ON *vefr*) from the working area up to and around the warp-beam (hence the kenning 'hanging cloud of the warp-beam' for 'web').

A literal translation of the Latin on which Gray based his poem is given below. The line numbers correspond to those in Mason. The 'friendly women' of l. 8 are the Valkyries, who were called 'the friends of Odin'.

> Wide is spread
> Before the slaughter to come
> The cloud of arrows:
> Blood rains down:
> Already to spears is fastened   5
> The death-pale
> Warp of men
> Which the friendly women are weaving
> With the red woof
> Of Randver's death.   10
>   This web is woven
> Of human entrails,
> And to the warp are tightly tied
> Human heads,
> Bedewed with blood are   15

Spears for treadles,
Weaving instruments of iron
And arrows for shuttles:
With swords will we beat tight
This web of Victory. 20
There are working at the weaving Hilda
And Hiorthrimula,
Sangrida and Swipula;
With drawn swords
The spear shall be shattered 25
The shield split
And the sword
Shall be splintered by the shield.
   Let us weave, let us weave
The Web of Darrad* 30
This (Sword) the Young King
Formerly owned.
Let us go forth
And enter among the cohorts
Where our friends 35
Fight with weapons.
   Let us weave, let us weave,
The Web of Darrad;*
And then unto the King
Then let us cling! 40
There they saw
Shields spattered with blood—
Gunna and Gondula
Who were guarding the King.
   Let us weave, let us weave 45
The Web of Darrad!*
When the arms clash together
Of Warlike Men
Let us not permit him
To be deprived of life: 50
The Valkyries have
Rule over slaughter.
   Those Peoples shall rule the lands
Who in desert headlands
Formerly dwelt. 55

*See introductory note. The phrase *vef darraðar* appears three times in the
original poem (ll. 30, 38, 46). The Latin translator has rendered it *Telam Darradi*
in l. 30 and *Telam Darradar* in ll. 38 and 46. Apparently he was led to think that
darraðar was a proper noun by the title, and, recognizing the form as a genitive
singular, rendered it first by a Latin genitive form (*Darradi*) but retained the ON
genitive form in the later two lines. The editors have rendered the Latin each
time 'Web of Darrad' to enable the reader to see the errors in the text that Gray
was working with.

I say that over the mighty King
Death hangs.
Already his Comrade has fallen to the arrows;
   And to the Hibernians
Pain shall come   60
Which never
Among men will be ended.
Now the web is woven.
Truly the field (with blood) bedewed;
Through the lands shall rush   65
The strife of Warriors.
   Now it is horrible
To look about
For a Cloud of Blood
Flies through the air: 70
The air shall be dyed
With the blood of men
Before our incantations
Shall all fall to the ground.
   We sing well   75
Of the young king
Many chants of victory:
May we prosper as we sing.
Moreover let that one learn,
Who is listening,   80
Many chants of War
And relate them to men.
   Let us mount our horses
Since we are carrying drawn swords
From this place.   85

Advertisement. The 'Friend' is Mason, and the plan was abandoned when Gray learned that Thomas Warton, Professor of Poetry at Oxford, was writing a *History of English Poetry*.

Preface. In *Njáls Saga*, Dorruðr (the 'Native of Caithness') saw twelve persons ride to a *dyngja*, originally in Icelandic a room for weaving, often wholly or partially underground.

‡*Note*) The *Valkyriur* were female Divinities, Servants of *Odin* (or *Woden*) in the Gothic mythology: their name signifies *Chuser[s] of the slain*. they were mounted on swift horses with drawn swords in their hands, & in the throng of battle selected such as were destined to slaughter, & conducted them to *Valhalla*, the hall of *Odin*, or paradise of the Brave, where they attended the banquet, & served the departed Heroes with horns of mead & ale. *Gray. Valhalla* is spelled *Valkalla* in *P* and *M*, for Dodsley evidently misread Gray's hand here, a natural error since this is supposedly the first use of the word in English. For additional information in *CB*, see textual notes.

‡3. [The Latin translation renders the original *rifs reiðiský* ('the hanging cloud of the warp-beam' according to Cleasby & Vigfusson, *An Old Icelandic Diction-*

ary, s.v. *rifr*) by *nubes sagittarum*, an error which Gray incorporated into his poem.]

> How quick they wheel'd & flying behind them shot
> Sharp sleet of arrowy shower[s]—

Milton Par[adise]: Reg[ained]. [iii. 323–4] *Gray.*

‡4. The noise of battle hurtled in the air. Shakesp: Jul: Caesar [II. ii. 22]. *Gray.*

8. *Orkney. Sigurd. Randver.* Tovey states that according to Phelps and Kittredge, the Latin translation (*Randveri mortis*) is a mistranslation of the Icelandic 'the friends of the slayer of Randverr [*sic*]', a poetic phrase meaning 'the friends of Odin' (i.e. 'the Valkyriur'). There seems to have been some misunderstanding here: in the original, ll. 8–10 read 'er þaer vinur fylla (which the friendly women are filling) / rauðum vepti (with the red woof) / Randvés bana (of Randver's slayer)'. Bayerschmidt and Hollander interpret ll. 9 and 10 *together* as a kenning for 'blood', construing *Randvés bana* with *rauðum vepti*, which seems more likely in view of its position.

9–12. See the textual note to the Preface.

32. *King.* Sictryg (Silitric or Sihtric).

37–40. The tribe which has hitherto been confined to the sea-coast shall rule over rich provinces in the interior of Ireland. *Br.* Gray evidently assumed that the battle was a victory for Sictryg, although this is hardly the modern interpretation. See *Shorter Cambridge Medieval History*, i. 412.

41. *Earl.* Sigurd.

44. *King.* Brian.

THE DESCENT OF ODIN

See introductory matter and explanatory notes to *The Fatal Sisters*. Gray's paraphrase of the Icelandic was written, like *The Fatal Sisters*, in 1761 and based largely on a Latin translation from Bartholinus, which is reprinted in *M.* Mason (ii. 103–4) appended additional notes culled from the *CB* and here indicated as *GM*. Mitford summarizes the legendary background of the poem as follows: '. . . Balder, one of the sons of Odin, was informed that he should soon die. Upon his communication of his dream, the other gods, finding it true, by consulting the oracles, agreed to ward off the approaching danger, and sent Frigga to exact an oath from every thing not to injure Balder. She, however, overlooked the Misletoe, with a branch of which he was afterwards slain by Hoder, at the instigation of Lok [ON *Lokr*, often translated as *Lok, Loki,* or *Loke*]. After the execution of this commission, Odin, still alarmed for the life of his son, called another council; and hearing nothing but divided opinions among the gods, to consult the Prophetess, "he up-rose with speed". Vali, or Ali, the son of Rinda, afterwards avenged the death of Balder, by slaying Hoder, and is called a "wondrous boy, because he killed his enemy, before he was a day old; before he had washed his face, combed his hair, or seen one setting-sun". See Herbert's Icelandic Translations, p. 45.'

The original title is *Baldrs Draumar* ('Balder's Dreams') in the Codex Arna-magnaeanus, no. 748, the only ancient source. In paper MSS., the first of which dates from 1670, the title is *Vegtamskviða* ('The Ballad of Vegtam', a name meaning 'Traveller' assumed by Odin in the poem). It is clear that the first section is missing from the Codex, which has only one stanza before *Upp reis Oðinn*, &c. To remedy this defect, between 1643 (when Bishop Sveinsson dis-covered the *Codex Regius*) and 1670, some scholar, whom Vigfusson and Powell (*Corpus Poeticum Boreale*, i. 181) 'guess' to have been Paul Hallson (*ob.* 1662), made an introduction, giving in brief form the story repeated above of the threat to Balder's life and the exaction of a pledge from all things not to harm him.

A literal translation of the Latin version by Bartholinus upon which Gray relied is as follows (the line numbers correspond to those in Mason, ii. 101–2):

> Odin sprang up
> Greatest of men
> And Sleipner
> With the saddle decked.
> Down he rode   5
> Toward Niflhel.
> On the road he met the Whelp
> Coming up from the dwellings of Hela
> Spattered with blood were his
> Breast in front   10
> Gaping mouth that longs to bite
> And lower jaw:
> He barked
> And snarled
> At the Father of Sorcery,   15
> And long he barked.
> Odin rode on
> (The earth shook beneath)
> Until he came to the deep
> Dwelling of Hela.   20
> Then Odin rode
> To the Eastern Side of the gate
> Where the Prophetess'
> Grave he knew to lie.
>   To the Wise Woman incantations   25
> That arouse the dead he chanted,
> He looked to the North
> He traced letters [on the grave]
> He began to utter speech
> He demanded answers   30
> Until she arose, despite her desire,
> And spoke in the language of the dead.
> PROPHETESS. What one of men
> To me of no account
> Presumes to make my   35

Soul unhappy?
With snow have I
Been blanketed, and lashed with rain
Bedewed with gentle drops
Long have I lain dead.   40
ODIN. I am called Traveller
The Son of Warrior am I.
Relate to me what things are being done in the dwellings of Hela:
I (will tell) you what things on earth.
For whom are these seats covered with gold,   45
Beautiful couches,
With gold adorned?
PR. Here for Balder mead
Already prepared, is set forth,
A Pure Potion   50
But a shield has been placed over it.
Surely the divine offspring
Will be affected by pain.
These words I have spoken against my will,
And now I will cease to speak.   55
O[DIN]. Do not, O Prophetess, remain silent.
I desire to question you
Until I shall know all.
I still desire to know
Who unto Balder   60
Will bring death,
And the Son of Odin
Deprive of life?
PR. Hoder* bears aloft
In honour his Brother to this place.   65
He unto Balder
Will bring death,
And the Son of Odin
Will deprive of life.
These words I have spoken against my will,   70
And now I will remain silent.
O[DIN]. Do not, O Prophetess, remain silent.
I still wish to question you
Until I shall know all.
I still desire to know   75
Who unto Hoder*
Will requite the hatred
Or the murderer of Balder
Will make ready for the pyre by killing him.
PR. Rinda will bring forth a Son   80
In the dwellings of the West:
He, the Son of Odin,

* In Mason *Hodus*.

When only one night old, will use weapons;
He shall not wash his hand
Nor comb his head   85
Until he has placed on the pyre
The enemy of Balder.
These words have I spoken against my will,
And now I will remain silent.
O[DIN]. Do not remain silent, O Prophetess,   90
Still I wish to ask you
Who the Virgins are
Who because of Thoughts weep
And to the Sky cast
The robes from their shoulders?   95
This one thing you must tell me,
For you shall not sleep until you do.
PR. You are no Traveller,
As I formerly believed;
But rather Odin,   100
Greatest of Men.
O[DIN]. No Prophetess are you,
Nor Woman of Wisdom,
But rather of three
Giants the Mother.   105
PR. Ride home, Odin,
And glory in this:
No one in like fashion shall come
To seek knowledge
Until Lok   110
Shall be freed from bonds
And to the Twilight of the Gods
The Destroyers shall come.

Motto: *gautr* is of uncertain meaning.

2. *steed. Shipner* was the Horse of Odin, wch had eight legs. *Gray (CB).* This
is probably a slip of the pen for the more usual *Sleipner* or *Spleipnir.*

‡4. *Hela* [the Latinized form of ON *Hel*]. *Niflheimr,* the hell of the Gothic
nations, consisted of nine worlds, to which were devoted all such as died of
sickness, old-age, or by any other means, than in battle: over it presided *Hela*, the
Goddess of death. *Gray.* [See note to l. 16 below.] *Hela* is described with a
dreadful countenance, & her body half flesh-colour & half blew. *Gray (CB).*

5. *Dog.* The Edda gives this dog the name of Managarmar; he fed upon the
lives of those that were to die. *M.* Mason is mistaken here. The dog who guards
the gate of Hel is Garm (ON *Garmr*). Managarm (ON *Managarmr,* 'Moon-
hound') is another name of Hati, one of the two wolves, offspring of an unnamed
giantess, who pursue the sun and moon and who will devour them at the end of
the world ('the Ragna-rok' is a more exact term). See Snorri, *Gylfaginning,* ch. xii.
Because these wolves are spoken of as *Fenriss kindir* in *Voluspa,* l. 111, it is

sometimes stated that Fenrir is their father; however, other editors and commentators believe that the phrase is merely a kenning for 'wolves'. (Cf. Snorri, *Gylfaginning*, ch. xii.)

16. *portals nine.* The ancient literature does not give a specific number. Gray, as his note on Hela (l. 4) indicates, thought that the underworld of Norse mythology comprised nine 'worlds' (i.e. regions). This belief apparently rests on Snorri's statement (*Gylfaginning*, ch. xxxiv) that Odin gave Hel 'power over nine worlds'. However, this would seem more likely to refer to the nine worlds that composed the universe as mentioned in *Voluspa*, st. 2 (Asgard, the world of the Æsir; Vanaheim, the world of the Vanir; Alfheim, the world of the elves; Midgard, the world of Men; Jotunheim, the world of the giants; Muspellsheim, the world of fire; Svartalfaheim, the world of the black elves [dwarfs?]; Niflheim, the world of the dead; and a ninth that seems to have no name). In other words, it is a poetic statement of the common Germanic belief in the mortality of the physical world and all its inhabitants—all are in the power of the Goddess of Death. The editors have not been able to determine whether Gray got the idea directly from Snorri or from some secondary source.

24. The original word is *Vallgaldr*; from *Valr* mortuus, & *Galdr* incantatio. GM.

27. There are no superscriptions indicating the speakers in the original.

37. In the original, Odin says that he is Vegtam ('Traveller'), son of Valtam ('Fighter'). Odin frequently assumed false names.

52. *Prophetess.* Women were looked upon by the Gothic nations as having a peculiar insight into futurity; and some there were that made profession of magic arts and divination. These travelled round the country, and were received in every house with great respect and honour. Such a woman bore the name of Volva[,] Seidkona[,] or Spakona. The dress of Thorbiorga, one of these prophetesses, is described at large in Eirick's Rauda Sogu [*Eiriks Saga Rauða*, ch. iv], (apud Bartholin. lib. i. cap. iv. p. 688.) She had on a blue vest spangled all over with stones, a necklace of glass beads, and a cap made of the skin of a black lamb lined with white cat-skin. She leaned on a staff adorned with brass, with a round head set with stones; and was girt with a Hunlandish belt, at which hung her pouch full of magical instruments. Her buskins were of rough calf-skin, bound on with thongs studded with knobs of brass, and her gloves of white cat-skin, the fur turned inwards, &c. GM.

65. *Boy.* Vali, son of Odin by Rind (ON *Rindr*).

66. Vows not to clip or comb one's hair are not uncommon in Germanic literature.

75. *Virgins.* These were probably the Nornir or Parcæ [Fates], just now mentioned: their names were Urda, Verdandi, and Skulda; they were the dispensers of good destinies. As their names signify Time past, present, and future, it is probable they were always invisible to mortals: therefore when Odin asks this question on seeing them, he betrays himself to be a God; which elucidates the next speech of the Prophetess. *M.* Mason's identification of the 'Virgins' with the Norns is unlikely, although this may well have been what Gray thought

the lines implied. The Norns dwell in heaven, in a palace by the Well of Urdr (Snorri, *Gylfaginning*, ch. xv). Later editors and translators seem to agree that the words refer to the waves and that the text as we have it is corrupt. For example, Vigfusson and Powell (*Corpus Poeticum Boreale*, i. 499) think that a conundrum, to which 'the waves' is the answer, has somehow replaced the original text: Henry A. Bellows in *The Poetic Edda* (New York, 1923) also adopts the explanation that the waves, the daughters of Ægir, the God of the Sea, are meant; however, he credits Bugge with the explanation and is content merely to say that the original lines are obscure and that there may be 'a hiatus' here.

86. In the Latin 'Mater trium Gigantum'. He means, therefore, probably Angerbode, who, from her name, seems to be 'no Prophetess of good', and who bore to Loke, as the Edda says, three children; the Wolf Fenris, the great Serpent of Midgard, and Hela, all of them called Giants. . . . *M*. Mason has jumped to two conclusions to arrive at this note. The Latin *trium gigantum mater* is a literal rendering of the *þriggia þursa móðir*, but there is no clear proof in the original that the Prophetess is a giantess and even less that Angrboda is specifically meant. Because the meaning of the passage is so obscure, the present editors thought that the 'three giants' might be a kenning-like allusion to the three responses that the Prophetess has given; however, Professor Ursula Brown does not believe that such a meaning of *þurs* can be sustained from its uses in other ON literature.

‡90. *Lok*. *Lok* is the evil Being, who continues in chains, till the *Twilight of the Gods* approaches, when he shall break his bonds; the human race, the stars, & sun, shall disappear; the earth sink in the seas, & fire consume the skies: even Odin himself & his kindred-Deities shall perish. for a farther explanation of this mythology, see Mallet's Introduction to the History of Denmark, 1755. 4ᵗᵒ. *Gray*. (A slightly more detailed draft of this note is in *CB*.)

91–94. If we had only the poem on which to base a judgement, we should think that Gray had here rendered the original (*ragna rök*) more accurately than Bartholinus, who, like many early students of the Old Norse literature, confuses *rök* ('doom's-day' or 'final judgement') with *rökr* ('twilight'). See Cleasby and Vigfusson, *Icelandic–English Dictionary*, s.v. *rökr*. Unfortunately, his note to l. 90 indicates that he accepted Bartholinus's mis-translation (see translation of Bartholinus above, ll. 112–13).

THE TRIUMPHS OF OWEN

The poem was probably written in 1760 or 1761 (see T & W, Appendix M); and, as when writing the *Death of Hoël*, Gray relied mainly upon a Latin translation by Evan Evans of Gwalchmai's *Ode to Owen Gwynned*. In his notes (ii. 104–5) Mason prints Evans's English version (which probably Gray had also seen in MS.) from *Some Specimens of the Poetry of Antient Welsh Bards*, p. 25, with this comment, '. . . it will appear that nothing is omitted, except a single hyperbole at the end, which I print in italics':

Panegyric upon Owain Gwynedd, Prince of North-Wales, by
Gwalchmai, the son of Melir, in the year 1157.

1. I will extol the generous Hero, descended from the race of Roderic, the
bulwark of his country; a prince eminent for his good qualities, the glory of
Britain, Owen the brave and expert in arms, a Prince that neither hoardeth
nor coveteth riches.

2. Three fleets arrived, vessels of the main; three powerful fleets of the first rate,
furiously to attack him on the sudden: one from Jwerddon [*Mason's note*: Ire-
land], the other full of well-armed Lochlynians [*Mason's note*: Danes and Nor-
mans], making a grand appearance on the floods, the third from the transmarine
Normans, which was attended with an immense, though successless toil.

3. The Dragon of Mona's Sons was so brave in action, that there was a great
tumult on their furious attack; and before the Prince himself there was vast
confusion, havoc, conflict, honourable death, bloody battle, horrible con-
sternation, and upon Tal Malvre a thousand banners; there was an outrageous
carnage, and the rage of spears and hasty signs of violent indignation. Blood
raised the tide of the Menäi, and the crimson of human gore stained the brine.
There were glittering cuirasses, and the agony of gashing wounds, and the
mangled warriors prostrate before the chief, distinguished by his crimson
lance. Lloegria was put into confusion; the contest and confusion was great;
*and the glory of our Prince's wide-wasting sword shall be celebrated in an
hundred languages to give him his merited praise.*

There is, incidentally, a translation of a Welsh epitaph on Prince Madoc 'by a
young lady . . . daughter of . . . a divine of the Church of England . . . [wife of]
a young gentleman of Gl[amo]rganshire' in the *Gentleman's Magazine*, x (1740),
409, which illustrates the contemporary interest in medieval Welsh:

Here lies the mighty Owen's Heir
In glorious Death, as well as Birth.
I scorn'd of Lands the menial Care,
And sought thro' Seas a foreign Earth.

Advertisement. Owen (Owain, d. 1170) succeeded his father in 1137, not 1120.
The date of the battle is 1157.

3. *Roderic*. Rhodri Mawr (Roderick the Great), king of Gwynedd, A.D. 844–78.

‡4. *Gwyneth* [Gwynned or Gwynedd]. N[orth]: Wales. *Gray*.

‡14. *Lochlin*. Denmark. *Gray*.

15. *Norman*. Warriors from Norway, not northern France.

‡20. *The Dragon-Son*. The red Dragon is the device of Cadwallader, wch all
his Descendents bore on their banners. *Gray*.   *Mona*. Anglesey.

25. *Talymalfra*. Moelfre, a small bay on the north-east coast of Anglesey. *Br*.

28. *Meinai*. The Menai Strait.

31. From this line to the end, most of the poem is Gray's work entirely, for
very little of the material appears in the original.

ELEGY WRITTEN IN A COUNTRY CHURCH YARD

Although Mason believed that the poem was begun as early as 1742, most scholars date its composition between 1745 and 1750. (For a detailed discussion see T & W, Appendix I, pp. 1214–16, and Stokes's edition of the *Elegy*.) Gray sent a copy to Walpole, who appears to have circulated it rather freely. In any event, to Gray's annoyance an imperfect copy was acquired by a journal which he disliked; consequently he wrote to Walpole (11 Feb. 1751, T & W no. 157): 'As you have brought me into a little Sort of Distress, you must assist me, I believe, to get out of it, as well as I can. yesterday I had the Misfortune of receiving a Letter from certain Gentlemen (as their Bookseller expresses it) who have taken the *Magazine of Magazines* into their Hands. they tell me, that an *ingenious* Poem, call'd *Reflections* in a Country-Churchyard, has been communicated to them, wch they are printing forthwith: that they are inform'd, that the *excellent* Author of it is I by name, & that they beg not only his *Indulgence*, but the *Honor of his Correspondence*, &c: as I am not at all disposed to be either so indulgent, or so correspondent, as they desire; I have but one bad Way left to escape the Honour they would inflict upon me. & therefore am obliged to desire you would make Dodsley print it immediately (wch may be done in less than a Week's time) from your Copy, but without my Name, in what Form is most convenient for him, but in his best Paper & Character. he must correct the Press himself. . . if he would add a Line or two to say it came into his Hands by Accident, I should like it better. . . . If you behold the Mag: of Mag:^s in the Light that I do, you will not refuse to give yourself this Trouble on my Account, wch you have taken of your own Accord before now. . . . If Dodsley don't do this immediately, he may as well let it alone.' Dodsley brought out the first edition of the *Elegy*, anonymously, on 15 Feb., one day before the *Magazine of Magazines* printed it with the author named as Mr. Gray of Peterhouse. Walpole prefaced to the first edition this statement:

Advertisement.

The following POEM *came into my hands by Accident, if the general Approbation with which this little Piece has been spread, may be call'd by so slight a term as Accident. It is this Approbation which makes it unnecessary for me to make any Apology but to the Author: As he cannot but feel some Satisfaction in having pleas'd so many Readers already, I flatter myself he will forgive my communicating that Pleasure to many more.*

The EDITOR.

Despite his sensitivity to the criticisms of his friends, Gray expressed considerable indifference to the opinions of the reading public in general (T & W no. 156, to Wharton, 18 Dec. 1750): 'On the other hand the Stanza's [the *Elegy*], wch I now enclose to you, have had the Misfortune by M^r W[alpole]:^s Fault to be made still more publick, for wch they certainly were never meant, but it is too late to complain. they have been so applauded, it is quite a Shame to repeat it. I mean not to be modest; but I mean, it is a Shame for those, who have said such superlative Things about them, that I can't repeat them. I should have been glad, that you & two or three more People had liked them, wch would have satisfied my ambition on this Head amply.' Mason, although the accuracy of his statement is open to some suspicion, claimed to be responsible for the title: 'I persuaded him first to call it an ELEGY, because the subject authorized him so to do; and the alternate measure, in which it was written, seemed peculiarly fit for that species of composition. I imagined too that so capital a Poem, written in this measure, would as it were appropriate it in future to writings of this sort; and the number of imitations which have since been made of it (even to satiety) seem to prove that my notion was well founded' (*M*, ii. 108).

There have been innumerable notes designed to explain the meaning or to indicate the sources of the *Elegy*. It seems to the editors unnecessary to repeat them here. The editions of Mitford, Bradshaw, and Tovey are rich in material of this sort, and the bibliographies of Northup and Starr list many additional sources.

‡1. *tolls*. [Era gia l' ora, che volge 'l disio
    A' naviganti, e 'ntenerisce 'l cuore
    Lo dì ch' han detto a' dolci amici addio:
    E che lo nuovo peregrin d' amore
    Punge, se ode] squilla di lontano,
    Che paia 'l giorno pianger, che si muore.

[(It was already the hour which turns back the desire
    Of the sailors, and melts their hearts,
    The day that they have said good-bye to their sweet friends,
    And which pierces the new pilgrim with love,
    If he hears) from afar the bell
    Which seems to mourn the dying day.]

                      Dante. Purgat. 8. [i–vi.] *Gray.*

35. *Awaits . . . hour*. The subject of the verb *awaits* is *hour*. Such inverted structure is fairly common in Gray's verse.

53–56. Many parallels have been cited for this passage. Perhaps the closest (*if* Gray had read it, and the concept and phrasing are not unusual) is the one by Celio Magno (1536–1602) cited in O. Shepard and P. S. Woods, eds., *English Prose and Poetry, 1660–1800* (Boston, 1934), pp. 1007–8:

    Ma (qual in parte ignota
    Ben ricca gemma altrui cela il suo pregio,
    O fior, ch' alta virtù ha in se riposta
    Visse in sen di castità nascosta,)
    In sua virtute e 'n Dio contento visse,
    Lunge dal visco mondan, che l' alma intrica.

[But (as in an unknown place
    A very rich gem conceals its value from its neighbour,
    Or a flower, which has great virtue reposed in it,
    Has lived hidden in the bosom of chastity,)
    He lived content in his virtue and in God
    Far from the worldly birdlime which entangles the soul.]

57. *Hampden*. John Hampden (1594–1643).

63 ff. See *The Alliance of Education and Government*, ll. 17–18, and *Agrippina*, l. 77.

73. *madding.* Wild, furious. See *Agrippina*, ll. 83–84.

‡92.   Ch'i veggio nel pensier, dolce mio fuoco,
                       Fredda una lingua, & due begli occhi chiusi
                       Rimaner doppo noi pien di faville.

                       [For I see in my thoughts, my sweet fire,
                       One cold tongue, and two beautiful closed eyes
                       Will remain full of sparks after our death.]
                             Petrarch. Son. 169 [170 in usual enumeration]. *Gray.*

93–94. *thee ... tale.* The 'thee' who relates the 'artless tale' is somewhat ambiguous. Presumably Gray is referring to the unnamed individual who is writing the *Elegy*, but he may have had in mind merely an idealized rustic poet who is described in the succeeding stanzas. When he first began the poem it is likely that he had the former interpretation in mind, but as he revised it over a rather long period he may have changed his views and also, because of the very intensity of the care which he lavished on minor revisions, may very likely have overlooked the ambiguous reference of 'thee'.

100 ff. See textual notes. Mason adds, concerning the rejected stanza: 'I rather wonder that he rejected this stanza, as it not only has the same sort of Doric delicacy, which charms us peculiarly in this part of the Poem, but also compleats the account of his whole day: whereas, this Evening scene being omitted, we have only his Morning walk, and his Noon-tide repose' (*M*, ii. 110).

116 ff. See textual notes. Mason says of this 'redbreast' stanza: 'Between this line [l. 116] and the Epitaph, Mr. Gray originally inserted a very beautiful stanza, which was printed in some of the first editions, but afterwards omitted; because he thought (and in my own opinion very justly) that it was too long a parenthesis in this place. The lines however are, in themselves, exquisitely fine, and demand preservation' (*M*. ii. 110–11).

118. See Gray's translation *From Propertius, To Mecænas*, Lib. II, El. 1, l. 65, and *Agrippina*, ll. 38–39.

‡127.——paventosa speme [——fearful hope]. *Petrarch. Son.* 114 [115 in usual enumeration]. *Gray.*

A LONG STORY

The Dowager Viscountess Cobham, whose father had bought the Manor House at Stoke Poges, when she learned that the author of the *Elegy* was a neighbour, sent two friends, Miss Henrietta Jane Speed (later the Countess de Viry) and Lady Schaub, the French wife of Sir Luke Schaub, to call on Gray. Since he was not at home, they left a note, and Gray returned the call. A friendship quickly developed, and as a result Gray wrote this poem. Gray wrote to Beattie (T & W no. 457) concerning the omission of the poem from Dodsley's *P*: '[I] added, that I would send him a few explanatory notes, & if he would omitt entirely the *Long Story* (wch was never meant for the publick, & only suffer'd to appear in that pompous edition [*B*] because of Mr Bentley's designs, wch were not intelligible without it) I promised to send him some thing else to print instead of it. . . .' Although *CB* is dated Aug. 1750, Gray must still have been revising the poem as late as October, as his note to l. 120 indicates. For further details concerning the individuals mentioned see T & W, pp. 330–4. As Mason and Mitford note, the style owes a marked debt to Prior.

3. *Huntingdons*. The Earl of Huntingdon rebuilt the manor in the time of Elizabeth. It was later held by the Hatton family, but it is not certain that Sir Christopher Hatton lived there.

6. *achievements*. Representations of (heraldic) arms.

‡11. *Lord-Keeper*. [Sir Christopher] Hatton [Lord Chancellor], prefer'd by Queen Elizabeth for his graceful Person and fine Dancing. *Gray*. *Brawls*. Brawls were a sort of figure-dance, then in vogue, and probably deemed as elegant as our modern Cotillions, or still more modern Quadrilles. *M*.

12. *Seal, and Maces*. The symbols of Sir Christopher's office borne before him by subordinates.

23. *buff*. A military coat, usually whitish-yellow, originally made of ox-hide. Here there is also a pun on the other meaning of *buff*—bare skin.

25. *The first*. Lady Schaub.

29. *The other*. Miss Speed, who had been brought up by the Cobhams.

35. *Melissa*. A kindly enchantress in Ariosto's *Orlando Furioso*.

37. *capucine*. A hooded cloak.

41. *Mr. P - - - t*. [Robert Purt, Rector of Settrington.] I have been told that this Gentleman, a neighbour and acquaintance of Mr. Gray's in the country, was much displeased at the liberty here taken with his name; yet, surely, without any great reason. *M*.

80. Fancy is here so much blended with the humour, that I believe the two stanzas, which succeed this line, are amongst those which are the least relished by the generality. The description of the spell, I know, has appeared to many persons absolutely unintelligible; yet if the reader adverts to that peculiar idea which runs through the whole, I imagine the obscurity complained of will be removed. An incident, we see, so slight as the simple matter of fact, required something like machinery to enliven it: Accordingly the author chose, with propriety enough, to employ for that purpose those notions of witchcraft, ghosts, and enchantment, which prevailed at the time when the mansion-house was built. He describes himself as a daemon of the lowest class, *a wicked imp who lamed the deer*, &c. against whose malevolent power Lady Cobham (the Gloriana of the piece) employs two superior enchantresses. Congruity of imagery, therefore, required the card they left upon the table to be converted into a spell. Now all the old writers, on these subjects, are very minute in describing the materials of such talismans. Hence, therefore, his grotesque idea of a composition of transparent bird-lime, edged with invisible chains in order to catch and draw him to the tribunal. Without going further for examples of this kind of imagery than the Poet's own works, let me instance two passages of the serious kind, similar to this ludicrous one. In his Ode, entitled the Bard,

'Above, below, the rose of snow, &c.'

And, again, in the Fatal Sisters,

'See the griesly texture grow.'

It must, however, be allowed, that no person can fully relish this burlesque, who is not much conversant with the old romance-writers, and with the Poets who formed themselves on their model. *M.*

‡103. *Styack*. The House-Keeper. *Gray*. Bradshaw notes that in the Sharpe, 1826, edition it is pointed out that the name on her gravestone is Tyacke, and that Gray probably on hearing the name 'Mrs. Tyacke' understood it to be 'Mrs. Styack'.

‡115. *Squib*. [James Squibb] Groom of the Chambers. *Gray*. See textual note to l. 115.

‡116. *Groom*. The Steward. *Gray*.

‡120. *Macleane*. A famous Highwayman hang'd the week before. *Gray*. James Maclean, a spectacular robber who once almost killed Horace Walpole, when asked by the judge if he had anything to say, could only reply, 'My Lord, I cannot speak.' Since he was hanged on 3 Oct. 1750, Gray's note indicates that he was still engaged in at least the revision of the poem at that time. See textual note to l. 120.

129. *hagged*. [T]he face of a witch or Hag; the epithet Hagard has been sometimes mistaken, as conveying the same idea; but it means a very different thing, viz. wild and farouche, and is taken from an unreclaimed Hawk, called an Hagard; in which its proper sense the Poet uses it finely on a sublime occasion:

> Cloath'd in the sable garb of woe,
> With hagard eyes the Poet stood.
>
> Vid. Ode 6th [*Bard*]. *M.*

133. Here the story finishes; the exclamation of the Ghosts which follows is characteristic of the Spanish manners of the age, when they are supposed to have lived; and the 500 stanzas [see l. 140 below], said to be lost may be imagined to contain the remainder of their long-winded expostulation. *M.*

140. *500 Stanzas*. In her letter of thanks (T & W no. 155) Miss Speed wrote: '. . . and Lady Cobham was the first, tho' not the last that regretted the loss of the 400 stanzas. . . .' The *400* may be a slip of the pen or the figure in a lost first draft.

ODE FOR MUSIC

Augustus Henry Fitzroy (1735–1811), third Duke of Grafton and Prime Minister, in July 1768 had obtained the Regius Professorship of Modern History at Cambridge for Gray, probably through the prompting of Gray's friend Richard Stonhewer, who was Grafton's private secretary (although the Duchess later said that the appointment was her husband's unsolicited gift). Grafton was elected Chancellor of the University in Nov. 1768; and, although Gray disliked occasional poetry, he felt that gratitude obliged him to offer, unasked, to write the ode to be performed when Grafton was installed on 1 July 1769. He finished the poem, the last one he wrote, in April. He wrote to Stonhewer (12 June 1769, T & W no. 497): '. . . as somebody was necessarily to do this, I did not see why Gratitude should sit silent and leave it to Expectation to sing, who certainly would have sung, and that *à gorge deployée* ['with an open throat', 'excessively'] upon such an occasion.' Gray did not have a high opinion of the poem, as he told

Beattie (16 July 1769, T & W no. 501): 'I do not think them worth sending you, because they are by nature doom'd to live but a single day, or if their existence is prolong'd beyond that date, it is only by means of news-paper parodies, & witless criticism. this sort of abuse I had reason to expect, but did not think it worth while to avoid it.' His expectations were fulfilled when the following item appeared in the *London Chronicle* of 27–29 July:

As a certain Church-yard Poet has deviated from the principles he once profest, it is very fitting that the necessary alterations should be made in his epitaph.—*Marcus.*

EPITAPH

Here rests his head upon the lap of earth,
　　One nor to fortune nor to fame unknown;
Fair science frown'd not on his humble birth,
　　And smooth-tongued flatt'ry mark'd him for her own.

Large was his wish—in this he was sincere—
　　Fate did a recompence as largely send,
Gave the poor C[u]r four hundred pounds a year,
　　And made a d[irt]y Minister his friend.

No further seek his deeds to bring to light,
　　For, ah! he offer'd at Corruption's shrine;
And basely strove to wash an Ethiop white,
　　While Truth and Honour bled in ev'ry line.

See also Nicholls's *Reminiscences*, T & W, Appendix Z, pp. 1300–1. For poetic echoes, especially of Milton, see Mitford, Bradshaw, and Tovey.

11. See the *Eton* ode, l. 3.

14. *th' indignant lay.* The previous verses which the poet feigns to have heard said by sages and bards as they look down on their old University, 'indignant' lest Comus, Ignorance, etc., should profane the 'holy ground'. *Br.*

18. *accomp.* Stanza 2 [is] 'Recitative' throughout, but accompanied at the sixth line. *M.* This means that though the recitative was held the next nine lines were also accompanied. *Phelps and Tv.*

21. See *Alliance of Education and Government*, l. 12.

27. *brown.* Shadowy.

27–34. This stanza, being supposed to be sung by Milton, is very judiciously written in the metre which he fixed upon for the stanza of his Christmas-hymn. 'Twas in [It was] the winter wild, &c. [*On the Morning of Christ's Nativity: The Hymn*, l. 29] *M.*

39. *Edward.* Edward the Third [1312–77]; who added the fleur de lys of France to the arms of England. He founded Trinity College. *M.* He actually founded King's Hall, which much later was one of the foundations consolidated into Trinity.

41. *Chatillon*. Mary de Valentia [Marie de Castillon], Countess of Pembroke, daughter of Guy de Chatillon Comte de St. Paul in France; of whom tradition says, that her husband Audemar de Valentia [Aymer de Valence], Earl of Pembroke, was slain at a Tournament on the day of his nuptials. She was the Foundress of Pembroke College or Hall, under the name of Aula Mariæ de Valentia. *M.*

42. *Clare*. Elizabeth de Burg, Countess of Clare, was Wife of John de Burg, son and heir of the Earl of Ulster, and daughter of Gilbert de Clare, Earl of Gloucester, by Joan of Acres, daughter of Edward the First. Hence the Poet gives her the epithet of 'Princely'. She founded [actually rebuilt] Clare Hall. *M.*

43. *Anjou's Heroine*. Margaret of Anjou [1430?–82], wife of Henry the Fifth [Sixth], foundress of Queen's College. The Poet has celebrated her conjugal fidelity in the former Ode: V: Epode 2d, Line 13th [*Bard*, l. 89]. *M.*   *the paler Rose*. Elizabeth Widville [Woodville, *c.* 1437–92], wife of Edward the Fourth (hence called the paler rose, as being of the House of York). She added to the foundation of Margaret of Anjou. *M.*

45. *Henry*. Henry the Sixth [1421–71] and Eighth [1491–1547]. The former the founder of King's, the latter the greatest benefactor to Trinity College. *M.*

46. *Saint*. See *Eton* ode, l. 4, and *Bard*, l. 90.

48. See note to l. 18.

51. *Granta*. A name for the River Cam, especially the upper portion.

54. *Fitzroy*. Grafton, so named because of his illegitimate descent—see note to l. 70.

66. *Marg'ret*. Countess of Richmond and Derby; the Mother of Henry the Seventh, foundress of St. John's and Christ's Colleges. *M.*

70. The Countess was a Beaufort, and married to a Tudor: hence the application of this line to the Duke of Grafton, who claims descent from both these families [by way of an illegitimate child of Charles II]. *M.*

84. *Cecil*. [William Cecil (1520–98), first Lord Burghley.] Lord Treasurer Burleigh was Chancellor of the University [1559], in the reign of Q. Elizabeth. *M.*

EPITAPH ON MRS. CLERKE

Jane Clerke (1726–57), the wife of John Clerke (1717–90), Fellow of Pembroke and later a physician at Epsom, died in childbirth, according to Gosse (although Tovey questions the circumstance). Her husband presumably asked Gray to write the epitaph.

ON LORD HOLLAND'S SEAT NEAR MARGATE, KENT

Henry Fox (1705–74), first Lord Holland, a dissipated and corrupt politician, during his career was Secretary of State and Paymaster of the Forces. An ally of the Earl of Bute for a time, he finally was deserted by his political adherents. He specifically denounced Rigby, Shelburne, and Calcraft in a caustic poem, *Lord Holland Returning from Italy*, privately printed, 1767. Although personally a rather attractive man, he was probably the most thoroughly hated statesman of the age and consequently much embittered in his last years. He built an imitation classical villa at Kingsgate near Margate and constructed many artificial ruins (which became much more extensive when some of the buildings collapsed accidentally) near the villa. Gray wrote the poem while on a visit to Robinson at Denton, Kent, in the summer of 1768 and by an oversight left it in his dressing-table; it was returned to him later. He clearly wished it kept secret, for he wrote to Mason (T & W no. 489, 29 Dec. 1768), who must have mentioned or shown it: 'Oh wicked Scroddles! there you have gone & told my *Arcanum Arcanorum* to that leaky Mortal Palgrave [see explanatory notes to *Invitation to Mason*], who never conceals any thing he is trusted with; & there have I been forced to write to him, & (to bribe him to silence) have told him, how much I confided in his taciturnity, & twenty lies beside, the guilt of wch must fall on you at the last account. seriously you have done very wrong . . . hitherto luckily nobody has taken any notice of it, nor (I hope) ever will.' The text used by Mitford is almost certainly corrupt and the identifications he suggests (see textual note to l. 18) incorrect. For a detailed account of the poem see T & W, Appendix T, and Whibley, *TLS*, 9 Oct. 1930, p. 805.

6. *Godwin . . . sand.* The Goodwin Sands at the entrance to the Straits of Dover, according to tradition, mark a sunken island, Lomea, which in the eleventh century belonged to the great Saxon Earl Godwin.

17. *Bute.* John Stuart (1713–92), third Earl of Bute, Secretary of State and Prime Minister. Holland was in his cabinet.

18. *Shelburn.* William Petty Fitzmaurice (1737–1805), second Earl of Shel-burne, first Marquis of Lansdowne, later First Lord of the Treasury, was originally a protégé of Bute. *Rigby.* Richard Rigby (1722–88), Vice-Treasurer of Ireland and then Paymaster of the Forces, was a notorious politician who first supported and later deserted Holland. *Calcraft.* John Calcraft (1726–72) was another politician of unsavoury repute, who, after being a follower of Holland, turned against him.

22. *London's hated walls.* Holland was particularly unpopular in London, where a petition later brought against several Ministers singled him out as 'the public defaulter of unaccounted millions'.

TRANSLATION OF A PASSAGE FROM STATIUS

Thebaid, vi. 646–88

Publius Papinius Statius (*c.* A.D. 45–96) in his epic *Thebais* celebrated the un-successful legendary expedition of the Seven (Adrastus, Polynices, Tydeus, Amphiaraus, Hippomedon, Capaneus, and Parthenopaeus) against Thebes, the object of which was to restore Polynices to the throne that his brother Eteocles (son of Oedipus) had usurped. Gray's translation was made in 1736.

1. *King.* Adrastus, King of Argos, was the only one of the Seven to survive the expedition.

5. *Pterelas.* A prince of Taphos, one of the Ionian Islands.

12. *Pisa*. A town in western Greece near the River Alpheus (*not* the Italian city). *Ephyre*. An old name for Corinth.

13. *Nesimachus's Son*. Hippomedon, one of the Seven.

30–31. See *Progress of Poesy*, ll. 52–53.

32. *Phlegyas*. Son of Mars, father of Ixion, and king of the Lapithæ.

35–45. Here the translation is unusually free even by the standards of this translation. Gray follows neither the sequence nor the association of Statius' phrases. A literal translation of Statius, vi. 668–84, follows: 'Phlegyas of Pisa begins the contest and at once draws all eyes to himself: so much promise of strength was there in the sight of his body. And first he roughens the discus and his hand with earth, then shakes off the dirt and turns the discus around, to see which part best suits his fingers and which fits more securely on the middle of his arm, not without skill: this sport he had always loved, not merely when he was attending the sacred games that brought fame to his country; but it was his regular habit to measure the distance between the opposite banks of the Alpheus and to hurl the discus over the waters where they were widest, without even wetting it. Therefore, confident of his abilities, he does not at once measure the rough acres of the plain, but the sky with his right arm, and after he had pressed both knees to the ground and gathered his strength, he whirls the discus above himself and hides it among the clouds. It flies aloft swiftly, and like one that is falling gains speed as it goes; then at last, exhausted, it returns more slowly to the ground from on high and buries itself in the fields.'

49–52. Here Gray renders but vaguely the paradoxical hyperbole of the original. Statius says, in effect, that the discus was hurled aloft with such force that it seemed to be falling when it was rising and that its fall back to earth seemed slow in contrast. See translation in note above.

58. *Æmonian Hag*. In Statius 'at Thessala victrix / ridet anhelantes audito carmine bigas'. (But the Thessalian woman who has conquered the moon [i.e. witch] laughs triumphantly at the panting steeds [of the moon-goddess] when they obey her spell.) Eclipses of the moon were popularly believed to be caused by Thessalian witches, who by their incantations could draw the moon from the sky. Aemonia is a variant of Haemonia, a poetic name of Thessaly.

TRANSLATION OF A PASSAGE FROM STATIUS

Thebaid, vi. 704–24

A copy of this passage was sent to West in May 1736, shortly after the poem had been written. Gray had also made a translation of ll. 689–703, but it is no longer extant. Mason comments (i. 9 n.) that here Gray is imitating 'Dryden's spirited manner'.

4. Gray apparently confused Menestheus, a Greek, with Mnestheus, a Trojan and friend of Aeneas. Mason may have made the error in transcribing, but the metre seems to require the incorrect *Mnestheus*. Although Phlegyas had done well in a preliminary attempt (see preceding translation, ll. 39–52), in his official throw the discus slipped from his hand and fell at his feet. Menestheus had made a fine throw (Statius, ll. 688–703).

23. Gray omits three lines of Statius (719–21) which are usually included in modern texts, but generally regarded as spurious.

TRANSLATION FROM STATIUS

Thebaid, ix. 319–26

The date of these verses is unknown, but their nature and Walpole's statement that they were written when Gray was very young suggest that they may have been a school exercise composed when he was at Eton (*c.* 1725–34). If so, they are probably his earliest extant English verse.

1. *Crenaeus*. The episode which these lines introduce seems to be the only account in Latin of the legend of this Crenaeus. Others of the same name are (1) a centaur mentioned by Ovid (*Metamorphoses*, xii. 313), (2) a brother of Hypsipyle murdered by the frenzied women of Lemnos (Statius, *Thebaid*, v. 221), and (3) a youth killed by the Argonauts (Valerius Flaccus, *Argonautica*, iii. 178).

14. *Whither*. Sixteenth–seventeenth-century variant of 'whether'.

TRANSLATION FROM TASSO

Torquato Tasso (1544–95) was the author of the Italian epic *Gerusalemme Liberata*, which dealt with the capture of Jerusalem by Godfrey of Bouillon during the First Crusade. The chief imaginary hero of the poem is Rinaldo d'Este.

In March 1737 Gray wrote that he was learning 'Italian like any dragon, and in two months am got through the 16th book of Tasso . . .' (T & W no. 37). Mason (i. 36–37 n.) states that the translation was made before Sept. 1738; and his opinion is confirmed by the date '1738' in *CB* (see textual notes).

1. *they*. Carlo the German and Ubaldo, who have been sent by Godfrey to recall Rinaldo to the Christian camp, which he had left as a result of a quarrel. The Saracen enchantress Armida had transported him to her bower of bliss.

12. *The wondrous Sage*. He is known simply as 'the good magician'.

DANTE

Ugolino della Gherardesca, count of Donoratico, was involved in the Guelf–Ghibelline struggles of thirteenth-century Italy and finally became the Guelf governor of Pisa. In 1288 the Ghibellines led by Archbishop Ruggieri degli Ubaldini revolted and during a parley which had been arranged with Ugolino incited a riot and treacherously seized him, his sons Gaddo and Uguccione, and his grandsons Ugolino and Anselmuccio. They were imprisoned and left to starve. When the bodies were examined they were found to be badly bitten by rats; in fact it was also suggested that the family had practised cannibalism, especially on the hands and arms. The theory has been advanced that Dante either attempted to explain the mutilations by Ugolino's biting of his own hands (ll. 63–64) or wished to suggest cannibalism directly (l. 81). The translation is a rather free one: many adjectives are added and the dream sequence has been enlarged. The only indication of the date of the translation is the comment prefixed to the Mitford version, but Gray had started to learn Italian late in 1736 or early in

1737 (see his letter to West, Mar. 1737, T & W no 37) and made the translation of Tasso in 1738. It seems probable that this poem was written at about the same time or a little later.

1. *Fellon.* Ugolino.

10. *thou.* Dante.

13–14. *Ruggieri . . . this.* The head on which Ugolino is gnawing is that of Archbishop Ruggieri.

30. *Lucca.* A Guelf city north-east of Pisa.

31. *Wolf.* Ugolino.

32–33. *Lanfranc . . . Sigismundo . . . Gualandi.* Leaders of the Ghibelline faction in Pisa.

35. *Chief.* Ruggieri.

69. *nor.* Probably a slip of the pen for *not* and so emended by Bradshaw.

79. *Hunger . . . my eyesight.* It was questioned in the nineteenth century that hunger could produce this effect, but some of the events of the Second World War indicate that it is quite possible.

IMITATED FROM PROPERTIUS: TO MECÆNAS

Sextus Propertius (*c.* 50 B.C.–post 15 B.C.), a friend of Virgil and Ovid, wrote amatory elegies to his mistress Hostia, who appears in his poems as Cynthia. His friend Gaius Cilnius Maecenas (b. 74–64 B.C., d. 8 B.C.) was a Roman statesman and a famous patron of letters. The correct number of the Elegy is 1. Gray sent the translation to West in a letter dated 23 Apr. 1742. He evidently had started the poem just after West had, unintentionally, discouraged him from proceeding with *Agrippina*.

9. *Coan.* A light transparent dress woven on the island of Cos, called by the Romans *coæ vestis* or *coa.* Cf. e.g. Horace, *Satires*, i. 2. 101–2: 'Cois tibi pæne videre est / Ut nudam. . . .' (In her Coan dress you can almost see her nude.)

31 ff. Maecenas is supposed to have attempted to divert Propertius from his customary poetic theme of love to subjects of more national interest.

34. *sculptured Carr.* The triumphal chariot. See note to ll. 47–52.

43–46. *Mutina* (43 B.C.) . . . *Sicily* (37–36 B.C.) . . . *Alexandria* (30 B.C.) . . . *Philippi* (42 B.C.). It is thought that Maecenas played some part in these victories of Octavian. During Actium, Maecenas was Octavian's vice-regent.

47–52. Here Propertius is describing a Roman triumph, during which the spectators shouted, 'Io (Hurrah) triumphe!' In celebration of a naval victory, the rams or prows of captured vessels might be displayed.

56. *Phlegra.* 'The place of burning' where the giants were blasted by a bolt of lightning while fighting against the gods.

62. *proper.* In the Latin sense of 'one's own' or 'appropriate'.

67–70. These lines are adapted from two lines (45–46) that Scaliger took from Propertius ii. 3 and inserted here. His text was followed by Broekhuyzen. West and Gray commented on the matter in T & W nos. 105–7. *T & W.*

81. *Melian . . . Machaon*. Philoctetes, a Malian, suffered for years from a snake bite which was cured only when he was brought to the Greek camp before Troy, where Machaon, the son of Aesculapius, healed him. Sophocles, *Philoctetes*, ll. 4–5, refers to Philoctetes as τὸν Μηλιᾶ / Ποίαντος υἱὸν [the Melian (i.e. Malian), son of Poeas]. Sophocles, whom Gray was probably following, uses the Old Attic Μηλιῆς (Μηλιᾶ is accusative); in later Attic the Doric form Μαλιεῖς was used (e.g. Aristotle, *Politics*, 4. 13. 9) and the same variation appears in the name of the district. Most modern works use the Doric forms (*Malis, Malian*).

83. Phoenix was blinded by his father, Amyntor, because he had won the affections of the latter's mistress. Phoenix fled to Peleus, and his sight was restored by Chiron, the centaur.

84. *Phoebus' Son*. Aesculapius often raised the dead, as he did in the case of Androgeon, son of Minos.

90. See explanatory note to *Imitated from Propertius, III, 5*, l. 47.

IMITATED FROM PROPERTIUS,

Lib: 3: Eleg: 5

In the *CB* the poem is dated Dec. 1738. See also explanatory notes to *From Propertius: To Mecænas*.

45. *Earth's monster-brood*. Certain of the 'venerable deities' (Titans, Cyclopes, Hecatoncheires, Giants) were imprisoned in the earth or in Tartarus.

46. *Alecto*. 'The unwearied pursuer', one of the Furies or Erinyes, whose function was to punish the guilty. Alecto's hair was formed of vipers.

47. *Tityus*. A giant condemned to Tartarus, where two vultures perpetually dined on his liver, which grew again after each meal. Prometheus suffered from a like inconvenience.

48. *triple dog*. Cerberus.

50. *pendent rock*. The rock of Sisyphus.

58. *Crassus*. Marcus Licinius Crassus (*c.* 115–53 B.C.) was crushingly defeated by the Parthians at Carrhae in 53 B.C. The standards (and some prisoners) were finally recovered by Augustus in 20 B.C.

THE DEATH OF HOËL

Aneurin (Aneirin, *fl. c.* 570–603) in the *Gododin* lamented the battle of Catraeth (probably Catterick or Cataractonium) in north-east Yorkshire, in which the army of his prince, Mynyddawg of Edinburgh, was defeated, *c.* 603, by the Saxons. None of the individuals mentioned in the poem can be identified. Gray's rendering of this passage was based, late in 1760 or in 1761, on the Latin translation of Aneurin sent to him by Evan Evans (published as *Some Specimens of the Poetry of the Antient Welsh Bards*, London, 1764), since his own knowledge of the Celtic languages was superficial. A literal translation of Evans's Latin follows:

> If it were permitted to me to work my will on the people of Deira,
> Like a flood I would overwhelm them all in a single slaughter;
> For recklessly I have lost a friend

Who was firm in resisting.
A man of great spirit, he sought no dowry from his father-in-law,
The son of Cian, sprung from vigorous Gwyngwyn.
Warriors went to Cattraeth, and they were glorious,
Wine and mead from golden cups was their drink,
Three hundred and sixty-three were distinguished by golden collars;
But of those who rushed into battle besotted with too much drink,
Only three came forth, who made a path with their swords,
The Warrior of Aeron and Conan Daearawd
And I myself (Aneurin the Bard) red with blood,
Else I should not have survived to compose this song.

3. *Deïra*. A northern Saxon kingdom near and to the east of the city of York.

12. *Twice*. The exact figure given by Evans is 363. See above.

CARADOC

The date when Gray wrote *Caradoc* and *Conan* is not known, but it was probably about the time when he produced his other Welsh poems—1760 or 1761 (see T & W, Appendix M). Mason (ii. 106) introduces the poems with this explanation: 'I find amongst Mr. Gray's papers, a few more lines taken from other parts of the Gododin [of Aneurin, *fl. c.* A.D. 570–603], which I shall here add with their respective Latin versions [from Evan Evans]. They may serve to shew succeeding Poets the manner in which the spirit of these their antient predecessors in the Art may best be translated into a modern imitation of them.' The Latin version is as follows:

> Quando ad Bellum properabat Caradocus,
> Filius apri silvestris qui truncando mutilavit Hostes,
> Taurus aciei in pugnae conflictu.
> Is lignum (i.e. hastam) ex manu contorsit.
>
> [When Caradoc was rushing into Battle,
> The Son of the wild boar who mangles his enemies by slashing,
> A Bull in the confusion of the flashing battle,
> He hurled the log (i.e. spear) from his hand.]

4. The accent should be on the second syllable of Caradoc. See T & W no. 240 and *The Bard*, explan. note to l. 102.

CONAN

See explanatory notes to *Caradoc*. Evans's Latin version as given by Mason is this:

> Debitus est tibi cantus qui honorem assecutus es maximum,
> Qui eras instar ignis, tonitrui, et tempestatis,
> Viribus eximie, eques bellicose, Rhudd Fedel, bellum meditaris.
>
> [A song is due to you who have attained highest honour,
> Who were like fire, thunder and tempest;
> Superb in strength, valorous knight, Rhudd Fedel, you are
>   exercising yourself in war.]

LINES SPOKEN BY THE GHOST OF JOHN DENNIS
AT THE DEVIL TAVERN

Whibley describes the *Lines* as the 'earliest original poem by Gray now extant'. It was sent to Walpole on 8 Dec. 1734, with this introductory statement: 'I . . . had too much modesty to venture answering . . . in the Poetical Strain myself: but, when I was last at the DEVIL, meeting by chance with the deceased Mr Dennis there, he offer'd his Service, &, being tip'd with a Tester, wrought, what follows—.' John Dennis (1657–6 Jan. 1734), an enemy of Pope and an important early eighteenth-century critic, was frequently in need of money.

4. *Celadon.* The pastoral pseudonym applied to Walpole in the Eton days of the 'Quadruple Alliance'. The others were Orosmades (Gray), Almanzor (Thomas Ashton), and Favonius or Zephyrus (Richard West).

11. . . . Farewel happy Fields / Where Joy for ever dwells. . . . *Paradise Lost*, i. 249–50.

13 ff. Probably an echo of the Emperor Hadrian's lines to his soul:

Animula vagula blandula	Ah, little soul, sweet wandering mite,
hospes comesque corporis,	Dear charmer of each day and night,
quæ nunc abibis in loca	Guest and companion of my clay,
pallidula rigida nudula,	To what strange places will you stray,
nec ut soles dabis iocos!	Pale and stiff and naked too—
	You'll not then jest as now you do!

34. *Nicolini.* Nicolino Grimaldi, a famous opera singer of the early eighteenth century.

41. *Orozmades.* See note to l. 4.

42–51. These concluding lines, in which the individuals named either reverse their ordinary roles in life or 'still keep their Passions, / But differ something from the world [that is, their own world as well as Gray's] in Fashions', involve several plays on words. For example, *Lucrece* (l. 42) and *Nun* (l. 43), in addition to their normal meanings, were also sometimes used as general designations for a prostitute.

43. *Mrs Oldfield.* Anne Oldfield (1683–1730), the actress, was the mistress of Arthur Mainwaring and later of General Charles Churchill. The final stanza of 'G— Ch—ch—ll's Prayer to Venus', *Gentleman's Magazine*, xi (1741), 48, may possibly contain a commentary on Mrs. Oldfield as well as on the general:

> Let florid *youth* attend thy train
> Much wanted by thy crazy swain,
> And, gentle *Venus*, prithee,
> To crown thy gifts and ease my pain,
> (Since *Ward* has laboured long in vain)
> Let *Mercury* come with thee.

50–51. *Artemisia.* Sister, wife, and successor (*reg.* 352–350 B.C.) of King Mausolus of Caria. According to legend she mixed ashes in her drink every day as a sign of her grief at the death of her husband. Here she is of course paralleled in her altered 'fashions' by Alexander the Great, who now wears an ornate wig (Ramillie) instead of, presumably, his helmet.

HYMN TO IGNORANCE

The poem is one of the few mock epic passages in heroic couplets which Gray wrote. The debt to *MacFlecknoe* and the *Dunciad* is evident; and, like the latter poem, this contains several Miltonic echoes. Since Gray left Cambridge in Sept. 1738 and returned in Oct. 1742, the poem was written—if ll. 11–12 are taken literally—in the autumn of 1741, perhaps soon after he arrived in England from the Continent. Mason, however, dates it *c.* 1743, which is probably too late.

3. *rushy Camus.* Jam nec *arundiferum* mihi cura revisere *Camum,* [Now I have no anxiety to see reed-crowned Camus again.] Milton, *Elegia* I, l. 11. *Br.*

4.   . . . where Rivers now
         Stream, and *perpetual draw thir humid traine.* Milton, *Paradise Lost*, vii, [305–]6. *Br.*

36–38. See also Young's *Love of Fame* (Satire V), J. Philips's *Blenheim* (As curst Sesostris, proud Egyptian King, / That monarchs harnessed to his chariot yoked), Pope, *Temple of Fame*, ll. 113–14 (High on his car Sesostris struck my view, / Whom sceptred slaves in golden harness drew). *Br.*

Sesostris, according to Greek legend, was a pharaoh who conquered huge areas in Africa and Asia; he is possibly a memory of Ramses II or Senusert III.

LINES ON DR. ROBERT SMITH

The stanza was first printed by Gosse in his revised edition of Gray's poems, where he introduced it as

written on the occasion of the threatened destruction of the Chestnuts at Trinity by Dr. Robert Smith (1689–1768), Master of that college, and author of a treatise on Optics, in consequence of which he got the nickname of Old Focus. They were preserved by Prof. Adam Sedgwick.

Gosse appends to the poem the note 'There was a second stanza' but gives no further information of any sort.

There is a Chestnut Walk at Trinity College, Cambridge, but a search of the records by the librarian and the archivist has revealed no indication that Dr. Smith ever threatened its destruction. See Hendrickson and Starr, *Notes and Queries*, viii (Feb. 1961), 57.

Dr. Robert Smith, Master of Trinity 1742–68, was the author of *A Compleat System of Opticks*, Cambridge, Printed for the Author, 1738.

TOPHET

This poem, according to Whibley, was written about 1749 under a sketch of the Rev. Henry Etough drawn by Mason and etched in 1769 by Michael Tyson, a friend of Gray and Mason. See textual notes and Whibley, *TLS*, 9 Oct. 1930, p. 805.

1. Although *Tophet* is the name of a place, the combination of unpleasant associations and similarity of sounds made it an obvious nickname for a parson named Etough.

2. Etough was generally disliked and feared because of his 'intimate knowledge . . . of the private and domestic history of all the great families in the kingdom', including that of Sir Robert Walpole. *Br.*

4. Professor Maxwell has pointed out to the editors that this line is an echo of Pope's *Epistle to Dr. Arbuthnot*, l. 140: 'Even mitred *Rochester* would nod the head.'

SATIRE ON THE HEADS OF HOUSES

Previous editors have said little about the contents or date of this poem. Gosse thought it written 'about 1765', but did not give his reasons. As far as the present editors have been able to discover, there is no adequate evidence for determining the date, but what little is available would seem to indicate that the poem may be earlier than Gosse imagined. James Marriott became Master of Trinity Hall on 10 June 1764, and it is possible that the somewhat ambiguous exclusion of Trinity Hall (ll. 35–36) from the list of colleges led Gosse to choose a date after 1764, for Gray was rather fond of Marriott (T & W no. 429). On the other hand, the couplet may merely refer to the low ebb to which the college had sunk in the mid-eighteenth century (see *Victoria History of the Counties of England*, vol. iii: *The City and University of Cambridge*, ed. J. P. C. Roach. Oxford, 1959, p. 365). In his letters, most of Gray's unfavourable reflections upon the personalities, administration and politics of the University begin about 1743 and continue through the 1740's. He objects to the 'Power of Laziness' he sees about him (T & W no. 115, 26 Apr. 1744; no 149, 25 Apr. 1749), the tendency of members of the University to follow in the same pattern ('. . . when the Tone was once given the University, who ever wait for the Judgement of their Betters, struck into it with an admirable Harmony', no. 150, 8 Aug. 1749), and gives mock-heroic accounts of such squabbles as the dispute between the Master and Fellows of Pembroke, comparing it to the 'barrel'd Cod' clause in the treaty with France—the latter phrase is somewhat reminiscent of the sub-title of this poem (no. 148, 9 Mar. 1749). When the Duke of Newcastle became Chancellor in 1748 the situation seems to have been particularly unfortunate: 'Heads and fellows of colleges wanted to be on the winning side in order that they might share in the spoils which the victors had to bestow . . .' (*V.C.H.* iii. 220). Since the subject of the poem is the sheep-like docility of the Masters in following the same path, it seems unlikely that the satire was written during the period (1763–4) when Sandwich was attempting to become High Steward (see explanatory notes to *The Candidate*), for at that time the support of the Masters was divided between him and Newcastle's nominee. What little evidence there is, therefore, suggests that the poem was written in the late 1740's or early 1750's. However, as Whibley remarks (*TLS*, 9 Oct. 1930, p. 805 n.), the verses are primarily a *tour de force* in rhyming the names of the colleges rather than a personal satire with direct individual application.

SKETCH OF HIS OWN CHARACTER

4. Mason printed the line in capitals to emphasize Gray's religious opinions.

6. *Charles Townshend and Squire.* Charles Townshend, 'the Weathercock' (1725–67), was a successful politician, Chancellor of the Exchequer in 1766–7. Samuel Squire (1713–66), Fellow of St. John's College, Cambridge, became Bishop of St. David's. Neither was famous for the austerity and inflexibility of his principles. 'This last line needs no comment for readers of the present time, and it surely is not worth while to write one on this occasion for posterity' (*M*, i. 264 n.).

THE CANDIDATE

In Nov. 1763, when the first Earl of Hardwicke, High Steward of Cambridge, was evidently about to die, John Montagu (1718–92), fourth Earl of Sandwich, a corrupt politician and one of the most viciously debauched men of the century, announced his candidacy for the High Stewardship, to the horror of Gray and many other members of the Cambridge community. He at this time had acquired an even more unenviable notoriety by piously denouncing to the House of Lords his friend John Wilkes (whose private life, though the very reverse of spotless, was almost angelic if compared to Sandwich's) for gross immorality. As a result, at the next performance (probably on 16 Feb. 1764) of *The Beggar's Opera*, when Macheath spoke the line 'That Jemmy Twitcher should peach me, I own sur-priz'd me', the audience delightedly hailed Sandwich as Jemmy Twitcher, and he was frequently referred to by that name for the rest of his career. Despite his utter unsuitability for the office, the Court supported his candidacy, for Thomas Pelham-Holles (1693–1768), Duke of Newcastle, Chancellor of the University, was out of favour at Court and the King wished to destroy his influence at the University. Newcastle, to maintain his authority, supported Philip Yorke (1720–90), Lord Royston, the Earl of Hardwicke's eldest son. A long and bitter contest followed (the details of which are in T & W, Appendix P), and Sandwich was finally defeated. Although Gray felt little enthusiasm for Newcastle and the Yorkes, Sandwich's character was such that Gray and his friends strongly sup-ported Royston. *The Candidate* was probably written between late Feb. 1764 (see C. C. Walcutt, 'The Ghost of Jemmy Twitcher', *N & Q*, 24 July 1937, pp. 56–62), and 30 Mar. 1764. In Sept. 1774 Walpole, who had heard Gray recite the poem much earlier, found a copy in Gray's hand and at some later date may have printed it.

1. *smugg'd. To smug* is defined by Francis Grose (*Classical Dictionary of the Vulgar Tongue*, 1785, p. 151) as 'to make neat or spruce'.

4. *guttle.* Gorge or guzzle.

9. Probably a reference to certain physical ailments that a man of Sandwich's personal habits would be likely to contract. (Sandwich is supposed to have said to Wilkes, 'Wilkes, you will die of a pox or on the gallows'—and Wilkes replied, 'That depends, my Lord, on whether I embrace your principles or your mistress.')

12. *Rochester*. John Wilmot (1647–80), Earl of Rochester, is said to have died of venereal disease contracted, according to some accounts, when he was in his teens. Here Walpole noted in *WY*: 'Ld Sandwich was [great-]grandson of Lord Rochester & resembled his portraits.'

14. 'Lady Sandwich was confined for lunacy, but Lord S'[s]. enemies said, she was still shut up after she recovered her Senses—at least she never appeared again in the world.' *WY*.

19. *Divinity*. Gray was particularly annoyed by the hypocritical support which so many divines, headed by the Bishop of Chester, had given Sandwich. Among them, Gray commented on Zachary Brooke (D.D., Lady Margaret Professor of Divinity and Chaplain to the King), Lawrence Brockett (B.D., Professor of Modern History), and Roger Long (D.D., Vice-Chancellor, Master of Pembroke).

24. *catches*. 'Ld S. instituted the Catch-Club.' *WY*.

27. *prophet of Bethel*. See 1 Kings xiii. 18.

34. Previous editors have never supplied the missing final word; it is, however, given in the Yale edition of the Walpole–Mason *Correspondence* (W. S. Lewis ed., i. 170), where it appears as *stitches* ('lies with a woman'). This reading is printed from Walpole's holograph *WM*, in which the final couplet is legible although it has been crossed out.

Although the appearance of *stitch* in *WM* would seem to be conclusive, the present editors are not entirely satisfied that this is the term actually used by Gray. The correspondence of Walpole and Mason clearly indicates their strong feeling that the poem could not be allowed to end as Gray had written it. Walpole wrote to Mason (see Yale ed., i. 170–1) in the letter which evidently contained a copy of the poem (*WM* is a separate MS.): 'Methinks I wish you could alter the end of the last line, which is too gross to be read by any females, but such cock bawds as the three dames in the verses—and that single word is the only one that could possibly be minded', and suggests, 'Might it not do thus? "Damn you both! I know each for a Puritan punk. / He is Christian enough that repents when he's drunk".' Mason replied, '. . . I think with you (and always did) that the lines ought to be altered', and suggested, 'Damn ye both for two prim puritanical saints! / He's Christian enough that both whores and repents! (or) that drinks, whores and repents.'

In view of these experiments, it does not seem altogether impossible that Gray wrote some word other than *stitches*, and that *WM* ends with a later substitute for the final word, provided by either Walpole or Mason, which required a minimal change in Gray's words and yet removed the 'grossness' that offended his friends. If *stitches* is a euphemistic substitute, the obvious alternatives are *switches* and *twitches*. One eminent eighteenth-century scholar has informed the editors that he and several of his colleagues privately believe the word to be *twitches*. Unfortunately, there is no definite evidence on which to base a choice of any of these alternatives, and it is quite possible that none of them is correct. See Starr and Hendrickson, *N & Q*, n.s. viii (Feb. 1961), 58–59.

WILLIAM SHAKESPEARE TO MRS. ANNE

Mason was much interested in Shakespeare and apparently had expressed some of his views, probably on the text, to Gray. This poem, sent in a letter of *c.* 8 July 1765, is Gray's reply. The latter evidently regarded Mason's editorial capacities with doubts which were amply justified some ten years later when Mason produced his edition of Gray's poems and letters. For more detailed annotation see Tovey and T & W, pp. 879–80.

When he wrote ll. 5–7, Gray probably had in mind at least some of the following editors and commentators on Shakespeare: Thomas Rymer (1641–1713); Sir Thomas Hanmer (1677–1746), Bart.; Sir Thomas Pope Blount (1649–97), Bart.; Nicholas Rowe (1674–1718), Poet Laureate; Lewis Theobald (1688–1744), who wished to be Poet Laureate; Thomas Edwards (Lincoln's Inn) and John Holt (Gray's Inn), each of whom, in 1748 and 1750 respectively, wrote on the text of the plays; Warburton, who edited the plays in 1747, and John Upton, who attacked Warburton's edition, both clergymen.

10. *dovelike.* Mason's 'meekness' seems to have been a standing joke between him and Gray. See T & W nos. 230, 317.

12. Mason was, rather reluctantly, living at York at this time and had been suffering from eye trouble for at least a month. He was engaged to Mary Sherman, whom he married—after some hesitation—on 25 Sept. 1765.

21. *Clouët.* The famous French chef of the Duke of Newcastle. Gray owned and annotated Verral's *Complete System of Cookery*, to which the chef had contributed.

IMPROMPTUS

Edmund Keene (1714–81), Bishop successively of Chester and Ely and a supporter of Lord Sandwich (see explanatory notes to *The Candidate*), was not a favourite of Gray and his friends. The date of the verses on him and his wife is uncertain, but obviously they were composed after his accession to the see of Chester in 1752 and his marriage in 1753 and before he became Bishop of Ely on 9 Jan. 1771. Since there are several references to him in Gray's letters during the years 1769 and 1770 and comparatively few during the earlier years of his bishopric, it seems likely that these verses were composed in the late 1760's.

Mrs. Keene's attraction for her husband, if one may judge by Walpole's remarks (see T & W no. 143, n. 3), seems to have been based more securely on her considerable private fortune than on her physical charms.

Raby Castle, in Co. Durham, was the seat of Henry Vane (*c.* 1705–58), Lord Barnard, created first Earl of Darlington. A similar view of his abilities is reflected in a poem sent by Walpole to Gray (T & W no. 211):

ON LD DARL[INGTON]'S BEING MADE JOINT PAYMASTER [OF THE FORCES, 1755]

> Wonders, Newcastle, mark thy ev'ry hour;
> But this last Act's a plenitude of pow'r:
> Nought but the force of an almighty reign
> Could make a *Paymaster* of Harry V[ane].

The tense of 'lives' perhaps should not be taken literally to suggest that the poem was written before Vane's death in 1758, for Gray was not far from Raby Castle when he visited Thomas Wharton at the latter's home, Old Park, in July 1762, July–Aug. 1765, July–Sept. 1767, and Aug.–Sept. 1769. Although any of these dates is possible, one may conjecture that the summer of 1767—when Gray visited another Vane estate, Barnard Castle (26 July, T & W no. 449), and when he was somewhat preoccupied with the subject of epitaphs (see T & W nos. 447–51)—is the most likely period of composition. Since all these impromptus have been written on consecutive sheets by Wharton (including *A Couplet*, concerning which nothing is known), it may be that the entire group was written in the summer of 1767.

PARODY ON AN EPITAPH

Gray evidently visited the church at Appleby with Wharton about 3 Sept. 1767 (see T & W nos. 453, n. 3 and 511 A, n. 31) and saw there the following epitaph by Anne Clifford, Countess of Dorset, Pembroke, and Montgomery (1590–1676) on her mother, Margaret Russell, Countess of Cumberland:

> Who Faith, Love, Mercy, noble Constancy
> To God, to Virtue, to Distress, to Right
> Observed, expressed, showed, held religiously
> Hath here this monument thou seest in sight,
> The cover of her earthly part, but passenger
> Know Heaven and Fame contains the best of her.

Gray must have composed his burlesque epitaph for Lady Dorset, who is also buried in the church, within the next few days.

3. *Broom . . . Brough.* Four of the countess's castles in Westmorland.

INVITATION TO MASON

In a letter (T & W no. 461) of 8 Jan. 1768 Gray urged Mason to pay a visit to Pembroke and expressed his and their friends' disappointment at Mason's failure to be there earlier: 'Here are, or have been, or will be all your old & new Friends in constant expectation of you at Cambridge, yet Christmas is past, & no Scroddles [Gray's somewhat unlovely name for Mason] appears!' The poem follows.

1. *Hurd.* Dr. Richard Hurd (1720–1808), Bishop of Lichfield and Worcester, author of *Letters on Chivalry and Romance*. *Palgrave.* William Palgrave (1735–99), Fellow of Pembroke, Rector of Thrandeston and Palgrave. In T & W no. 484 (Aug. 1768) Mason says, ' . . . I mean to call . . . on Mr Wedell [William Weddell of Yorkshire; see textual notes] & Proud Palgrave . . . .'

2. *Stonhewer.* Richard Stonhewer (*c.* 1728–1809), Fellow of Peterhouse and later private secretary to the Duke of Grafton, probably was largely responsible for Gray's appointment to the Regius Professorship of Modern History at Cambridge. *Delaval.* Edward Hussey Delaval (1729–1814), Fellow of Pembroke, was a well-known linguist, classical scholar, and scientist. Gray remarks more than once that he had a loud voice.

3. *Powel.* William Samuel Powell (1717–75), Fellow and Tutor of St. John's. *Marriot.* Sir James Marriott (*c.* 1730–1803), Master of Trinity Hall.

4. *Glyn.* Robert Glynn (1719–1800), Fellow of King's College and Gray's doctor during his fatal illness, was 'eccentric in manner and dress'. *cut phizzes* (faces). Probably 'cut out portrait silhouettes' or 'grimaced'. *Nevile.* Thomas Nevile, Fellow of Jesus and classical scholar, suffered from a speech impediment.

5. *Brown.* James Brown (1709–84), President (later Master) of Pembroke, was one of Gray's closest friends. The line may refer to his very small stature or, possibly, to the way he wore his spectacles.

6–7. *Widow . . . Nanny . . . Nelly.* The women who worked at the Coffee-house in Cambridge.

8. *Balguy.* Thomas Balguy (1716–95), Fellow of St. John's, Archdeacon of Winchester, seems to have been thought of by Gray and Mason as rather ambitious and mercenary. However, he declined the bishopric of Gloucester in 1781. The phrase used here is an adaptation of a seventeenth-century expression applied to those of Popish sympathies: 'He has a Pope in his belly.'

LINES WRITTEN AT BURNHAM

Gray wrote to Walpole of the area around Burnham: ' . . . both Vale & Hill is [*sic*] cover'd over with most venerable Beeches, & other very reverend Vegetables, that like most ancient People, are always dreaming out their old Stories to the Winds.' The first four lines then appear, and T & W (p. 47, n. 7) add, 'These lines have not been traced; presumably they are Gray's own.' After them Gray continues: 'At the foot of one of these squats me I; il Penseroso, and there grow to the Trunk for a whole morning,'[the last two lines appear here] like Adam in Paradise, but commonly without an Eve, & besides I think he did not use to read Virgil, as I usually do there. . . .' T & W (p. 48, n. 9) suggest that the last two lines are an echo of *Paradise Lost*, iv. 340–5:

> . . . About them frisking playd
> All Beasts of th' Earth, since wilde, and of all chase
> In Wood or Wilderness, Forrest or Den;
> Sporting the Lion rampd, and in his paw
> Dandl'd the Kid; Bears, Tygers, Ounces, Pards
> Gambold before them. . . .

See also *Aeneid*, vi. 282–4:

> In medio ramos annosaque bracchia pandit
> Ulmus opaca, ingens, quam sedem Somnia volgo
> Vana tenere ferunt, foliisque sub omnibus haerent.

[In the midst a gloomy elm spreads its branches and aged limbs, a huge tree, which, the legends say, idle dreams make their home, and cling beneath every leaf.]

The first two lines, like those quoted above from Virgil, are reminiscent of Dodona, the oracle of Zeus where Fates were revealed by the rustling of leaves in the sacred oak trees.

AGRIPPINA

Agrippina was very likely composed during the winter of 1741–2. Gray wrote to West (T & W no. 62) that he had seen Racine's *Britannicus* (which he imitated in *Agrippina*) in Paris on 21 May 1739; Mason (i. 124, and T & W no. 62, n. 7) says that it was Mlle Dumesnil's performance at this time that influenced Gray to choose the death of Agrippina as his subject. The first scene was finished by 1 Apr. 1742. In a letter of that date (T & W no. 101), Gray wrote to West, 'I take the liberty of sending you a long speech of Agrippina . . . .' Mason (i. 124) says that this was the concluding speech of the first scene (i.e. ll. 82–190). See textual notes for explanation of the attribution of speeches as the text is here printed.

In the same letter, Gray continues: 'Aceronia, you may remember, had been giving quiet counsels.' This statement makes it seem certain that Gray had at some previous time sent West at least part, and more than likely all, of ll. 1–81. There is no clue to the date of the twelve lines of Otho's speech in Scene II, but it is not likely that they were composed later than 23 Apr. 1742, for in a letter of that date (T & W no. 105) Gray wrote to West, 'she [*Agrippina*] is laid up to sleep', and Mason, in a note on this passage, says (i. 145) that Gray never afterwards worked on the tragedy.

Apparently Walpole urged Gray to resume the composition, but Gray replied (T & W no. 130), 'Poor West put a stop to that tragic torrent he saw breaking in upon him:—have a care, I warn you, not to set open the flood-gate again, lest it should drown you and me and the bishop and all.' Gray never relented in his resolve to abandon the play, apparently having taken to heart and even exaggerated West's rather lukewarm opinion of its worth. The last time Gray mentions it is in his letter of 8 Feb. 1747 (T & W no. 131), to Walpole: 'Agripp:na can stay very well, she thanks you; & be damn'd at Leisure: I hope in God you have not mention'd, or shew'd to any Body that Scene (for trusting in it's [*sic*] Badness, I forgot to caution you concerning it). . . .'

5. *Lictor*. Upon his accession to the throne, Nero had granted his mother two lictors.

6. *Germanicus*. Germanicus Caesar (15 B.C.–A.D. 19), the elder brother of Claudius and the father of Agrippina and Caligula, was inordinately loved by the Roman people. Agrippina never ceased to invoke her father's name to gain her ends.

7. *Antium*. Anzio, a town in central Italy where Nero was born.

14. *Britannicus*. Claudius Tiberius Germanicus Britannicus (A.D. 41–55), the son of the previous Emperor, Claudius, and Messalina. He was poisoned by Nero at a banquet.

34–35. See *Elegy*, ll. 71–72.

38–39. See *Elegy*, l. 118.

44–47. The imagery of this passage is based on falconry, in which the young bird is unhooded and shown the quarry it is to attack.

71. *whiter*. More favourable or lucky.

82. Originally from this line the text 'was one continued speech . . . to the end of the scene' (*M*, i. 136 n.). Mason, however, altered it by giving some of the lines to Aceronia—see textual notes.

83. See *Elegy*, l. 73.

94. See *Progress of Poesy*, l. 53.

99–100. *Rubellius. . . Sylla*. Rubellius Plautus and Faustus Cornelius Sulla Felix both belonged to the imperial house, and both were later assassinated by the order of Nero, who commented with interest on their personal appearance when their heads were brought to him.

106–19. Mason's attribution of this material to Aceronia is particularly inappropriate.

112. *Corbulo*. Gnaeus Domitius Corbulo (II), an able general, was forced by Nero to commit suicide in A.D. 67.

115. *Masians*. This reference is unidentified. Tovey suggests that Gray wrote 'the Asians' (i.e. those [legions] of Asia), and Mason mistakenly copied it as 'Masians'. However, the present editors feel that the word may have been *Marsians* (the legions in Germany), who were considered the best infantrymen and whose name is often used as a generic term for all Roman soldiers, especially when a writer wishes to stress hardiness and courage (cf. Horace, *Odes*, i. 2. 39; ii. 20. 18); or—a more likely explanation—*Moesians* (Grays' *æ* and *œ* often look like *a*). Aceronia names first the western and eastern extremes of the empire (Germany and Armenia), where more or less active fighting was going on. She then names Egypt, on the south. Moesia (modern Serbia and Bulgaria) would complete the circle of border provinces where legions were normally stationed. 'Asians' would duplicate the four under Corbulo in Armenia.

118–19. *daughter . . . of . . . Caesars*. Agrippina was not daughter of an Emperor (as *Caesar* seems here to mean).

125–6. *Soranus . . . Cassius . . . Vetus . . . Thrasea*. Marcius Barea Soranus, Gaius Cassius Longinus (II), Lucius Antistius Vetus, and Publius Clodius Thrasea Paetus. Nero was responsible for the deaths of all of them save Cassius, who was merely banished.

148. See *Bard*, l. 69.

149. *Seneca*. The Emperor later forced him to commit suicide.

151. *Burrhus*. Sextus Afranius Burrus, like Seneca, a tutor and adviser of Nero, who later may have poisoned him.

179. *Syllani*. Agrippina was responsible for the deaths of the Silani brothers (Lucius Junius Silanus Torquatus [I] and Marcus Junius Silanus [II]), which were initiated by her desire to marry Nero to Octavia, the betrothed of the former and the daughter of her husband, the Emperor Claudius, whom she is said to have poisoned.

191 ff. Marcus Salvius Otho (A.D. 32–69), the lover of Poppaea, was Emperor in A.D. 69. Poppaea Sabina married Nero but is said to have died (A.D. 65) when her husband in a momentary fit of pique kicked her while she was pregnant.

194. See *Ode on a Distant Prospect of Eton College*, l. 29.

SONNET

Richard West (1716–42), called Favonius by his intimates, was Gray's closest friend. His health was always poor, and on 1 June 1742 he died of some form of respiratory disease. Like Gray, he was a very scholarly youth and one of the better Anglo-Latin poets of the century. This sonnet, the only one Gray is known to have composed, is one of the few written in the first half of the eighteenth century. It was composed very shortly after West's death. Book II ('Book IV' in many other editions) of the Latin poem *De Principiis Cogitandi* deals with the same subject.

THE ALLIANCE OF EDUCATION AND GOVERNMENT

In his letter (T & W no. 146) to Wharton of 19 Aug. 1748—presumably the year the poem was written—Gray explained that he was enclosing 'the Beginning of a Sort of Essay. what Name to give it I know not, but the Subject is, the Alliance of Education & Government; I mean to shew that they must necessarily concur to produce great & useful Men'. The poem was never finished, he told Nicholls (T & W, Appendix Z, p. 1291), because 'he had been used to write only Lyric poetry in which the poems being short, he had accustomed himself, & was able to polish every part; that this having become habit, he could not write otherwise; & that the labour of this method in a long poem would be intolerable; besides which the poem would lose its effect for want of Chiaro-Oscuro; for that to produce effect it was absolutely necessary to have weak parts'. Mason states, 'He was busily employed in it at the time when M. de Montesquieu's book was first published: On reading it, he said the Baron had forestalled some of his best thoughts; and yet the reader will find, from the small fragment he has left, that the two writers differ a little in one very material point, viz. the influence of soil and climate on national manners. [Note: 'See L'Esprit des Loix, Liv. 14. chap. 2, &c.'] Some time after he had thoughts of resuming his plan, and of dedicating it, by an introductory Ode, to M. de Montesquieu; but that great man's death, which happened in 1755, made him drop his design finally' (*M*, i. 192). Mason adds (pp. 201–3) that he found among Gray's papers other notes that he evidently intended to make use of in the poem and gives them as follows:

> Man is a creature not capable of cultivating his mind but in society, and in that only where he is not a slave to the necessities of life.
>
> Want is the mother of the inferior arts, but ease that of the finer; as eloquence, policy, morality, poetry, sculpture, painting, architecture, which are the improvements of the former.
>
> The climate inclines some nations to contemplation and pleasure; others to hardship, action, and war; but not so as to incapacitate the former for courage and discipline, or the latter for civility, politeness, and works of genius.
>
> It is the proper work of education and government united to redress the faults that arise from the soil and air.
>
> The principal drift of education should be to make men *think* in the Northern climates, and *act* in the Southern.

The different steps and degrees of education may be compared to the artificer's operations upon marble; it is one thing to dig it out of the quarry, and another to square it; to give it gloss and lustre, call forth every beautiful spot and vein, shape it into a column, or animate it into a statue.

To a native of free and happy governments his country is alway[s] dear:

'He loves his old hereditary trees.' COWLEY. [Apparently a misquotation of Cowley's essay *The Dangers of an Honest Man in Much Company*, in which there is a translation of 'aequaevumque videt consenuisse nemus' (Claudian, *Carmina Minora XX*, l. 16): 'A neighbouring Wood born with himself he sees / And loves his old contemporary Trees.'] While the subject of a tyrant has no country; he is therefore selfish and base-minded; he has no family, no posterity, no desire of fame; or, if he has, of one that turns not on its proper object.

Any nation that wants public spirit, neglects education, ridicules the desire of fame, and even of virtue and reason, must be ill governed.

Commerce changes intirely the fate and genius of nations, by communicating arts and opinions, circulating money, and introducing the materials of luxury; she first opens and polishes the mind, then corrupts and enervates both that and the body.

Those invasions of effeminate Southern nations by the warlike Northern people, seem (in spite of all the terror, mischief, and ignorance which they brought with them) to be necessary evils; in order to revive the spirit of mankind, softened and broken by the arts of commerce, to restore them to their native liberty and equality, and to give them again the power of supporting danger and hardship; so a comet, with all the horrors that attend it as it passes through our system, brings a supply of warmth and light to the sun, and of moisture to the air.

The doctrine of Epicurus is ever ruinous to society: It had its rise when Greece was declining, and perhaps hastened its dissolution, as also that of Rome; it is now propagated in France and in England, and seems likely to produce the same effect in both.

One principal characteristic of vice in the present age is the contempt of fame.

Many are the uses of good fame to a generous mind: it extends our existence and example into future ages; continues and propagates virtue, which otherwise would be as short-lived as our frame; and prevents the prevalence of vice in a generation more corrupt even than our own. It is impossible to conquer that natural desire we have of being remembered; even criminal ambition and avarice, the most selfish of all passions, would wish to leave a name behind them.

See textual notes for the additional couplet found in the MS. by Mason.

9. auras / vitalis carpis [You take in the air of life (i.e. live and breathe)], *Aeneid*, i. 387–8.

12. See *Ode for Music*, l. 21. *Br.*

17–18. See the *Elegy*, l. 63. *Br.*

46–47. See *Progress of Poesy*, ll. 52–53.

47. *Scythia*. Usually applied to the area now roughly comprised in south-

west Russia and Romania. Here Gray seems to have in mind the invasions which, more or less, originated in this district.

48. See Dryden's translation of Virgil's *Georgics*, i. 483 (And rolling onwards with a sweepy sway), and *Bard*, l. 75. *Mt, Br.*

77. *Zembla.* Novaya Zemlya ('New Land'), the mountainous and snow-covered pair of islands north of Russia and Siberia. See Boswell's use of the word (*Life of Johnson*, Hill–Powell ed., v. 392) which indicates that it was proverbial for distant, inaccessible places.

STANZAS TO MR. BENTLEY

Mason wrote of this poem (*M*, i. 226): 'While Mr. [Richard] Bentley was employed [in 1752] in making the Designs [for *B*] . . . , Mr. Gray, who greatly admired not only the elegance of his fancy, but also the neatness as well as facility of his execution, began a complimentary poem to him. . . .'

21–24. See the *Translation from Tasso*, ll. 69–70.

26–28. See textual notes for these lines.

28. *heave*, not *heaves* as Mitford suggested. Mason probably intended a subjunctive here.

SONG 1

Songs 1 and *2* are supposed to have been written for Miss Speed, who wished 'that she might possess something from his pen on the subject of love'. *Song 1* was first entitled 'Amatory Lines' by Mitford, whose selection has been followed in most later editions, although in *CB* only the word 'Song' heads the poem. The date is unknown, but see explanatory notes to *Song 2*.

SONG 2

See explanatory and textual notes to *Song 1*; this poem was also given to Leman by Miss Speed. The date of composition is uncertain, but Walpole mentions it in a letter of 28 Nov. 1761, commenting that it was written at 'Miss Speed's request, to an air of Geminiani: the thought is from the French'. Gray met Miss Speed in 1750.

ODE ON THE PLEASURE ARISING FROM VICISSITUDE

The poem was probably written about 1754, since Mason states that he found the following note in Gray's memorandum-book for that year: 'Contrast between the winter past and coming spring.—Joy owing to that vicissitude.—Many who never feel that delight.—Sloth.—Envy. Ambition. How much happier the rustic who feels it tho' he knows not how' (*M*, i. 235). The material in italics is added by Mason to complete the poem. Jean-Baptiste Louis de Gresset (1709–77) is apparently the principal source: 'I have heard Mr. Gray say, that M. Gresset's "Epitre a ma Soeur" (see his works in the Amsterdam edition, 1748, p. 180) gave him the first idea of this Ode: and whoever compares it with the French

Poem, will find some slight traits of resemblance, but chiefly in our Author's seventh stanza' (*M*, ii. 82). Mitford remarks: 'The following lines seem to have been in Gray's remembrance at this place:

> Mon âme, trop long tems flétrie
> Va de nouveau s'épanouir;
> Et loin de toute rêverie
> Voltiger avec le Zéphire,
> Occupé tout entier du soin, du plaisir d'être.'

> [My soul, too long withered,
> Will blossom again;
> And far from any reverie
> Will flutter in the breeze
> Completely occupied with the care, with the pleasure of existence.]

17–20. These lines were apparently rejected by Gray, but restored to the text by Mason, who then completed the stanza with four lines of his own. Since the entire stanza forms a rather illogical intrusion between l. 16 and l. 25, it is likely that the position as well as the presence of the lines is Mason's idea, not Gray's.

59. *crystalline*. So Milton accents the word:

On the crÿstălline sky, in sapphire thron'd. P.L. Book vi, l. 772. *M*.

EPITAPH ON A CHILD

The poem, according to Mason (i. 270 n.), was written to commemorate Robin Wharton (1753–58) at the request of his father, Dr. Thomas Wharton (1717–94), one of Gray's closest friends. Wharton had been a Fellow of Pembroke and was a London physician until he succeeded to his estate at Old Park. The passage to which Mason refers in his note is in a letter, 18 June 1758, to Wharton (T & W no. 271): 'You flatter me in thinking, that any thing, I can do, could at all alleviate the just concern your late loss has given you: but I can not flatter myself so far, & know how little qualified I am at present to give any satisfaction to myself on this head, & in this way, much less to you. I by no means pretend to inspiration, but yet I affirm, that the faculty in question is by no means voluntary. it is the result (I suppose) of a certain disposition of mind, wch does not depend on one-self, & wch I have not felt this long time.'

EPITAPH ON SIR WILLIAM WILLIAMS

Sir William Peere Williams, Bart. (*c*. 1730–61), M.A., Clare Hall, 1759, was fatally shot by a sentinel, 27 Apr. 1761, during the siege of Belle Île in the Bay of Biscay south of Morbihan; at the time he was a captain in Burgoyne's Dragoons. After his death his executor, Frederick Montagu, asked Gray to write an epitaph, which, Mason (ii. 62) says, was to be 'inscribed . . . on a Monument at Bellisle . . . but from some difficulty attending the erection of it, this design was not executed'. The poem was finished by Aug. 1761, since Gray sent a copy to Mason then. Gray, however, does not seem to have known Sir William well or to have regarded the poem with unmitigated enthusiasm: 'Montagu . . . has earnestly desired me to write some lines. . . . it is a task I do not love, knowing S^r W: W: so slightly as I did: but he is so friendly a Person, & his affliction seem'd to me so real, that I could not refuse him. I have sent him the following verses, wch I neither like myself, nor will he, I doubt' (To Mason, T & W no. 339).

5. *Aix.* The island at the mouth of the Charente River, where Williams was deputed to receive the capitulation.

10. *Victor.* Actually Williams was killed before the surrender of Belle Île.

EPITAPH ON MRS. MASON

Mrs. Mary Mason died on 27 Mar. (not May, as Whibley states) 1767, and her epitaph was inscribed on a monument in Bristol Cathedral. Nicholls writes in his *Reminiscences* (T & W, Appendix Z, p. 1294): 'The last four lines of Mason's epitaph on his wife were written by Gray, I saw them in his hand-writing interlined in the Mss which he shewed me . . . . [The four lines follow.] I do not now remember the lines of Mason which were effaced & replaced by these which have the genuine sound of the lyre of Gray. I remember that they were weak, with a languid repetition of some preceding expressions. Mr Gray said "That will never do for an ending, I have altered them thus".'

COUPLET ABOUT BIRDS

Nicholls introduces these lines with the following comment: 'I will set down after this [see *Latin Exercise from the* Tatler] another little fragment, two verses made by Mr Gray as we were walking in the spring in the neighbourhood of Cambridge.' Since Gray did not meet Nicholls until 11 June 1762 (see T & W no. 397, n. 1), the couplet was obviously composed after this date.

LATIN AND GREEK POEMS

LATIN EXERCISE FROM THE *TATLER*

Nicholls introduced the lines with this remark: 'I asked Mr Bryant who was next boy to him at Eton, what sort of a scholar Gray was he said a very good one & added that he thought he could remember part of an exercise of his on the subject of the freezing & thawing of words, taken from the Spectator, the fragment is as follows.' Bryant believed that Gray wrote the lines when he was 'rather low in the fifth form'. In reality, the theme, as Tovey notes (*Gray and His Friends*, p. 272), is based not on the *Spectator*, but on the *Tatler*, no. 254. Gray also may have had in mind *Aeneid*, xii. 284: ferreus ingruit imber [a shower of iron fell thick and fast].

PARAPHRASE OF PSALM LXXXIV

The only clue to the date of composition is the note of Mitford (see textual notes, *ad finem*). According to this, the poem must have been written while Gray was still at Eton; it may be his earliest complete work.

The stanzas printed in *GM* appear as part of a review of Robert A. Willmott's *A Journal of Summer Time in the Country*, in which the reviewer (anonymous) quotes at some length from Gray's 'Journals'. The stanzas are introduced in language almost word for word the same as Mitford's note in his MS. copy of the poem.

30. The comma after *Judææ* in *Mt* has been disregarded in the translation and has been omitted from the text. Gray's punctuation is often (and self-admittedly) erratic, and there seems to be no way of reconciling the punctuation with the sense of the passage.

TRANSLATION OF ODE

Mitford's transcription of this poem has been the sole authority for the text in previous editions. Mitford describes his source as 'written with ink by Mason over Gray's pencil'. The MS. transcribed by Mitford is in all probability the same one that has recently been discovered bound into a copy of Boswell's *Life of Johnson* (Lot 67 in Sotheby's Catalogue, Sale of 29 Feb. 1960). Mr. Charles W. Traylen (49–50 Quarry St., Guildford, Surrey) has kindly furnished us with a photostat. The hand seems definitely to be Gray's, although somewhat sprawling and ill formed as compared with his mature hand. This confirms earlier conjectures, based on the position of the poem in Mitford's Note-books and the immaturity of style, that the poem is a schoolboy exercise.

The author of the English ode which Gray translated freely into Latin can hardly be the (John) Gilbert Cooper (1723–69) whom Mitford and Tovey (who spells his name 'Cowper') apparently had in mind, since Cooper was only three years old when the poem was published, without identification of the author, by D[avid] Lewis in his *Miscellaneous Poems by Several Hands* (London: J. Watts, 1726), pp. 53–55, as

Translation from the Antient British.

I

Away; let nought to Love displeasing,
  My *Winifreda*, move your Care;
Let nought delay the Heav'nly Blessing,
  Nor squeamish Pride, nor gloomy Fear.

II

What tho' no Grants of Royal Donors
  With pompous Titles grace our Blood?
We'll shine in more substantial Honours,
  And, to be Noble, we'll be Good.

III

Our Name, while Virtue thus we tender,
　Will sweetly sound where-e'er 'tis spoke:
And all the Great ones, They shall wonder,
　How they respect such little Folk.

IV

What tho', from Fortune's lavish Bounty,
　No mighty Treasures we possess?
We'll find, within our Pittance, Plenty,
　And be content without Excess.

V

Still shall each kind returning Season
　Sufficient for our Wishes give:
For we will live a Life of Reason,
　And that's the only Life to live.

VI

Through Youth and Age, in Love excelling,
　We'll Hand in Hand together tread;
Sweet-smiling Peace shall crown our Dwelling,
　And Babes, sweet-smiling Babes, our Bed.

VII

How should I love the pretty Creatures,
　While round my Knees they fondly clung,
To see them look their Mother's Features,
　To hear them lisp their Mother's Tongue!

VIII

And, when with Envy Time transported
　Shall think to rob us of our Joys;
You'll, in your Girls, again be courted,
　And I'll go wooing in my Boys.

2. *et.* This word, which is metrically superfluous, makes a simple passage difficult, and has been ignored in the translation. The editors suspected a dittography in Mitford's transcription, perhaps caused by the echo of the last syllable of *exulet*, before the holograph MS. became available, but the *&* is unmistakably present in *Bos*.

The line apparently puzzled Tovey, who changed *tuo* to *meo* and *cara* to *caro*; these emendations have been reproduced by Bradshaw and in subsequent printings. Since *caro* introduces a false quantity into a line that was previously correct and *meo* makes a difficult line more difficult, the editors are unable to imagine what Tovey thought he was accomplishing by his emendations.

6. *titulis.* Strictly, the inscriptions at the base of a statue or bust, giving the name, ancestry, magistracies, and exploits of the person represented; but often, as here, the nobility of the families that displayed them.

12. *Tales.* The holograph, with *e* and *i* superimposed (see textual notes), does not establish clearly which form Gray intended here. To the present editors it seems that the *e* was written over the *i* and that *tales* makes a better reading in sense also. We have, therefore, respectfully disagreed with former editors. Also see 'Ode', st. iii.

13. *Diva.* Perhaps Fortuna, perhaps Juno Moneta, in whose temple at Rome money was coined. See 'Ode', st. iv.

14. *nostros.* Mitford transcribed this incorrectly as *nostras*; Tovey, Bradshaw, and others have perpetuated the error.

18. *expleret.* This is clearly the reading of *Bos*; unfortunately it is a secondary tense of the subjunctive in a clause where a primary tense is required. Tovey's *explerit*, copied by Bradshaw (see textual note), removes this difficulty, but is not without a certain awkwardness of its own; Tovey's version may, however, not be an emendation but merely a misreading of *Mt* (see explanatory note to l. 29 on the difficulty of Mitford's hand).

29. *inviderit.* Gray clearly wrote *inviderit* in *Bos* and Mitford copied the word correctly in his Note-book, but the latter's peculiarities of handwriting (especially in *e* and *i* where the loop of the former is frequently closed and the dot of the latter usually appears over one of the following letters) caused Tovey to misread it as *inséderit*. For a more detailed explanation of the causes of this see Hendrickson and Starr, *N & Q*, n.s. viii (Feb. 1961), 55–56.

31. *vestris.* An obvious error for *tuis*. This is the only specific example of the 'peculiarities' cited by Tovey in support of his contention that the poem is 'an early work'.

32. *amabo.* Scanning final long *o*'s as short is characteristic of Latin poetry of the Silver Age.

LATIN VERSES AT ETON

The poem is heavily indebted to Pope's *Essay on Man* (see Starr, *Bibliography of Gray*, no. 525, for a detailed study). This fact enables us to fix the date of composition as some time between the spring of 1733, when the first three books of Pope's poem were published, and the summer of 1734, when Gray left Eton (see textual notes).

12. *liquidos . . . odores.* This phrase normally means 'perfumed water or oil' in Classical Latin (e.g. Horace, *Odes*, i. 5. 2). However, *liquidus* also means 'bright', 'pure', 'unmixed', or 'unadulterated' in other contexts; Gray evidently has in mind these other meanings here.

13. *Olympum.* See note to l. 52 of *Ad C: Favonium Aristium.*

17. Line repeated in *Luna Habitabilis*, l. 13.

21. Hiatus, probably after *rimari*, required to make line scan.

23. *serventque tenorem.* Lucretius uses *tenorem* twice, once with *servare* (iv. 632) and once with *conservare* (v. 508). The latter passage—(unum labendi conservans usque tenorem—'steadily preserving a smooth, gliding movement in a single direction') is echoed in the *Elegy*, l. 76.

27. Virgil, *Aeneid*, vi. 270: sub luce maligna [with scanty light].

49. Lucretius, v. 1387: per loca pastorum deserta atque otia dia.

51. Virgil, *Georgics*, iii. 117: gressus glomerare superbos [to prance proudly].

52. Virgil, *Georgics*, iv. 247: laxos in foribus suspendit aranea casses [the spider has hung loose webs in doorways].

HYMENEAL

In his letter of 24 May 1736 (T & W no. 23), West says, 'Your Hymenêal I was told was the best in the Cambridge Collection [i.e. *Gratulatio*, &c.] before I saw it, and indeed, it is no great compliment to tell you I thought it so when I had seen it . . . .'

The marriage which was the occasion of the *Gratulatio* was solemnized on 27 Apr. 1736 between Frederick Louis, Prince of Wales, and Princess Augusta of Saxe-Gotha.

1. *Aeneid*, iv. 65: Heu, vatum ignarae mentes [Alas, the benighted minds of prophets].

6. *Aeneid*, iv. 33: nec dulces natos Veneris nec praemia noris? [will you know neither sweet sons nor the rewards of Love?].

12. This verse obviously does not scan. As Mitford (p. 174 n.) points out, it is formed by combining parts of two lines from the *Aeneid*: xii. 336 (Iraeque Insidiaeque, dei comitatus, aguntur) and iv. 67 (interea et tacitum vivit sub pectore vulnus). In view of Gray's usual care, it is not unlikely that the printer let something drop out of Gray's text.

14. *Aeneid*, vi. 274: Luctus et ultrices posuere cubilia Curae.

21. *ne finge metum*. Not very clear. The phrase *ne finge* is apparently taken from Virgil, *Aeneid*, iv. 337–8 (Neque ego hanc abscondere furto / speravi, ne finge, fugam. . . . [I have not hoped to hide this flight in secrecy—do not imagine that I have. . . .]), where Aeneas tells Dido not to imagine that he is trying to slip away without telling her. But that is just what Aeneas was trying to do; Dido was afraid of a very real and imminent possibility. What it is that the Prince is supposed not to fear is vague to the point of obscurity.

31. Horace, *Odes*, i. 3. 11: Commisit pelago ratem.

33. *Aeneid*, iv. 697: subitoque accensa furore [inflamed by sudden madness].

36. *Aeneid*, iii. 514: explorat ventos, atque auribus aera captat.

38. *Aeneid*, v. 138: laudumque arrecta cupido.

52. *Pygmaliona*. The version of the Pygmalion story told by Ovid (*Metamorphoses*, x. 243–97) is probably the one Gray had in mind. See Mitford for echoes of Ovid's phrases.

IN DIEM 29^{AM} MAII

There is no information on the date of composition of this poem nor on that of *In 5tam Nov*. On the basis of style and tone, the editors would guess that both were written later than the Eton exercises but before *Ad C: Favonium Aristium*, i.e. about 1736–7.

Title: Charles II was born 29 May 1630, and entered London on his thirtieth birthday at his restoration.

1. The line is taken from Lucan, *Civil Wars*, i. 1:

> Bella per Emathios [Thessalian] plus quam civilia campos.

Lucan calls the wars 'worse than civil (wars usually are)' because the principal antagonists, Caesar and Pompey, were not merely fellow citizens but kinsmen. Gray's reason for so characterizing the Rebellion is not so clear.

12. *patri*. Charles I (1600–49).

13. *Vigornia*. Milton (in *Defensio Secunda pro Populo Anglicano*, vi. 320) uses *Vigornium* as the name of Worcester, the scene of Charles II's defeat in Sept. 1651.

15. *Arbor*. The Boscobel oak in which Charles is said to have hidden after his defeat.

20–21. The allusion is to the Roman *corona civica*, which was made of oak leaves and bestowed on persons who had saved the life of a Roman citizen in war.

IN 5ᵀᴬᴹ NOVEMBRIS

See introductory note to *In D[iem]: 29ᵃᵐ Maii*.

Title: 5 Nov. is Guy Fawkes' Day, commemorating the plot to blow up the King and Parliament on 5 Nov. 1605. It was not uncommon for students at the universities to contribute Latin verses as part of the ceremonies of thanksgiving for the delivery of the nation.

2. *judice*. This use of the simple ablative with the gerundive to denote the agent is not found in good Latin. One occasionally finds an ablative with *ab* so used, especially if an ambiguity might result from the use of the dative, the usual construction.

4. *nobilitaret honos*. Both used ironically.

6. This line is obscure; at first glance it seems to mean 'the first and the later Nero . . .', but such a rendering would, among other difficulties, seem to duplicate the reference to Domitian in l. 8 (cf. Juvenal, iv. 38) or even to suggest the most unlikely possibility that such a classical scholar as Gray attributed the anecdote concerning Caligula (l. 7) to Nero. The editors believe that Gray meant 'the first tyrant (possibly Romulus, more likely L. Tarquinius Superbus, *reg*. 534–510 B.C.) and 'the later tyrant, Nero'.

7. Probably Caligula (Gaius Caesar, *reg*. A.D. 37–41), who marched his troops to the shore of the Channel, drew them up in battle order, and then commanded them to gather sea-shells, which he called the spoils of Ocean.

9. *Phalaris*. Tyrant of Agrigentum (modern Girgenti) in Sicily, *c*. 570–564 B.C. He had a brazen bull constructed in which he roasted his victims alive.

Trinacria. The ancient name of Sicily, derived from the triangular shape of the island.

10. Presumably Gray means that Phalaris set fire to a temple of Diana, but the editors have been unable to find any authority in ancient literature for such a tale.

31–34. The translation represents what the author apparently intended to say.

LUNA HABITABILIS

The poem was written later than 29 Dec. 1736, and before 17 Mar. 1737. On the former date Gray wrote to Walpole (T & W no. 35), 'The Moderatour has asked me to make the Tripos-Verses this year. . . .' Since the Moderators were responsible for providing the verses issued at the Comitia Posteriora, which in 1737 were held on 17 Mar. (T & W no. 37, n. 1, and Appendix B, p. 1198), the poem must have been in print by the latter date. No known copies of this printing are extant. The poem was republished in 1755 in *Musae Etonenses*. So far as the editors are aware, the first complete translation is given here. See Starr, *Bibliography of Gray*, nos. 481, 482, 483, 486.

1–2. The lines have a pronounced Epic flavour, but seem to be Gray's own. Mitford's citation from Claudian seems little more than a verbal coincidence.

4. *Musa*. Perhaps Urania, Muse of Astronomy; perhaps a rather vaguely defined personification of poetic inspiration. (See notes to ll. 72 and 77.)

13. The same line appears in *Latin Verses at Eton* (l. 17).

15. *Aeneid*, iv. 451: . . . taedet caeli convexa tueri [(Dido) is weary of looking at the vault of heaven].

21. *Aeneid*, iv. 493: . . . magicas invitam accingier artis. *Accingere*, which appears in *ME*, is obviously wrong; it is probably a printer's 'correction', since the correct form *accingier* was less familiar. The correct form appears, without comment, in Mitford. The editors have been unable to determine who first restored it to the text.

22. *Thessalicos modos*. See Gray's translation of Statius, vi. 646–88, explanation note to l. 58.

24. Virgil, *Aeneid*, ii. 773: visa mihi ante oculos, et nota major imago.

29. Virgil, *Aeneid*, iv. 177: ingrediturque solo et caput inter nubila condit [she walks on the ground and hides her head among the clouds].

31. Virgil, *Aeneid*, iii. 127: Et crebris legimus freta consita terris [we sail through straits strewn with many lands]. Some good MSS. have *concita* instead of *consita*.

35. See Mitford's note on the propriety of *imbibit* in this passage.

40. *tela diei*. This figure occurs in Lucretius (e.g. i. 147) and often in the works of later poets.

41. This line is repeated in *De Principiis Cogitandi*, i. 200.

49. Ovid, *Metamorphoses*, xiv. 838: . . . pictos delapsa per arcus.
   Thaumantias. Iris, Goddess of the Rainbow.

53. *Martem invadunt*. This combination of metonymy with a daring extension of the inner object (cognate accusative) construction is Virgil's (*Aeneid*, xii. 712: invadunt Martem . . .).

54–55. Virgil, *Aeneid*, i. 461–2: sunt hic etiam sua praemia laudi; / sunt lacrimae rerum et mentem mortalia tangunt [here too glory has its fit reward; tears are shed for sorrows, and mortal chances affect the mind].

72. *nostra*. The choice of possessive is puzzling. The speaker is the *Musa* of l. 4, the *Dea* of l. 18, but Gray here has her speak as if she were the Goddess of the Moon, Phoebe, or Luna. No doubt, as has been suggested, *nostra* means 'British'; the whole passage means that the Moon astronomers observe the Earth and its countries, call them by their own names, and swagger about as if they owned them.

Aeneid, i. 140: . . . illa se iactat in aula.

77. *Soror*. It is impossible to tell who or what is meant. Presumably a sister of the speaker is one of the eight other Muses, but there is no clue to tell us which one. Perhaps Gray is merely saying in a poetic way that it is time for him to end his poem and give another poet a chance to speak.

83. A hypermetric verse.

85. Virgil, *Georgics*, iii. 198: . . . campique natantes (cf. also Lucretius, v. 488: . . . camposque natantis).

88. *turmas biformes*. Literally, 'squadrons of two shapes', i.e. a blend of man and horse. *Biformis* is applied to a centaur by Ovid, *Amores*, ii. 12. 19.

89. *Aeneid*, ii. 237–8: . . . machina . . ./ feta armis; vi. 590: . . . et non imitabile fulmen.

95. *Aeneid*, i. 285: . . . ac victis dominabitur Argis.

GRATIA MAGNA

'On p. 83[–85] vol. iii of Mitford's MSS. is a MS. Poem which has no other description or designation, but which seems, from the place in which it is found, to be Gray's. Compare the English Poem of West on p. 109 [of *Gray and His Friends*]. The Latin may also be West's; it is obviously in the rough.' *Tovey*. Tovey believed that West's English poem was the basis of the Latin verse. See notes on individual passages for illustrations of the roughness of the poem.

4. Although the thought is impeccably classical (cf. e.g. Horace, *Odes*, i. 5. 13–16), the expression is less so. *Appensa* in the meaning 'hang from' is late and largely ecclesiastical; *suspensa* is the usual classical expression. Moreover, *in* would not normally be used here; one finds *suspendere in fumo* ('hang in smoke') and *suspendere in carnario* ('in a larder' or 'in a drying-frame'), but *ab* or *ex* would be more idiomatic in the present phrase.

5. *Nunquam . . . . uror*. *Nunquam* is appropriate to the past or future, but not to the present; *non jam* ('no longer') seems to be intended. It is not impossible that Mitford made an error in copying this particular passage, but the negative particles are used rather loosely throughout the poem; moreover, this passage is plainly only a rough, unfinished draft.

5. *doloso*. Horace, *Odes*, ii. 1. 7–8:

incedis per ignes
Suppositos cineri doloso. [You are walking over fires buried
in treacherous ashes.]

In his poem, Horace has used a fine and appropriate image, for he is warning
Pollio, who is about to write a history of the Civil Wars, that the flames of passion
only seem to be extinguished and that the apparently cold ashes may at any
moment burst into flame. In the present poem, the image is much less appropriate,
for the author's main point is that not a trace of fire remains in the ashes.

17. *eburnea.* Three syllables by synizesis.

18. *laudo.* The shortening of -*o* is characteristic of Silver Latin.

25. *labelli.* This word should be neuter (*labella*), but *illi* shows clearly that the
error is the author's.

26. *immemores.* The meaning 'causing forgetfulness' is confined to later
writers (e.g. Statius).

29–34. Both sentences in these lines leave much to be desired. The roughness
mentioned by Tovey is particularly evident here.

51–52. Propertius, ii. 1. 43–44.

Navita de ventis, de tauris narrat arator,
enumerat miles vulnera, pastor oves . . . .

[The sailor talks about winds, the ploughman about oxen;
the soldier counts his wounds, the shepherd his sheep . . . .]

56. *notas.* The censor placed a mark (*nota*) beside the name of a citizen who
was to be removed from the list or demoted from one of the higher classes. The
word came to mean the act that caused the mark to be used, and, finally, any disgraceful act.

AD C: FAVONIUM ARISTIUM

'I choose to call this delicate Sapphic Ode the first original production of
Mr. Gray's Muse; for verses imposed either by schoolmasters or tutors ought
not, I think, to be taken into consideration.'—*Mason.*

Perhaps Mason had otherwise undisclosed private information that the composition of this poem preceded that of the *Alcaic Fragment* (O lachrymarum fons)
which is contained in the same letter (T & W no. 53, June 1738).

The poem was written while Gray and West intended to study law together in
the Inner Temple. The setting is in part more literary than actual: Gray was at
Cambridge, not in Italy, as some details suggest, and it seems rather forced to
speak of the winds rising and the summer growing old (st. viii) in June. How
much of the wish to die in twilight splendour (st. xii) is due to youthful romanti-
cism rather than to any actual melancholy is more difficult to determine.

Title: *Favonius* was West's designation in the Quadruple Alliance. Gray has
here playfully added the *Gaius* and the *Aristius* to form a Roman-sounding name,
influenced in part, perhaps, by the name of Horace's friend Aristius Fuscus.

1–4. This opening was probably suggested by Horace, *Odes*, ii. 6. 1–4, with the added attraction of the word-play on *aedes*: (*Inner*) *Temple*.

> Septimi, Gadis aditure mecum et
> Cantabrum indoctum iuga ferre nostra et
> Barbaras Syrtis, ubi Maura semper
> Aestuat unda . . . .

6. *temeré*. Mitford has a long note trying to establish that Gray is incorrect in making the final *e* long. He says that the final *e* is always elided in Virgil, Horace, and the other poets of the best period. So far as the editors can determine, this statement is substantially correct; the word does occur unelided in Plautus and Terence (e.g. *Phormio*, iv. 5. 2), but unfortunately in places where it is impossible to determine from the metre whether the vowel is long or short. From this fact Mitford draws what appears to us to be the unwarranted conclusion that the word *could not* be used in hexameter verse unless the final syllable were elided, because it consisted of three successive short syllables, and that, therefore, the final *e* must have been short. Not only is Mitford's argument fallacious, but there is ample precedent in the host of adverbs in *-ē*.

7. Horace, *Sermones*, ii. 6. 61–62:

> Nunc veterum libris nunc somno et inertibus horis
> Ducere sollicitae iucunda oblivia vitae?

[To induce sweet oblivion of a troubled life, sometimes with the works of ancient writers, sometimes with sleep and idle hours.]

9. Horace, *Odes*, i. 22. 10–11: Dum . . . ultra / Terminum curis vagor expeditis [while I was wandering outside the boundary with my cares laid aside].

10. *Camœnam*. The Camoenae were nymph-like nature spirits of the ancient animistic religion of Italy, but in later Roman poets often identified with the Muses.

18. Virgil, *Georgics*, i. 376: . . . captavit naribus auras.

23. Horace, *Odes*, iv. 3. 18: . . . dulcem quae strepitum, Pieri, temperas [You, Pierian Maid, who modulate the sweet sound] . . . .

27. *Favoni*. Favonius was the personified West Wind, but also, of course, in the private language of Gray, Richard West. Here Gray seems to have the wind primarily in mind, but, as often, there is also an indirect reference to West.

30. *Clytie*. A daughter of Oceanus, changed into the plant heliotrope. See Ovid, *Metamorphoses*, iv. 256–70.

35. *Eoos*. From Eos, Goddess of Dawn, hence 'Eastern'.

40. *Calpen*. Mt. Calpe (Spain) and Mt. Abyla (Africa) form the Pillars of Hercules.

49. *multâ*. Mitford says, 'Mason has improperly accented this word.' The mistake, if it is a mistake, is Gray's; the accent is quite clear in *CB*. Mitford is probably correct in assuming that this is *multa* (neuter accusative plural) used 'adverbially' (i.e. an inner object with *flagranti*), but that would not necessarily make the accent an error.

52. *Aeneid*, x. 216: ... Phoebe medium pulsabat Olympum. Virgil borrowed the phrase from Ennius (*Annales*, i, fr. 1).

ALCAIC FRAGMENT

This poem comes at the end of the same letter to West (T & W no. 53) which begins with *Ad C: Favonium Aristium*. In his reply, West refers to the poem as 'your little Alcaic Fragment' (T & W no. 55), the title under which it has appeared in most previous editions. Despite a personal feeling that this title does the poem less than justice, the present editors have bowed to tradition and retained it.

In his *Poems in Latin* (London: Oxford, 1941), p. xi, John Sparrow praises the 'exquisite charm' of this poem, which is, he says, 'at once perfectly Horatian and wholly unlike Horace: so Horace would have said what Horace could never have felt.'

For further comment, see the 'Introduction to the Latin Poems' of the present edition.

1. Sophocles, *Antigone*, 803:

. . . ἴσχειν
δ' οὐκ ἔτι πηγὴν δύναμαι δακρύων.

[I can no longer hold back the stream of tears.]

FROM PETRARCH

There is no clue to the date of composition, but the poem probably belongs to the period of the translations from Italian into English; see explanatory notes to these translations.

Motto: The 'some one' is Laura.

1. *io*. Although this interjection usually indicates triumph or joy, it does not always do so. See, for example, Tibullus, ii. 4. 6: 'Uror, io, remove saeva puella faces! [Alas, I am on fire; cruel girl, take the flames away!]'

FROM GENOA

Gray left Turin on 18 Nov. 1739 (see T & W no. 74, last sentence) and wrote to West on 21 Nov. 1739, from Genoa, beginning his letter with the present poem (T & W no. 75). The tense of *advehor* (l. 3) suggests that he wrote the poem during the journey.

2. *Taurini*. The Taurini inhabited the district around modern Turin (ancient *Augusta Taurinorum*).

3-4. *Genuæque ... soles*. The same words in the same order and position end the first stanza of *Oh Ubi Colles*. See explanatory note thereto.

ELEGIAC VERSES

1. *Trebiæ*. Scene of the first major defeat of the Romans by Hannibal, 218 B.C. Virgil, *Georgics*, iv. 182: ... et glaucas salices.

5. *Maurorum*. Strictly, 'Moors', but used by the Romans to designate any Africans.

6. *Ausonidum*. Strictly, the inhabitants of Ausonia, or Lower Italy, named for Auson, the son of Ulysses and Calypso, but used by Roman writers as a poetic name for all Italians.

AD C: FAVONIUM ZEPHYRINUM

Sent to West in a letter (T & W no. 87) dated May 1740.

Title: *Favonius* is the designation of West, with the addition of *C:* (i.e. Gaius) and the redundant *Zephyrinus* to form a Roman-sounding name; cf. *C: Favonius Aristius*.

1. *Mater rosarum*. Probably Flora, Goddess of Flowers. Her festival, the Floralia, was celebrated 28 Apr.–3 May; Ovid (*Fasti*, v. 183) calls her 'mater florum [mother of flowers]' and a few lines later (v. 194) says of her 'dum loquitur vernas afflat ab ore rosas [while she speaks, the perfume of vernal roses breathes from her mouth]'; he then tells (*Fasti*, v. 201–6) how she was first raped and later married by Zephyrus.

2. Lucretius, i. 11: . . . et reserata viget genitabilis aura Favoni [and the life-giving breeze of Favonius, freed from its prison, blows strongly].

6–7. Horace, *Odes*, ii. 13. 26–27: Et te sonantem plenius aureo, / Alcaee, plectro . . . .

10. *Tusculi*. Tusculum was a very ancient town of Latium, situated on a hill near the site of modern Frascati.

12. *Palladiæ Albæ*. Alba was given the epithet *Palladia* after Domitian caused the Quinquatria, the festival of Minerva (i.e. Pallas Athena) to be celebrated there; see, e.g., Martial, v. 1. 1.

14. *Anio*. A tributary of the Tiber; at Tibur it forms a cataract (hence the epithet *praeceps* [headlong] in Horace, *Odes*, i. 7. 13: . . . et praeceps Anio, ac Tiburni lucus).

17. *Tibur, et Æsulæ*. Tibur and Aesula (or Aefula) were ancient hill-towns not far from Rome.

20. *Naiasin*. Since both holograph MSS. agree on this form (and *Naiades* in l. 21), there seems to be no doubt that Gray used them deliberately. We cannot, therefore, accept Mitford's emendations to *Naisin* (and *Naides*), which have been frequently reprinted in subsequent editions.

The difficulty is that *Naiasin* (and *Naiades*) cannot be pronounced as the Romans would have done and fit the metre. The Greeks had two forms of the word: Νāïás and Νāΐs. The Roman poets borrowed both forms, but for the most part merely transliterated them, preserving the Greek pronunciation and declensional forms: e.g., *Nāïdes* (Virgil, *Eclogues*, x. 10); *Nāïades* (Ovid, *Metamorphoses*, xiv. 328); *Nāïadum* (Virgil, *Eclogues*, vi. 21), with Latin -*um* instead of Greek -ων, but preserving the separation of *a* and *i*. Gray (probably influenced by English *naiad*) followed the practice of the Romans in transliterating Greek forms (*Naiasin* is Greek dative plural; *Naiades* is Greek nominative plural), but pronounced them *Nai-a-sin* and *Nai-a-des*.

21. *Naiades*. See previous note.

24. *Venusinus ales.* Apparently Horace (65–8 B.C.), who was born at Venusia, a town on the borders of Apulia and Lucania.

31–32. 'There is no instance in Horace of a broken word ending the third line of the Alcaic stanza. . . .' *Mt.*

33. *Aeneid*, vi. 283–4:   . . . quam sedem Somnia vulgo
       Vana tenere ferunt, foliisque sub omnibus haerent.

THE GAURUS

The poem was begun in June or early July 1740 (see textual notes), and sent to West in a letter (T & W no. 94) of 25 Sept. 1740. Gray cites 'Sandy's [*sic*] Travels' [George Sandys (1578–1644), *The Relation of a Journey Begun an. Dom. 1610, in Four Books*, London: W. Barrett, 1615] as the source of his factual information. His primary concern, however, was to give an imaginative and sympathetic reconstruction of the terrors of the eruption and their effects on the people involved in them.

1. *Gaurus.* A mountain in Campania between Cumae and Naples, now Monte Barbaro. In classical literature it is usually spoken of as covered with vines and the source of a very good wine; Sandys describes it as 'stony and desolate'. Gray's actual subject is not so much the Gaurus as the volcanic eruption of 1538, during which a new mountain, Monte Nuovo, arose from the site of the Lucrine Lake; it is this mountain that Gray is speaking of in ll. 35–39 and 49–51. At some other points he seems to be confusing the Gaurus and the new mountain.

4. Virgil, *Eclogues*, vii. 58: pampineas . . . umbras.

8. *deo.* Presumably Somnus, the personification and God of Sleep, but Gray may be merely generalizing.

10. *Aeneid*, iii. 674: curvisque immugiit Aetna cavernis.

12. *Parthenopæa.* This seems to be a slip on Gray's part. Parthenope was a Siren who, because of grief at the departure of Odysseus, threw herself into the sea and was washed ashore at the site where Naples was later built. For this reason, Naples was sometimes called *Parthenope* or *Parthenopeia* (*urbs*). There does not appear to have been any form *Parthenopaea*.

17. Virgil, *Georgics*, i. 330: terra tremit; fugere ferae.

22. *notasque.* The *-que* seems to be solely for the sake of the metre.

25. *fumumque.* The *-que* is counted as long, probably on the analogy of Virgil's occasional practice before stop plus liquid (e.g. *Aeneid*, vii. 186; *Georgics*, i. 164).

31. Virgil, *Georgics*, i. 397: tenuia nec lanae per caelum vellera ferri [thin fleeces of wool to be borne through the sky—i.e. thin fleecy clouds]. *Aeneid*, xi. 62–63 (solacia luctus / exigua ingentis), shows the classical idiom.

32. 'I should conceive the proper phrase to be "colligere in unum".' *Mt.* See his note for citations supporting this view.

47. Horace, *Satires*, ii. 8. 26: indice monstraret digito.

FAREWELL TO FLORENCE

Gray sent the poem to West in his letter of 21 Apr. 1741 (T & W no. 97), with the following introductory sentence: 'Yet the place [Florence] and the charming prospects demand a poetical farewell, and here it is.'

Actually, the poem describes Fiesole, not Florence; only 'Arni de valle' in l. 5 and 'longe' in l. 7 so much as hint at Florence. Nevertheless, the usual title is 'Farewell to Florence', largely on the basis of the sentence quoted above. See also expl. note on 'Faesulae' in *Oh Ubi Colles*.

1. *Fæsulæ*. Despite Gray's comma, this has been construed as genitive singular, not as vocative plural. The Latin name of Fiesole is usually *Faesulae*, but Silius Italicus (*Punica*, viii. 477) gives it as *Faesula*. Since Gray read Silius Italicus for the first time in 1739, on his trip into Italy (T & W no. 74), and since his punctuation is self-admittedly erratic, the editors feel that Mason's text represents Gray's intention better than the reading in *CB*.

2. Fiesole is some 900 feet higher than Florence, and therefore is, or at least is supposed to be, cooler.

5. Virgil, *Eclogues*, i. 76–77: non ego vos posthac . . . / videbo.

7. Horace, *Epodes*, i. 29–30: neque ut superni villa candens Tusculi Circaea tangat moenia [nor that a gleaming villa may be near the Circaean walls of lofty Tusculum].

IMITATED FROM BUONDELMONTI

The poem was probably written in Apr. 1741. Gray sent it to West in a letter dated 21 Apr. 1741 (T & W no. 97), together with the original 'sonnet' of Buondelmonti. Gray also copied both poems into *CB*, clearly identifying the Italian as Buondelmonti's. Some editors, e.g. Mitford, give the impression that the Italian as well as the Latin poem was composed by Gray.

Gray refers to the author of the Italian poem (*CB*, i. 139) as 'Sig:r Abbate Buondelmonti. Fiorentino.' He is identified in T & W no. 97, n. 4, as 'Giuseppe Maria Bondelmonti (1713–57), of the ancient family of that name'. Mason gives the name as 'Buondelmonte'—a spelling that has appeared in a number of subsequent editions. The name is spelt 'Buondelmonti' in the *Enciclopedia italiana* (viii. 117), as Gray gives it.

The following text of the Italian poem is taken from *CB*, i. 139:

> Spesso Amor sotto la forma
> D'amistá ride, e s'asconde:
> Poi si mischia, e si confonde
> Con lo sdegno, e col rancor.
> In pietade ei si trasforma;
> Par trastullo, e par dispetto:
> Má nel suo diverso aspetto
> Sempr' egli é l' istesso Amor.

We are indebted to Professor James D. Powell for the following translation:

Often Love laughs and hides
Under the form of friendship:
Then he mixes and confuses himself
With disdain and with malice.
He transforms himself into Pity;
He seems a toy and he seems an annoyance;
But in his various aspects
He is always the same Love.

The acute accents in Gray's text should be grave.

ALCAIC ODE

Bradshaw, p. 153, says that the original in the Grande Chartreuse was destroyed during the French Revolution by a mob from Grenoble. Gray wrote the poem in the album of the monastery on his second visit, in Aug. 1741, when he was returning alone from Italy.

In his note on this poem, Bradshaw (p. 281) quotes from Gray's letter of 25 Sept. 1740 (T & W no. 94) to West, 'There was a certain little ode set out from Rome, etc.' The ode mentioned in this letter is certainly not the present poem; the passage is generally taken to refer to *Ad C. Favonium Zephyrinum*. Bradshaw's note implies that Gray had composed the Grande Chartreuse ode and sent a copy to West more than a year before he wrote it in the monks' album; however, the usual assumption, which the present editors share, is that the poem was composed in Aug. 1741.

6. The caesura does not conform to the practice of Horace. In the first two lines of the Alcaic strophe, Horace regularly has a diaeresis at the end of the second full foot (i.e. after the fifth syllable); in 630 verses, there are only four exceptions (*Odes*, i. 37. 5; i. 37. 14; ii. 17. 21; iv. 14. 17). In none of the exceptions does the sense permit a caesura.

9. Horace, *Odes*, iv. 1. 20: ponet marmoream sub trabe citrea.

10. Martial, vi. 73: Phidiaca manu.

11. Horace, *Odes*, i. 32. 14–16: o laborum / dulce lenimen medicumque, salve / rite vocanti.

OH UBI COLLES

This poem, in the Sapphic metre, was probably written soon after Gray's return from his tour of the Continent in Sept. 1741.

1. *Fæsularum*. Faesulae (*Faesula* in Silius Italicus, viii. 477, and in Gray's *Farewell to Florence*), city of Etruria, modern Fiesole, an older and separate town, 3–5 miles north-east of Florence.

2. *Palladis curæ*. Since Pallas Athena (Minerva) was the Goddess of Wisdom, Learning, and the Arts, the epithet is particularly appropriate to Florence.

3. *Genuæ*. Gray frequently testifies to his delight in the beauty and climate of Genoa. See e.g. his letter to West (T & W no. 75) which begins with 'Horridos tractus'.

3–4. *Genuæque ... soles*. Cf. *From Genoa*, ll. 3–4.

SOPHONISBA MASINISSAE. EPISTOLA

The sole source of this poem is an obviously conflated letter (T & W no. 110; see introductory note thereto) published by Mason. Apparently the poem was sent to West some time between 15 May and 27 May 1742.

Although the general conception of the poem and some lines are worthy of Gray, there are many weaknesses and even some outright errors. In view of Gray's usual mastery of Latin, the obvious conclusion would seem to be that Mason copied incorrectly or even 'completed' a rough draft that he found among Gray's papers. The present editors were at first inclined to this view, but finally concluded that the poem, with all its faults, is probably what Gray wrote.

A detailed examination of a single point will indicate the need for restraint in attributing to others all the errors in Gray's early work, especially in compositions that he probably had no intention of publishing. The correct spelling and quantities of *Masinissa* are shown by Ovid, *Fasti*, vi. 769: postera lux melior: superat Masinissa Syphacem [the next day is luckier: on it Masinissa defeated Syphax]; Mason's text has *Massinissa*. With this spelling, the verse can be forced to scan only by lengthening the -*i*- in the antepenult; we must assume that Gray did this. In his note on l. 7, Mitford (i. 201) hints strongly that the mis-spelling was introduced by Mason in an unsuccessful effort to correct the scansion. However, the same spelling, unquestionably in Gray's hand, occurs in a genealogical table in *CB*, i. 87. There can be little doubt, therefore, that the error in spelling is Gray's; in all probability this defective line must be attributed to him, not to Mason.

Other errors cannot be so definitely attributed to Gray, but there is no reason to suppose that they are not his.

The episode that forms the basis of the poem is told by Livy in Book XXX, chaps. 12 and 14; there is additional background material in other portions of Livy's work, which has been incorporated into individual notes below.

Sophonisba (or Sophoniba) was the daughter of the Carthaginian general Hasdrubal, Son of Gisco. All that is known of her life is related in the poem and the accompanying notes.

1. *Munus.* Among its many meanings, *munus* often denotes 'last service' (i.e. funeral or burial). Both here and in l. 14, the double meaning gives a pathos that is not likely to be accidental.

3. *luce vel una.* Something of a poetic licence. Masinissa married Sophonisba on the day he entered Cirta in triumph, being, as Livy puts it, 'like all Numidians, quick to fall in love'. His hasty marriage, however, as Livy also says (XXX. 12), was apparently undertaken as a calculated risk, in the hope that, as the wife of an ally, she would be spared by Scipio instead of being treated as part of the spoils taken from Syphax. It was not until Masinissa had returned to Scipio's base camp, several days later, that he was presented with the choice of delivering Sophonisba to the Romans or allowing her to escape by drinking the cup of poison.

4. *Stygios . . . lacus.* Circumlocutions like this are common in place of the simple name (Styx).

5. Ovid, *Fasti*, v. 156: virgineo nullum corpore passa virum [who had yielded her virgin body to no man].

7. *Masinissa*. Having gone to Spain to fight in the service of Carthage, he came over to the Romans. Gray says that he did so because of anger at the marriage of Sophonisba, who had been betrothed to him, to Syphax; but the more likely, if less romantic, reason is that, having lost the throne of Massylia to Syphax, he had been abandoned by the Carthaginians and had turned to an alliance with Rome as the means of recovering his kingdom.

13. *Scipiadae*. The form *Scipiades* is made by means of the Greek patronymic suffix, on the analogy of names like Πηληιάδης (Son of Peleus, i.e. Achilles). It performed a double service: it gave the poets a name that could be used in dactylic hexameter verse, as the oblique cases of *Scipio* could not; and, more important at certain times, it conveyed a delicate compliment to the powerful Scipios by likening them to the great heroes of Homer.

18. *Eliseas*. Adjectival form derived from Elisa (or Elissa), a poetic name for Dido.

20. Ovid, *Fasti*, ii. 468: hostiles credit adesse manus.

23–26. Apparently Sophonisba is referring to an earlier victory of Masinissa over Syphax (*c.* 216–214 B.C.), which, she implies, he celebrated by a triumphal procession in Carthage, although the details are largely those which Livy relates about the encounter when Masinissa took Cirta in 203 B.C., with due allowance for poetic freedom. However, since Masinissa was born about 238 B.C., the subsequent reference to his extreme youth, and *primitias* and *antiquae* in this passage, are better suited to the earlier date. On the other hand, Livy (XXX. 12) insists that Sophonisba met Masinissa for the first time when he captured Cirta. The whole basis of the poem is better romance than history, so that there is no way of reconciling all conflicts between the poet and the historian.

23. *Syphacis*. Syphax was king of the Massaesylians, the western group of Numidians. He and the family of Masinissa fought over a period of years to gain the rule of the whole tribe. At first Masinissa, leading the armies of Gala, his father, was victorious, but later Syphax gained the upper hand.

27. Mitford's violent objection to Gray's counting the *-o* of *ego* as long seems a bit captious. It is true, as he says, that the *-o* is short in the best poets of the classical period, but it is not uncommon to find it long in pre- and post-Augustan poets. The long *-o* is the older form (cf. Greek ἐγώ), so that its use in early Latin and its revival in post-Augustan Latin is not surprising or unusual.

32. *Aeneid*, iii. 597: aspectu . . . haesit.

34. Ovid, *Amores*, ii. 440: et enim fusco grata colore Venus.
fuscus. Masinissa was a Numidian. Horace, *Sermones*, ii. 8. 14, applies *fuscus* to a slave from India.

37. *Aeneid*, ix. 181: ora puer prima signans intonsa juventa.

46. Ovid, *Tristia*, ii. 520: saepe oculos etiam detinuisse tuos.

DE PRINCIPIIS COGITANDI, LIBER PRIMUS

It is impossible to determine exactly when the poem was composed. Gray states (*CB*, i. 129) that it was begun at Florence in 1740, but he was there from 7 July 1740 until 27 Apr. 1741. On 21 Apr. 1741 he wrote to West (T & W no. 97), '. . . I send you the beginning not of an Epic Poem, but of a Metaphysic one.' Mason (i. 116 n.) states that the fragment sent with this letter comprised the first 53 lines. There seems to be no good reason for doubting the implication of the opening lines of Book II that Book I was finished about the time of West's death in June 1742. Gray does not mention the poem again until 26 Apr. 1744, when he wrote to Wharton (T & W no. 115), 'Master Tommy Lucretius . . . is but a puleing Chitt yet, not a bit grown to speak off [*sic*], I believe, poor Thing! it has got the Worms, that will carry it off at last.' This implies, though not very strongly, that he had not yet completely abandoned the work, or at least the idea, but there is no certainty.

Gray states that Book II was begun at Stoke in June 1742 (*CB*, i. 286); he sent a copy to Walpole in a letter (T & W no. 131) of 8 Feb. 1747, in which he refers to it as 'the Beginning of the fourth Book' (see textual notes).

There is no doubt that Gray intended to do for Locke's *Essay concerning Human Understanding* what Lucretius had done for the doctrines of Epicurus. However, he never progressed beyond a general statement of Locke's theory and the working out of a few examples, for the first book—despite its length—is still a fragment, and the second is essentially a threnody on the death of West. The influence of Lucretius appears mainly in the general purpose of the work and the use of a few terms and mannerisms of style. So far as the work has gone, there is none of the crusading atheism or moral fervour of Lucretius; of course, in eighteenth-century England, the need to defend a rational approach to human problems did not exist as it did in Lucretius' day.

Although the point is by no means clear, it seems that Gray was at least partially influenced by the meanings attached by Lucretius to the terms *primordia*, *principium*, and *foedus*. Lucretius (i. 55–61) defines *primordia* as follows: '*primordia* ("atoms", "first-beginnings") . . . from which Nature creates all things, feeds them and makes them grow; and into which she resolves all things again when their existence is over; these (atoms), in setting forth my explanation, I am wont to call "matter" [*materies*] and "generative bodies of things" [*genitalia corpora rebus*] and "seeds of things" [*semina rerum*], and sometimes to refer to them as "primary bodies" [*corpora prima*] because from them as primary elements all things are made'.

Principium in Lucretius sometimes means merely 'beginning' (i. 339); sometimes it means 'basic law or doctrine' (i. 149); sometimes it means 'basic element' (i. 707) and is indistinguishable from *primordia*. Gray seems to have all three meanings more or less in mind, especially in the title of his poem. The editors have chosen *elements* as the word that most nearly renders the Latin word, but the reader should keep in mind that the poem attempts to set forth the basic elements of thought, the way it begins and grows, and the laws which govern that development.

Lucretius implies in various passages that there is a natural law which determines what things can and cannot come into existence and the powers of those which do. The law itself he refers to by *Natura gubernans*, v. 77, and *Natura creatrix*, i. 629; its terms and conditions by *foedus* or *foedus Naturaï*. For example, in i. 584–7, he says: 'Now, moreover, since a definite limit of growing and retaining life is fixed for things each according to its kind and since it has been immutably decreed what each can do in accordance with the covenants of Nature [*foedera Naturaï*]—and conversely what each cannot do— ....' The editors have assumed that Gray was aware of these meanings in their translation of ll. 32–33.

In searching the text of Lucretius for particular words and forms, the editors have relied primarily on Johannes Paulson's *Index Lucretianus* (Leipzig, 1926).

Title. *Favonium*. Richard West.

22. *vitaï*. Archaic genitive singular of the first declension, frequently used by Lucretius.

31. *Musa*. Gray does not seem to have any particular Muse in mind, merely a generalized personification of poetic inspiration.

aurea. Perhaps an echo of Pindar's χρύσεα φόρμιγξ. See note on *Progress of Poesy*, l. 20.

38. *cœlestis*. Since this is clearly genitive singular, modifying *flammæ*, the accent has been omitted. See textual notes.

43. See textual notes.

55. *Tamisis*. A slip of the pen for *Tamesis* 'the Thames'.

68. *pellisque*. Since this is clearly genitive singular, the accent has been omitted.

69. This line is repeated from *Latin Verses at Eton*, l. 53.

68–69. The editors are in some doubt about the correctness of the translation of *pellisque . . . vivit*. Because of the repetition of the line from *Latin Verses*, in which Gray is unquestionably speaking of the spider's web, it would seem that he intends to liken the network of nerves to such a web. However, this image is not completely compatible with the rest of the passage, and there is the difference that in the present poem *funditur* is used personally, with *ille* [i.e. *tactus*] as its subject.

75. *simul ac*. Gray's text has a comma between these words, but it seems to be an error. The words are not usually so separated, and the punctuation indicates a false caesura.

90. *Lepos*. Older form with -*s* for later -*r* and -*o*- still long. See note to l. 114.

109–26. This passage seems to need some revision. The 'Argument' given by Mason (i. 159) is: '. . . their [senses of sight and hearing] connection with the higher faculties of the Mind; Sense of Beauty and Order and Harmony annexed to them. From the latter, our delight in Eloquence, Poetry, and Music derived.' In Gray's marginal caption, the Argument has been modified to 'Ideas of Beauty, Proportion & Order'. In the text itself, 'Beauty' has completely vanished, and instead of 'Proportion' and 'Harmony' we find 'place' and 'combination'.

114. *honos*. The older form, with -*s* for later -*r* and unshortened -*o*-, is typical of Lucretius' fondness for archaic forms (e. g. *colos* for *color*, vi. 208), although he happens not to use this particular word in the nominative singular.

res accendere rebus. Cf. Lucretius, i. 1117: . . . res accendent lumina rebus ['things (already known) will light torches to illuminate things (as yet unknown)'].

123. *Libethrides undæ*. From Libethrum, a town on the slope of Mt. Olympus, sacred to the Muses, who are sometimes called *Libethrides*. The phrase appears to be Gray's own coinage as a variant for the more common 'Pierian springs'.

124. *Pater . . . canendi*. Probably Apollo. The editors have found no ancient example of this epithet; presumably it is Gray's invention, in imitation of Virgil's *pater ipse colendi* ('father of husbandry', an epithet of Jupiter) in *Georgics*, i. 121.

136. *Alma Parens*. Presumably the 'Natura creatrix' of l. 32, although it is a common epithet of Venus. Gray probably had in mind the fact that Lucretius makes Venus the personification of the creative forces of nature.

140. *capiat*. See textual notes. The word is badly blurred in *CB*, but looks more like *capiat* than like *cupiat*.

149. *eosdem*. Disyllabic by synizesis.

196. *semina rerum*. See p. 266.

198. *Fulgĕre*. This third conjugation form instead of the more common *fulgēre* is found in Lucretius (v. 1095; vi. 165) and in Virgil (*Aeneid*, vi. 826).

200. Line repeated from *Luna Habitabilis*, l. 41.

DE PRINCIPIIS COGITANDI, LIBER SECUNDUS

Despite the title, this is really an elegy on the death of West, not a part of *De Principiis Cogitandi*; Gray may have intended that it should be an introduction to a later book, but he never completed it. Gray tells us that the poem was begun at Stoke in 1742; it seems likely that it was finished shortly thereafter.

TRANSLATIONS FROM THE GREEK ANTHOLOGY

The work generally designated by the term 'Greek Anthology' comprises a group of poems, mostly epigrams, numbering about 4,100 and ranging in date from about 700 B.C. to A.D. 1000 or even later. These poems have come down to us in two Byzantine collections: that of Cephalas, a scholar of the tenth century, and that of Planudes, a grammarian of the fourteenth century. Although the collection of Cephalas is generally superior, the collection of Planudes was more popular and more widely circulated for about four centuries. Early in the seventeenth century a MS. of the anthology of Cephalas was discovered at Heidelberg, in the library of the Counts Palatine; this is known as the *Palatine Anthology* or, because it was in the Vatican Library for a time, as the *Vatican*. Each of these collections contains some poems not found in the other, and some variant readings of the poems found in both.

Modern editions, including that of W. R. Paton in the Loeb Library, are usually based on the Palatine MS., with those poems that occur only in the collection of Planudes added as an appendix (variously designated 'Planudean Appendix' or 'Book XVI').

The edition that Gray used (H. Stephanus, Paris, 1566) was based on the collection of Planudes. However, in the present edition the original Greek poems are cited by book number and poem as they appear in the Loeb Library edition, since it is now the most easily available. The editors have been unable to locate Gray's own copy of Stephanus, which Mathias informs us was interleaved and contained notes and conjectural emendations as well as the translations here given; we have, however, cited the original poems as they appear in a microfilm of a copy of Stephanus furnished to us by the British Museum.

There is no definite information on the date of composition; on the basis of style, the editors would surmise that these poems were composed rather late in Gray's Latin period, probably after his return from the Continent. However, there are two slight indications of an earlier date. First, Gray wrote a parody of the first line of a poem by Glycon (*Pal. Anth.* x. 124) in a letter (T & W no. 3) dated 17 Nov. 1734:

πάντα κόνις, καὶ πάντα πιὸς, καὶ πάντα τόβακκο
[all is dust, and all is pie, and all is tobacco].

Second, West sent Gray a translation into Latin elegiac couplets of a poem of Posidippus (*Pal. Anth.* vii. 170, where the poem is attributed to Callimachus; Stephanus, p. 220) in a letter written in Dec. 1737 or Jan. 1738 (T & W no. 43; see notes therein on date). Since Gray and West often engaged in a friendly rivalry, working on similar projects at the same time and exchanging the results of their efforts, perhaps Gray's translations should be assigned to an earlier date (*c.* 1738).

It may even be that West's translation prompted Gray to begin his own study of the Greek Anthology, for in his reply to West (T & W no. 47, dated 22 Jan. 1738), he says, '... unde hoc tibi sit depromptum, (ut fatear) prorsus nescio ... [whence you drew this, I am (to tell the truth) in complete ignorance].' Mason informs us, however, that Gray inserted West's translation into the MS. notes in his copy of Stephanus, presumably opposite the original epigram (*M*, i. 27 n.). At the very least, these facts permit us to infer that Gray knew the Greek Anthology more intimately at some later date than he did in January 1738.

After reaching the above conclusion independently, the editors have found that Professor William Powell Jones, on p. 52 of *Thomas Gray, Scholar* (Harvard, 1937), attributes the translations to an even later date, some time after the death of West on 1 June 1742.

Roman numbers have been prefixed to Gray's poems and to their translations. In the explanatory and textual notes, these numbers are used instead of titles to designate the individual poems.

I

Original poem: *Pal. Anth.* xi. 365 (Stephanus, p. 133).
In *Pal. Anth.* attributed to Agathias Scholasticus (*fl.* sixth cent. A.D.); in Stephanus, to 'unknown author'.

1. *Aristophanis.* In the original, Aristophanes the Astrologer.

3. *Sideris.* The word *sidus* has a wide range of meaning ('star', 'constellation', 'sun', 'moon', 'season'). The translation given herein is adopted because in folk wisdom the moon is supposed to exert a powerful influence on crops.

II

Original poem: *Pal. Anth.* xvi. 136 (Stephanus, p. 317).
Antiphilus of Byzantium flourished about A.D. 50.

The title of the poem in the anthology indicates that the picture that inspired it was in Rome.

Timomachi. Timomachus of Byzantium was a famous painter of portraits of contemporaries and of mythological personages; he probably flourished during the middle decades of the first century B.C.

6. *Colchidos*. Colchis was a country between the Euxine and the Caspian Seas.

III

Original poem: *Pal. Anth.* xvi. 57 (Stephanus, p. 296).

Paulus Silentiarius was a high official, head of the *Silentiarii* ('Gentlemen of the Bedchamber') in the court of Justinian (*reg.* A.D. 527–65).

Bacchae. The women (*Maenades*) who worshipped Dionysus.

1. *Maenas*. The nominative singular of *Maenades* (see above).

IV

Original poem: *Pal. Anth.* xvi. 119 (Stephanus, p. 314).

Posidippus flourished *c*. 250–225 B.C.

1. *Lysippe*. Lysippus of Sicyon was a contemporary of Alexander the Great, of whom he made many bronze statues; none have survived, although some extant busts are supposed to have been copied from the works of Lysippus.

V

Original poem: *Pal. Anth.* xvi. 129 (Stephanus, p. 315).

No author is given for this poem, but the one immediately following, on the same subject, is by Julianus Aegyptius, who wrote two epitaphs on Hypatius, who was put to death by Justinian in A.D. 532.

VI

Original poem: *Pal. Anth.* xvi. 164 (Stephanus, p. 323).

The attribution to Lucian (A.D. *c*. 120–*c*. 200) is doubtful. The present poem follows an epigram by him on the Aphrodite of Cnidos and stands among a group of epigrams on the same subject, but, unlike the others, it does not refer specifically to the statue by Praxiteles.

Mathias inserted 'A nymph' before 'offering' in the title; this error has often been reproduced by subsequent editors, even after Bradshaw correctly pointed out that the resultant reading did not fit the poem.

VII

Original poem: *Pal. Anth.* xvi. 211 (Stephanus, p. 332).

Nothing is known of Statyllius Flaccus; Flaccus is a Roman name, but it does not necessarily follow that the person was a Roman.

The next epigram (*Pal. Anth.* xvi. 212), which Gosse gives as the original, is similar in language and substance, but is by Alpheius.

Catullianam illam spirat mollitiem [it breathes the well-known tenderness of Catullus]. *Gray (Mt)*.

VIII

Original poem: *Pal. Anth.* xvi. 210 (Stephanus, p. 332).

Plato. Mitford identifies the author as 'the second of the name', but without citing any authority or specifying more precisely. Presumably he means Plato the

Comedian (*fl.* 428–389 B.C.), the contemporary and rival of Aristophanes. There is a tradition, supported by Meleager, that the great Plato (429–347 B.C.) wrote poetry when he was very young. There were also other poets of the same name about whom nothing is known.

The last line of the original poem has been emended in the Loeb Library edition, so that it differs from the reading in Stephanus and from Gray's translation.

Elegantissimum hercle fragmentum, quod sic Latine nostro modo adumbravimus [Certainly a very fine fragment, of which we have given an imperfect idea thus in Latin, in our usual way]. *Gray* (*Mt*).

IX

Original poem: *Pal. Anth.* ix. 627 (Stephanus, p. 354).
Marianus was a Byzantine lawyer (*fl.* A.D. 491–518).

The poem is one of a group on various Baths, many of which were called 'Eros' from the fact that statues of that god concealed the pipes from which the water flowed, making it appear that the water was flowing from the mouth or other parts of the anatomy of the statue. Some were built around hot springs, and a number of the poems give some version of the myth related in the present poem to account for the warmth of the water.

X

Original poem: *Pal. Anth.* xi. 391 (Stephanus, p. 186).
Lucilius was a grammarian at Rome, a pensioner of Nero (*reg.* A.D. 54–68).

Argus. The name of the miser in the Greek poem is Asclepiades, a name often assumed by physicians. For reasons that the editors have been unable to determine, Gray chose a completely different name. There seems to be no known person of either name who had the reputation of being a miser. The spelling in Gray's poem, as in Stephanus and many MSS., is *Lucillius*.

XI

Original poem: *Pal. Anth.* v. 215 (Stephanus, p. 452).
Posidippus. See note to poem IV. In the *Palatine Anthology*, this poem is attributed to Meleager, who flourished *c.* 100–70 B.C.

XII

Original poem: *Pal. Anth.* v. 125 (Stephanus, p. 482).
Lollius Bassus of Smyrna wrote an epigram on the death of Germanicus, which occurred in A.D. 19. This is the sole clue to his date.

XIII

Original poem: *Pal. Anth.* v. 74 (Stephanus, p. 452).
Rufinus. J. W. Mackail, in *Select Epigrams from the Greek Anthology* (London: Longmans, Green, 1906), p. 334, identifies the author as Rufinus Domesticus, an official of the court of Justinian (*reg.* A.D. 527–65); W. R. Paton, editor of the Loeb Library edition, thinks that the author is a different person of the same name, date uncertain.

ORDERS OF INSECTS

Gosse's prefatory statement (see textual notes) caused the present editors and Mr. M. J. C. Hodgart, Librarian of Pembroke College, Cambridge, to spend many fruitless hours searching in *CB*; the verses are certainly not in *CB* now, if they ever were. It seems likely that Gosse's statement as to his source is based on a hasty reading of the following footnote in Mathias (ii. 551): 'The editor [Mathias] desires to express his grateful acknowledgments to the Rev. Mr. Bright, (executor to the late Mr. Stonhewer), who obligingly communicated Mr. Gray's original interleaved volumes of the "Systema Naturae", whence the following specimens were selected.'

Gray composed these verses in the last years of his life, certainly not before 1758 and probably about ten years later than that date. The verses appear on leaves facing the text of Linnaeus in a very clean and clear copy; the sole correction is the crossing out of the *-o-* in *Chrysomela* (l. 11). The fragment published in this edition under the title *Additional Lines on Insects* makes it seem likely that Gray first worked out the present verses in the same way and then copied them into Linnaeus; something, perhaps his final illness, prevented him from completing his verses on the Aptera and copying them as he had those on the first six Orders.

The reader who wishes to correlate Gray's verses with the classifications of Linnaeus should note that other editions of Linnaeus classify the insects differently from the tenth.

9. *Coccionellae.* Gray's variant for Linnaeus's *Coccinella*, which cannot be fitted into a hexameter verse. Probably the same reason caused Gray to change *Chrysomela* to *Chrys'mela* (l. 11).

15. *Staphylis.* Linnaeus has *Staphylinus.*

30–37. Linnaeus's arrangement is *Cicada, Notonecta, Nepa, Cimex, Aphis, Chermes, Coccus, Thrips.*

31. Mathias, without explanation, emended *Fastigio* to *Remigio*, perhaps because of the problems of scansion presented by *fastigio*, perhaps because of the Virgilian echo (remigio alarum, *Aeneid*, i. 301), but in *GL fastigio* is clearly written in what is undoubtedly a clean copy and the editors have thought it best, therefore, not to emend the text.

46. *Hemerinus.* Linnaeus has *Hemerobius.*

51–59. Linnaeus's arrangement is *Cynips, Tenthredo, Ichneumon, Sphex, Vespa, Apis, Formica, Mutella.*

59. *Mutilla.* Linnaeus has *Mutella.*

ADDITIONAL LINES ON INSECTS

These lines give the first five genera of the order Aptera as they appear in *GL* (see textual notes to *Orders of Insects*), except that *Phthir*, a transliteration of the Greek word for 'louse' (φθείρ), is used instead of the Latin *Pediculus*. It is evident that Gray intended to treat the Aptera as he did the other orders, but abandoned the project for some reason, quite possibly his last illness (see explanatory notes to *Orders of Insects*).

The MS. containing these lines, with its numerous corrections, very likely gives a better insight into Gray's method of work than the clean copy of the verses that Gray transcribed into *GL*.

INSCRIPTION FOR A WOOD IN A PARK

The poem appears in a letter to West which Mason dated 27 May 1742 (T & W no. 110); Toynbee and Whibley suspect that this is one of Mason's conflations and that it combines two or three letters written between 15 May and 27 May. In any case, the present poem must have been composed some time in May 1742.

The language of the poem is a strange mixture of Epic, Doric, and Attic Greek. Probably Gray would urge in its defence that Pindar combined Epic, Doric, and Aeolic to form the purely literary dialect of his *Odes*.

1. ἐκηβόλου . . . Ἀνάσσας. Artemis, here represented as Goddess of the Chase. ἐκηβόλος is a frequently employed epithet of her brother Apollo also, particularly when he is conceived as the god who sends plagues (see, e.g., *Iliad*, i. 14).

3. κλαγγεῦσιν. Possibly a form coined by Gray, on the analogy of Epic and Ionic forms like ποιεῦσι for ποιέουσι (Attic ποιοῦσι); Goodwin, *Greek Grammar*, section 785. 1, states that all such forms are of doubtful authenticity.

4. Νυμφᾶν. A Doric genitive plural, as is ἀγροτερᾶν.

POEMS OF DOUBTFUL AUTHENTICITY

MARTIAL'S LIB. 10, EPIG. 13 [23] PARAPHRASED

The MS. of this poem, which sounds very much like a schoolboy's exercise, definitely is not, in the opinion of Professor W. P. Jones, in the hand of Gray, Walpole, or Mason, although it was described in the Sotheby sale of 6 Nov. 1951 as a holograph. It had been in the collection of John Bowyer Buchanan Nichols (1859–1939), a descendant of John Nichols (1745–1826), and is now at the Bibliothèque Martin Bodmer (Cologny, Genève). The only reason to believe that it may be by Gray is that it was so attributed in the Nichols papers, but no evidence for this attribution was given by Sotheby or the present owner. Certainly neither the rhymes *barr–care* (ll. 7–8), *pass–was* (ll. 16–17), *declare–year* (ll. 20–21), and *were–clear* (ll. 22–24), nor the archaisms of spelling *barr*, *steddy*, and *yett* (ll. 7, 13, 14) seem very characteristic of Gray.

The epigram paraphrased is actually Martial, Book X, Epigram 23, not Epigram 13. A literal translation of Epigram 23 follows: 'Antonius Primus, blest with a calm old age, now counts over the fifteen Olympiads [sixty years] that he has lived and, as he looks back upon the bygone days and years, finds them all safely his, nor does he fear the waters of Lethe that are now so near. As he thinks back, not a single day is unpleasing or burdensome; not one has there been that he is unwilling to remember. A good man multiplies the span of his life: to be able to take delight in one's past life is to live twice.'

10, 21. *ā* is an old abbreviation for *and*. Apparently the writer of the MS. at first intended to use the same abbreviation in l. 21 but went on to write out the rest of the word.

THE CHARACTERS OF THE CHRIST-CROSS ROW, BY A CRITIC, TO MRS. —

Gray sent a copy of this poem to Walpole in a letter (T & W no. 139) of about 15 June 1747, with this comment: '. . . I send you a Poem that I am sure they will read . . . a masterpiece—it is said, being an admirable improvement on that beautiful piece called Pugna Porcorum [*Pugna Porcorum per P. Porcium poetam Paracelses pro Potore*, Parisiis, 1589, is written entirely in words beginning with *p*] which begins

'Plangite [*Plaudite*, 'applaud', is the word in the poem] porcelli Porcorum pigra propago' [Plain, ye piglets, pokey progeny of pigs]; but that is in Latin . . . but indeed, this is worth a thousand of it, and unfortunately it is not perfect, and it is not mine.' Walpole was sure from the style that Gray had written many of the lines, but Gray denied the authorship. Probably the original poem was written by one of his friends, William Trollope (*c.* 1707–49), Fellow of Pembroke, and Gray assisted him in the revision. See T & W no. 139, n. 12. Christ-cross (criss-cross) row is the alphabet, before which a cross was usually placed in the old hornbooks. The reference to 'Mrs. —' is unidentified. See textual notes also.

17. *clews*. Literally, balls or clusters of yarn or threads.

20. *Grannam Osborne's Gazetteer*. James Pitt (1679–1763), who under the name of Francis Osborne conducted the *Daily Gazetteer*, in which he defended Sir Robert Walpole, was nicknamed 'Mother Osborne'.

31. *Pisgys*. Pixies.

52. *Queer Queensbury*. Lady Catherine Hyde (1701–77), later Duchess of Queensberry, was both beautiful and eccentric. She was dismissed from court in 1728 for soliciting subscriptions at St. James's for the second part of *The Beggar's Opera* after the Lord Chamberlain had forbidden its production. *T & W*.

VERSE FRAGMENTS

When Mason copied these lines into *CB*, it seems probable that he regarded them (with the possible exception of ''tis Ridicule . . .', which he enclosed in quotation marks) as by Gray (see *Ode . . . Vicissitude*, textual and explanatory notes, ll. 17–20). That Mason intended to imply that the verse was by Gray is all the more likely since he prefaced a later extract from the Pocket-book of 1754 (*CB*, iii. 1111) with the statement: 'It is not clear whether this is his [Gray's] or an extract from some Book.'

TRANSLATION OF PHILIPS'S *SPLENDID SHILLING*

'After some Latin Alcaics signed "Antrobus" comes in the 3rd volume of Mitford's Excerpts [Note-book, iii. 110–11] a Latin translation of Phillips's "Splendid Shilling", to which he does not assign the authorship'—*Tovey*.

Tovey gives no reason other than its position in the Note-book for attributing the poem to Gray; it has been included for the sake of completeness.

The first dozen lines of *The Splendid Shilling* (1701, 1705), a burlesque of *Paradise Lost* by John Philips (1676–1709), run as follows:

> Happy the man who, void of cares and strife,
> In silken or in leathern purse retains
> A Splendid Shilling: he nor hears with pain
> New oysters cried, nor sighs for cheerful ale;
> But with his friends, when nightly mists arise,   5
> To Juniper's, Magpye, or Town-Hall repairs:
> Where, mindful of the nymph whose wanton eye
> Transfixed his soul and kindled amorous flames,
> Chloe, or Phyllis, he each circling glass
> Wisheth her health, and joy, and equal love.   10
> Meanwhile he smokes, and laughs at merry tale,
> Or pun ambiguous, or conundrum quaint.

3. *Solidus*. Properly, a gold coin of the Roman Empire.

3–4. See Philips's original, l. 4.

6–7. See Philips's original, l. 6.

13. *non lateri parcit*. Besides the literal meaning, the author quite likely intends us to remember that the expression was also Roman slang (cf. Juvenal, vi. 37; Ovid, *Ars Amatoria*, ii. 413) for 'he is worn out by sexual intercourse'.

IMITATION OF MARTIAL

Edmund C. Mason, in 'Anecdote of Gray', *The Gentleman's Magazine*, lxxi (July 1801), 591, says that this poem was among the papers of his late relative William Mason, and supplies the following anecdote:

> Mr. Gray, after having proceeded to the degree of A.B. at Cambridge, was supposed to have contracted an affection for Miss D--me; at the same time that Mr. M was said to have felt the tender passion for Miss C--t--y, afterwards Mrs. H--g-m. On Mr. M's commending the superiority of his mistress, Mr. Gray penned the following lines, a very masterly imitation of Martial:

The present poem is then given, followed by a translation into Greek by a 'Mr. West'. This gentleman could not be Gray's friend, as Mitford seems to assume in noting the publication of the poem (i. lxxxiv); he is described by Mason as having just (i.e. 1801) returned from the Grand Tour. In the same notice, Mitford merely comments dryly, 'This gentleman [Ed. Mason], however, has not given any account of the authenticity of his manuscript.'

The only verifiable statement in the anecdote is untrue: Gray never received the degree of A.B. However, despite the patent spuriousness of the anecdote, the poem has been included because of the possibility that it itself may be genuine.

1. *Fulvia*. This and *Caelia* seem to be employed merely as typical Roman names; neither has any particular association that would make its choice in this poem essential.

INDEX

Since many of Gray's poems were not published during his lifetime and often did not have any title prefixed to them in surviving manuscripts, editors have felt at liberty to provide their own titles. These frequently differ greatly; and, to avoid confusion, the present editors have attempted to include most of these titles as cross-references in the index, although some have appeared in editions not sufficiently authoritative to justify inclusion in the textual notes. Such an entry as 'Sapphic Ode. See Ad C: Favonium Aristium.' is an example.

All entries beginning with the word 'O' or 'Oh' are alphabetized as if spelled 'Oh'—thus: 'O[h]'.

When there is appended to a title entry an additional number in italics, the reference is to the page on which the explanatory notes to that poem commence.

DATE DUE